Für Gerhard zur Erinnerung an
den Aufenthalt am CES
im Frühsommer 2012
Hans-Werner

© 2011 Verlag Lutz Garnies, Haar bei München
3rd, fully revised and expanded edition

EDITOR
University Executive Board, Ludwig-Maximilians-Universität München

EDITING COMMUNICATIONS AND MEDIA RELATIONS
Luise Dirscherl, Clemens Grosse, Christoph Olesinski

EDITING UNIVERSITY ARCHIVE
Dr. Ulla-Britta Vollhardt

TRANSLATED FROM THE GERMAN BY
Christopher Wynne

COPY-EDITING
Dr. Kathrin Bilgeri, Julia Wunderlich

DESIGN
Verlag Lutz Garnies – Verlag und Agentur.
www.vlg.de

ISBN 978-3-926163-64-6

LUDWIG-MAXIMILIANS-
UNIVERSITÄT MÜNCHEN

PAST AND PRESENT

*L*udwig-Maximilians-Universität (LMU) in Munich can look back over a more than 500-year history. Founded in 1472 in Ingolstadt by Louis the Rich, Duke of Bavaria, as a state university for the duchy, the university was moved to its present location in Munich in 1826 after a brief interval in Landshut. King Louis I's decision to move the university to the capital of Bavaria, led to Munich becoming an exceptional location of research and education. Today, the city and surrounding area are home to three universities, numerous colleges and renowned research facilities, such as the Max Planck Society with ten institutes, and the Helmholtz Zentrum München, among others. Within this high-caliber academic environment LMU is of particular importance. As a genuine universitas, it provides an established spectrum of disciplines, and is considered one of the best research universities in both Germany and Europe. This was proved in a convincing manner by LMU's success in the "Excellence Initiative," a competition launched by the German goverment to promote top-level university research. In the first round of proposals in 2006, LMU was already selected as "university of excellence" as one of just three universities in Germany.

LMU's strength as a place of research, its international reputation, and its enormous appeal for students and researchers has a long tradition. In its history, rich in challenges and decisive turning points, there have also been dark times, especially during the period under the National Socialists when LMU was largely brought into line with the "principles" of the Nazi Regime. To understand LMU's role during that period, a research project was initiated under the former president of the university, Andreas Heldrich. As a result, two anthologies and several monographs have since been published, which examine more closely the university`s involvement. On the other hand, one of the best-known resistance groups, still familiar to this day, was formed within university circles. Several students at LMU, centered around Hans and Sophie Scholl, set up the *Weiße Rose* (White Rose) group in 1942, together with others of a similar mind. Following an audacious and courageous leaflet campaign in the atrium of the main university building, the Scholl siblings were arrested in February 1943 and executed a few days later; show trials and death sentences for other members of the White Rose followed. The annual White Rose Memorial Lecture and a commemorative artwork in the paving outside the main university building act as a reminder of the Scholl siblings and the White Rose.

In the post-war period, the destruction wrought in World War II rendered it virtually impossible for regular teaching and research work to be carried out. The successful rebuilding of the university, however, was not least of all due to the help of many scholars and students, who laid the foundation stone for the positive development of their Alma mater anew. Reopened in 1946 with 7 faculties, LMU now comprises 18 faculties and more than 45,000 students, making it one of Germany's largest universities. For those at the university today, it is worth taking a look back at its history, to comprehend fully that one is not only studying, researching or working at a topflight, modern university, but at the same time at a very old one with a centuries-old tradition. This illustrated volume, now in a third, fully revised and expanded edition, is intended to contribute to this understanding. It traces the history of LMU in texts and pictures from its beginnings in Ingolstadt up to the present day.

I would like to take this opportunity to thank all those who have contributed toward the success of this new edition. First and foremost, of course, the Münchener Universitätsgesellschaft and its Chairman, Dr. Wolfgang Strassl, for their generous financial support. Special thanks are also due to the authors, who reworked or rewrote their articles.

I hope that this book provides a fascinating insight and gives great pleasure, not only to those connected to our university and their friends, but to everyone interested in LMU and its important role in the history of Bavaria and Munich.

Munich, Spring 2011

Bernd Huber

President, Ludwig-Maximilians-Universität München

CONTENTS

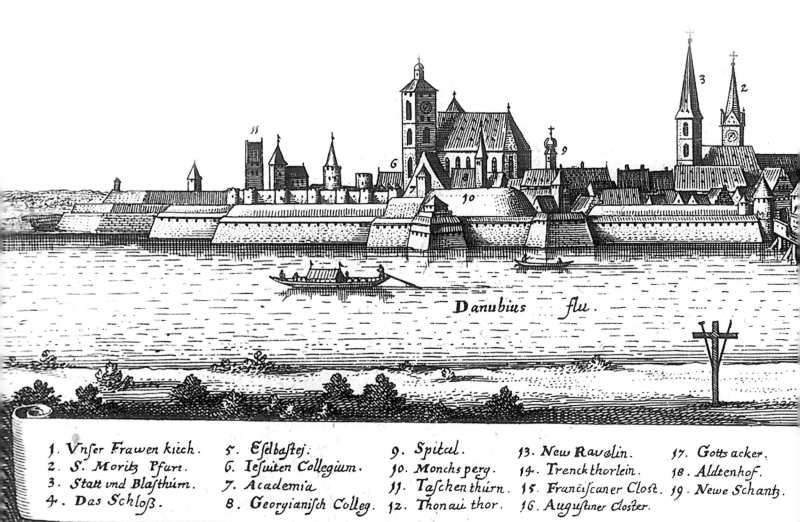

Danubius flu.

1. Vnser Frawen kirch.
2. S. Moritz Pfarr.
3. Statt vnd Blasthurn.
4. Das Schloß.
5. Eselbastej.
6. Iesuiten Collegium.
7. Academia.
8. Georgianisch Colleg.
9. Spital.
10. Monchsperg.
11. Taschenthurn.
12. Thonau thor.
13. New Ravelin.
14. Trenckthorlein.
15. Franciscaner Clost.
16. Augustiner Closter.
17. Gotts acker.
18. Aldtenhof.
19. Newe Schantz.

1472–1800

THE UNIVERSITY DURING THE INGOLSTADT EPOCH

WINFRIED MÜLLER

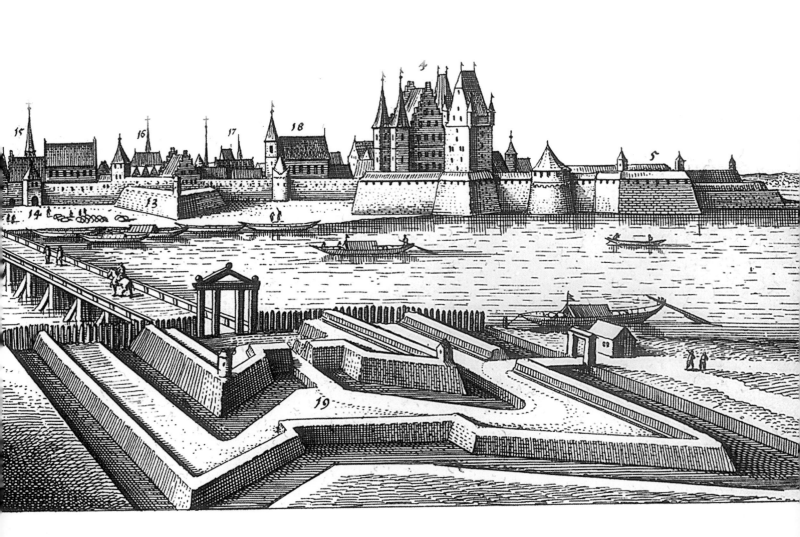

The so-called founder's folio from 1472 is bound in the oldest matriculation register (1472–1547) of the newly founded "Hohe Schule (Academy of Higher Learning) of Ingolstadt." It shows — seen from the viewer's perspective — the founder, Louis the Rich, Duke of Bavaria-Landshut, on the left before the Virgin and Child, patron of the university; on the right is the rector of the university, Christoph Mendel von Steinfels. The inscription immediately under the image lists the names of the figures: "Dux Ludwicus fundator / Christofferus Mendel doctor primus Rector 1472." Below this are the first entries in the matriculation register dated March 18, 1472.

previous double page:
Historical view of the fortified town of Ingolstadt. No. 1 marks the "Liebfrauenkirche" (Church of our Lady); no. 6 is the Jesuit college; no. 7 the "Hohe Schule" and no. 8 the Georgianum.

For Louis the Rich, Duke of Bavaria-Landshut (1417–1479), June 26, 1472 was an important day. While teaching had already started at the new *Hohe Schule* (Academy of Higher Learning)" founded by him in Ingolstadt in March that year, the official inauguration and opening of "his" university was held that day in June. The duke attended the ceremony in person together with illustrious guests, and listened to the inaugural speech given by the learned councillor Martin Mair, who extolled the virtues of education in an eloquent and practiced manner and swore the "amor scientiae."

FOUNDING OF THE UNIVERSITY AND AUTOCRACY

Admittedly, it was not just a love of scholarship that prompted Louis the Rich to establish his new foundation, but its practical uses as well. The University of Ingolstadt belongs to the so-called second wave of German universities founded between 1450 and 1550, for which territorial pragmatism was a supporting pillar of university policy just as much as an appreciation of the sciences.

For the secularly and religiously largely autonomous principalities united under the umbrella of the Holy Roman Empire of the German Nation, the founding of a state university was not only an expression of that particular ruler's quest for culture and prestige, but also of his claim for autocracy with regard to educational policies.

The territorial state in the early modern era needed educated clerks for the government and the church. A prerequisite for this was the existence of an adequate seat of learning. For this reason, Louis the Rich approached Pope Pius II back in 1458 with a request that the privileges of

Louis the Rich, Duke of Bavaria-Landshut (1417–1479) at the official inauguration of his foundation, the "Hohe Schule of Ingolstadt," on June 26, 1472.

Pope Pius II (1405–1464), a higly educated and accomplished writer, enabled the privileges of a "studium generale" be given to Ingolstadt. He was also particularly well-known as a humanist under his secular name Enea Silvio Poccolomini.

a "studium generale" be given to Ingolstadt. The pope met this wish by granting a foundation privilege on April 7, 1459.

There were several reasons for choosing Ingolstadt as a university seat. Bearing the division of the Wittelsbach territories since 1255 in mind — that for a time had led to the parallel existence of four independent, smaller, Bavarian duchies — the choice was politically motivated, as the duchy of Bavaria-Ingolstadt had been merged with Bavaria-Landshut following the death of Louis VII (The Bearded), Duke of Bavaria, in 1447. Ingolstadt had thus lost its position as a ducal seat. The founding of a university was intended to make up for this loss.

Ingolstadt's geographical location however also spoke in its favor. The town, which had a population approaching 3,000 at the time of the university's foundation, was centrally located, and with its good connections to the network of roads, filled a vacuum in the Bavarian-Franconian-Swabian area which was devoid of "Academies of Higher Learning." With such a wide catchment area, a sufficient number of students could be expected. At the beginning, there were in fact some 800 students, which then dropped to an estimated 300 to 500 scholars on average.

Last but not least, Ingolstadt could draw on favorable material resources for its new foundation, as the town had been blessed with a number of other foundations by Duke Louis VII in 1434. The endowment for 15 benefices, for example, that were to pray for the salvation of the duke's soul in particular, had already played a role in earlier considerations regarding the financing of the university.

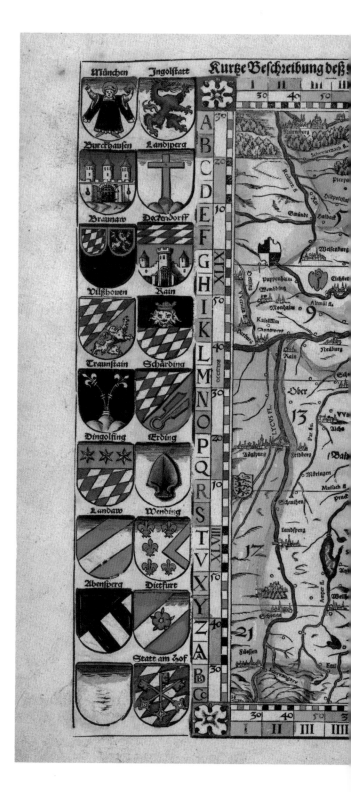

14

Bavaria in southern Germany as depicted on the famous map by Philipp Apian (1531–1589). It clearly shows Ingolstadt's attractive, central location in an area devoid of "Hohe Schulen" at that time.

The "Ingolstädter Gnad" in the choir of the minster. The devotional painting depicts the Virgin Mary on the throne and is based on a work in gold by a French craftsman that Louis VII (The Bearded), Duke of Bavaria-Ingolstadt (prob. 1368–1447), donated to the minster in 1438. It not only gave the Church of Our Lady its name, but is still to be found today in the seal of Ludwig-Maximilians-Universität. The exact appearance of the university seal was already laid down in the founder's charter of 1472.

The pope also approved the re-dedication of the foundation in favor of the future university in 1465, and until 1800 the benefice house served as the main building. In 1467, the Chapter in Eichstätt finally provided a canonry position to pay for one theology professor, who was also to be the priest of the *Liebfrauenkirche* (Church of Our Lady). The transformation of the *Liebfrauenkirche* into a collegiate church, in other words into a confraternity of lay priests, as an institute providing for the professors's needs, however, never came about.

Through this and other endowments the university already had a sound financial base in 1524, even before the incorporation of St. Moritz's Church — or rather its allocation to the university as a benefice. With an annual revenue of around 2,500 florins (guilders) from these endowments, Ingolstadt was one of the richest universities in Germany.

EARLY ORGANIZATIONAL AND ADMINISTRATIVE STRUCTURES

After a lengthy preparatory phase, accompanied by adverse circumstances elsewhere, the first lectures at the University of Ingolstadt were held on March 3, 1472. Organizationally, it was based on the ducal foundation charter of 1472, that was tied into the university structure — a protective covenant for each magister and scholar — that had become established in the Middle Ages.

At first it was planned to found a "universitas doctorum et studentium," subdivided into "nationes" or regional groups. This concept was however soon abandoned in favor of an adaption of the University of Paris model, with its division into four "facultates" and its rectorial constitution, that had reached Ingolstadt via Vienna. Following these lines, the University of Ingolstadt also had a chancellor who acted in a clerical supervisory capacity. During the entire Ingolstadt epoch, this office was

assigned to the Bishop of Eichstätt, as it formed part of that diocese. However, it was regularly delegated to a member of the Faculty of Theology, the pro-chancellor.

The "facultas artium," later the Faculty of Philosophy, that served as the propedaeutic "artes liberales," was therefore constituted in Ingolstadt. Its attendance was a prerequisite for studying in the three higher faculties, theology, jurisprudence, and medicine, each of which had its own dean. The rector held the highest position in the university, being elected every six months and later — but only since 1702 — annually. The "consilium generale" acted as the electoral body at

The foundation charter of the university from 1472. The founding of the "Hohe Schule" was not only an expression of a quest for culture and prestige, but also of a claim for autocracy.

In 1494, George the Rich, Duke of Bavaria-Landshut (1455–1503), gave the university the Georgianum, a college originally for eleven needy scholars of theology, named after him. In the ducal Georgianum, those training for the priesthood as well as priests are still given board and lodging to this day. Famous scholars include Joseph Ratzinger, now Pope Benedict XVI, and Sebastian Kneipp.

first. Originally an assembly with members from the whole university, it was restricted to chairs — the Senate — in the early 16th century.

The university's unique organizational structure was mirrored in a number of special privileges. These included immunity from taxes for dependants and so-called "relatives" of the university such as printers and apothecaries, the university's own academic jurisdiction for its members, identified as such by their entry in the register, and the right to have its own seal. Evidence of this is also most notably to be found in the statutory right, the right of amendment and the right to self-administration in the assemblies of the faculties and the whole university, that had already been laid down in the statutes in 1472.

Finally, the university's administration of its own assets, originally under the control of the rector, deserves a special mention. This duty had already been transferred to a treasurer in 1473, who was assigned a personal control instance in the form of the synod. When the autonomous administration of property was lost to the court treasury in 1676 as a result of financial problems attributed to the university, this was a distinct blow to the freedom of the seat of learning.

CAUGHT BETWEEN ACADEMIC FREEDOM AND OMNIPOTENT CONTROL

As much as this erosion of corporative rights was specific to the end of the 17th and especially the 18th century, this had been laid down in essence from the very outset, it being a foundation under public law. As a ducal foundation the university inevitably found itself caught between self-autonomy on the one hand and absolutist-like supervisory and regulatory wishes on the other. It was and remained under the supreme governance of the ruler and, as such, the freedom of the university was at risk.

The ruler insisted on the right to approve university statutes and to have a say in new appointments, among other things. Students and professors also had to swear an oath of allegiance. On the other hand however, the Wittelsbach rulers always made their own contribution to the prosperity and operational proficiency of the university.

One example of this is the foundation of a college in 1494, originally for eleven needy scholars of theology, by George the Rich, Duke of Bavaria. Named after its founder, the Georgianum is still affiliated to the university today. With regard to academic activities, the omnipotent patron took on the function of arbitrator for the university on repeated occasions. This was necessary for instance in the very first year of its foundation in connection with a philosophical dispute as whether to adopt the "via antiqua" or "via moderna," Realism or Nominalism. The controversy had actually led to a division within the "facultas artium" for some time. With the "nova ordinatio" of 1507, Albrecht IV tried to clarify precisely the correlation of both "routes."

The opinion of the ruler, in the person of the ducal advisor and chancellor under Duke William IV, Leonard von Eck, played a decisive role, not least of all during the institutional incorporation of new humanist disciplines.

CARTE BLANCHE FOR HUMANISM

The advancement of the "studia humanitatis" was considered a sign of the cultural open-mindedness of a university, which gladly expounded upon the rhetorical qualities of its humanists at public events. In Ingolstadt, the origins of a dedicated lecture reach back to 1477.

The important humanist Conrad Celtis (1459–1508) taught rhetoric and poetics in Ingolstadt. In 1487 he was awarded the title "poeta laureatus" by Emperor Frederick III.

The duke permitted the medic Erhard Windsberger to read "poetrej" in addition to holding his lectures on medicine. The actual recognition of humanist studies is linked to the names Conrad Celtis and Jakob Locher — who were both awarded the imperial "poeta laureatus" title.

Whereas Celtis only taught in Ingolstadt for a relatively brief period (1492–97), Locher worked at the Bavarian state university from 1498 through 1528. Both were particularly self-assured and zealous. Locher especially had hefty arguments with Gregor Zingel, who was known for his "barbaric" language and his outdated scholastic theological approach.

The altarpiece of 1572 in the Church of Our Lady in Ingolstadt by Hans Mielich (1516–1579) in the tradition of a Gothic triptych depicts the tension between science and religion on the reverse. The dispute between St. Catherine of Alexandria — the patron of the Faculty of Philosophy — and professors from the university can be seen on the three panels of the altarpiece. While Catherine represents faith in its purest form, the scholars argue in favor of science. It resulted in Catherine emerging victorious. This cannot be seen in the paintings, but that was intentional on the part of the person who commissioned the work. The triptych also conveys progress and tolerance. This is primarily shown in the fact that Catherine, as a woman, keeps the upper hand. According to legend, she converted no less than 50 philosophers in ancient times. The most important message of this work, however, is that the House of Wittelsbach, a member of which commissioned the piece, and the scholars are united in faith.

DECISION AGAINST THE REFORMATION

Admittedly, such controversies soon became obsolete and were overshadowed by the events of the Reformation. If the University of Ingolstadt distinguished itself as the antipode to Wittenberg University, then this was essentially due to the fact that Martin Luther's principal theological opponent, Johann Eck, taught in Ingolstadt.

Eck had recognized the explosive potential of Luther's teachings for the conventional order of the church at an early stage. He was therefore determined to plant his theological opponents firmly in the heretical camp during the Leipzig Debate of 1519. He wanted to ensure Luther's conviction at the court case that had already been opened in Rome. Not without personal ambition, Eck himself travelled to Rome in 1520, where he played a decisive role in drafting the papal bull "Exsurge Domini" threatening a ban. He subsequently went to lengths to have it published in Germany. Right up to his death, Eck — who incidentally recognized the shortcomings of the Old Church and wanted to redress these — actively fought against reformatory teaching in word and deed.

After the dukes of Bavaria had agreed on an unswerving counter-reformatory policy in the early 1520s in particular, the University of Ingolstadt developed into a bastion of the Old Church. For lecturers and those scholars who sympathized with the new teachings, this was to have grave consequences.

NEW THOUGHTS IN THE STRUGGLE AGAINST THE ESTABLISHED ORDER

The theologian Arsacius Seehofer and the medic and botanist Leonhart Fuchs, who became famous for his "New Herbal", had to leave Ingolstadt and went to Wittenberg and Tübingen respectively. The renowned historiographer Johannes Aventinus,

Luther's principal theological opponent, Johann Eck (1486–1543), taught theology at the "Hohe Schule" from 1510 onward. The University of Ingolstadt became a stronghold of the Counter-Reformation.

Leonhart Fuchs (1501–1566) is considered one of the fathers of botany. The fuchsia — which belongs to the Onagraceae family and comprises a large number of species — bears his name.

who had taught as a private tutor at the University of Ingolstadt in 1507, was temporarily imprisoned in 1528, after which time he retired to Regensburg. The path followed by the theologian Balthasar Hubmaier (1485–1528), who studied for his doctorate under Johann Eck, took an utterly different turn. He supported the views of the Anabaptists and was executed in Vienna in 1528.

Conversely, during the 16th century, Ingolstadt was often the place sought out by those who had left their native region for religious reasons. These included Robert Turner, in exile from England, who became regens of the Georgianum and rector of the university in 1584/85, as well as the professors Veit Amerbach, Rudolf Clenck, Martin Eisengrein, and Friedrich Staphylus, who had reverted to their old faith after briefly turning to the teachings of the Reformation.

They taught in the period following the death of Johann Eck (1543) — a time for the University of Ingolstadt that was marked by a number of signs that pointed to an ensuing crisis. First of all, the situation in general was difficult. The plague forced the *Hohe Schule* into exile in Kelheim, and Ingolstadt's dual role as a seat of learning and a garrison town also had a negative impact on the university. In 1546, during the course of the Schmalkaldic War, it was evacuated once again, and even 100 year later, it was still suffering from the effects of major political events when Ingolstadt was besieged by the Swedes in 1632 during the Thirty Years' War. More importantly, the existence of the faculty of theology was endangered from 1543 onward due to an acute shortage of teaching staff.

This was made all the more difficult since the dukes of Bavaria held steadfastly to Catholicism in their lands, and were reliant on a functioning and well-founded training for clergymen to consolidate the established faith. The university, as the "country's precious treasure," had to be led out of this crisis and equipped for a new role.

CATHOLIC REFORM:
THE JESUITS ARRIVE IN BAVARIA

Duke William IV went to great lengths to reform the Bavarian state university and the study of theology in particular. For this purpose, he negotiated with the Jesuit Order and instigated the delegation of several theologians to Ingolstadt.

With an instruction from the founder of the order, Ignatius of Loyola, in their pockets, the first three priest from the Society of Jesus, Petrus Canisius, Claudius Jajus, and Alfons Salmeron, arrived in Ingolstadt on November 13, 1549. Just three day later, on November 16, Canisius — the most important representative of the "Societas Jesu" during the initial period of its teaching in Ingolstadt — held his inaugural lecture. This act gained an epochal significance that extended far beyond that of the Bavarian state university, it being the first time at any university in Germany that professorships had been granted to Jesuits. Jesuit teaching in Ingolstadt actually marked the beginning of the Society of Jesus's development into an exceptional teaching order of the Counter-Reformation, a development that resulted in Jesuit professors teaching at 17 out of 18 Catholic universities in the Old Empire by 1648.

THE DEVELOPMENT OF THE
"SOCIETAS JESU" IN INGOLSTADT

The rise of the Jesuits in Ingolstadt was not without interruption. In 1552 they left the city as the erection of a college had been delayed. Following a marked drop in the number of students training for the priesthood, Duke Albrecht V hastily called them back with the assurance that a college would be built. For this, the Jesuits committed themselves to the provision of two honorary theology professors, one for dogmatic theory, the other for moral theology. This was to remain the situation until the order was dissolved in 1773, not taking the later esta-

Petrus Canisius (1521–1597) — one of three Jesuit priests summoned to Ingolstadt in 1549 by William IV, Duke of Bavaria (1493–1550). It was the first time that chairs at a German university were allocated to Jesuits.

ELECTIO.

Ad mensis Octobris diem XVIII, anni M.D.LXXXIX,
cunctis Senatorum suffragijs salutabar florentis.mæ
huius Academiæ Rector, Philippus, diuina proui-
dentia confirmatus Eps Ratisbon, Bauariæ Dux,
ingressus æt. annum XIV. Procurationem porò
causarum forensium Seren.mus meus parens, Princeps
Guilhelmus, certis de causis à me ac Dn. L.to Quirino
Leonino, Geldrio Ciuin Ratisbon, Cons. Theologo ac
præceptore nostro, in D.cem Steuartium Lesaium Prof.tum
Aplorum Coloniæ, professorem hic publicum, et
Parochum Mauritianum, transferri voluit.

Ab. Hic Philippus, Ser.mus Prin. et Rector Magnificen.mus eosdem off.i
& Pont. viri Card. S.R. E. ordinem cogitatis, discessit, ex dic
te magno totius Bauariæ mœrore, altera post Trinitatis, d.
5te Febr. Maij An. 1598.

RESIGNATIO.

Ab initio huius nri Rectoratus, Maximilianus
et Ferdinandus Comites pal. Rheni, vtriusq. Bauariæ
Duces, mei fratres dilectis. ac Christophorus Gustauus
Marchio Badensis, Ingolstadÿ per trienniy fecē
spacium, causa studiorum versabantur. VIII
vero Id. Febr. an. 1560. superuenit Ferdinandus
Ser.mi Archiducis Caroli Austriaci, Ducis Bur-
gundiæ, Styriæ, Carinthiæ, Carniolæ, auunculi
nri honorati princeps primogenitus. Similiter
insequentes albo Studiosorum nominatim accesserunt.
scrib. Phil. Ephus Ratisbon. Bauariæ Dux

According to the university constitution, the rector held the highest position in the university, being elected every six months and later annually. His election and assumption of office (eclectio) as well as his regnation (resignatio) belonged to the central academic rituals of the old university. In the matriculation register of the University of Ingolstadt from 1589–1613, the festive electio (on October 18, 1589) and the resignatio (at the end of the Michaelmas term 1589/1590) of the rector Philip William of Bavaria, aged just thirteen, is shown in the aula of the university in the presence of professors (in black robes) and noble students (in colored clothes). The miniatures by the painter Caspar Freisinger (1560–1599) of Ingolstadt are from around 1590.

In 1552 the Jesuits left Ingolstadt once again as the erection of a college had been delayed. Duke Albrecht V (1528 – 1579) hastily called them back in 1556. In 1585, the Jesuit college moved into new rooms, which Duke William V (1548–1626), not without reason called "the Pious," had had built for this purpose.

blishment of a professorship for scholasticism into account that was also given to the "Societas Jesu." Apart from the Jesuits, two other priests, who held the parishes of Liebfrauenkirche and St. Moritz, were always attached to the Faculty of Theology, one of whom acted as pro-chancellor.

TEACHING IN THE "FACULTAS ARTIUM" AND THE THEOLOGY FACULTY UNDER THE JESUITS

While the Jesuits only held a majority in the theology faculty, they could count the professorships in the "facultas artium" entirely their own. Since the 1520s, the number of students and doctoral candidates had been in continuous decline, to such an extent that is was bearly possible to recruit new academics from within their own ranks. This led to a shortage of lecturers until the Jesuits offered to provide a philosopher.

In 1561, the discipline of logic was then transferred from the duke to the "Societas Jesu"; in 1564, that of physics. In 1570, it was finally given a third chair, enabling it to hold a three-year course in its entirety, as laid down in the Order's constitution. For the "facultas artium," this dual approach of a Jesuit and secular philosophical course harbored the risk of the latter gradually being suppressed — something that, strongly criticized, actually happened. In 1585, the three remaining lay professors in the "facultas artium" were dismissed, and on January 27, 1588, the duke gave his formal confirmation to the "Societas Jesu" that "sy die patres allain und niemandts anders" — they and noone else were to appoint professors themselves "auf 'ewige Zeiten'" — for evermore. As a result, the "facultas artium" was finally integrated in the Jesuit course.

It just remains to mention that the Jesuits were also granted the chair of canon law in 1675 that came under the faculty of law — much to the annoyance incidentally of the lawyers in Ingolstadt.

STATE CONTROL AND DENOMINATIONAL COMMITMENT

The absolutist-like protection of the "Societas Jesu" was one major aspect in the use of the university for the purpose of reforming the Catholic church. The other was that it was placed under the control of the state more forcibly than before. The initial appointment of a superintendent by the ruler in 1560, basically speaking a ducal university inspector, can be seen as symptomatic. This office however did not become properly established, being revived in a modified form only in the 18th century with the university directorship.

Moreover, the fact that doctoral candidates and professors had to profess their faith by taking an oath to the Tridentine Mass in the course of a consolidated denominational divide in Ingolstadt as well as at other Catholic universities, was indicative of the absolutist-like policy. As a result, the mathematician and cartographer, Philipp Apian, for example, who had risen to fame on account of his map of Bavaria, was expelled from Ingolstadt for refusing to take the oath.

THE HEIGHT OF JESUIT TEACHING

Such measures and the dynamics of the Jesuit Order that unfurled through the interaction with the duke, were not just viewed positively within the university. The lawyers in particular and the medics, who had no choice but to take the Jesuit course for propaedeutic philosophy studies, fought — sometimes vehemently — against this.

Despite such early anti-Jesuit feeling, it should be acknowledged that, in many cases, excellent

The astronomer, mathematician, medic, and geographer Philipp Apian (1531–1589) was appointed professor at the University of Ingolstadt at the age of 21. However, he was later expelled for refusing to take an oath to the Tridentine Mass.

Even in the oldest statutes of the university, Duke Louis the Rich granted the rector of his "Hohe Schule" the right to use a staff of office. The old scepter no longer exists. The two scepters still extant — that of the "facultas artium" and that of the three Faculties of Theology, Medicine, and Jurisprudence, date from the mid 17th century. The upper part of the "facultas artium" scepter comprises a baldachin supported by four ornamentalized columns, under which St. Catherine of Alexandria, the patron of the faculty, and a scholar knee before the Virgin and Child. The scepter dates from 1642 and was made by the goldsmith Michael Freytag of Ingolstadt, as was the scepter of the three Faculties of Theology, Medicine, and Jurisprudence. The patrons of the faculties, the Evangelists Luke (theology) and John (medicine), and St. Ivo of Kermartin (jurisprudence) are depicted under the baldachin of this scepter that is supported on six columns. This picture shows the dean of the Faculty of Social Sciences, Professor Hans-Bernd Brosius, and the beadle, Helmut Stepper, who is carrying the the "facultas artium" scepter (2004).

Together with Johann Baptist Cysat (1585–1657) the astronomer Christoph Scheiner (1573/75–1650) discovered the sunspots, and is the only natural scientist from the University of Ingolstadt to have earned himself a place in the annals of European science.

scholars were delegated by the Jesuit Order to the University of Ingolstadt. The university could count two of the most important Catholic theologians of the 16th century among its teaching staff: Gregor de Valencia from Castile who belonged to the theology faculty from 1575 through 1592, and Jakob Gretser (1562–1625). From 1588 onward, Gretser lectured in Ingolstadt over a period of several decades and also made a name for himself as a philologist, historian, and playwright.

Another no less important representative of the late Jesuit scholastic period at the end of the 17th century, Adam Tanner (1572–1632) is worthy of mention. He came to notice through his sceptical verdict on witchcraft trials. Christoph Scheiner rose to fame through his trailblazing work in the field of optics, and together with Johann Baptist Cysat, was the first to discover sunspots in 1611 while in Ingolstadt, earning him a place in the annals of European science as the only natural scientist from the university.

The Faculty of Law at Ingolstadt gained international repute. It had survived the crisis in the 16th century unscathed and did not limit its activities solely to lectures and disputations. It's opinion was frequently sought by other courts and opposing parties in complex legal cases.

This reputation was consciously cultivated by the Bavarian dukes through their adoption of a dedicated — and costly — appointments policy. Distinguished law teachers from Italy and the Catholic region of the Netherlands followed the summons to Ingolstadt. In the 16th century, these were the civil law specialists Romuleus from Florence and Ossanaeus from Herzogenbusch; in 1587 Andreas Fachinäus from Italy was summoned — also a civil law specialist — as was Hubert Giphanius (1534–1604), who followed in 1590. The Everhards, a dynasty of Dutch professors, taught in Ingolstadt for many generations.

The botanical garden in Ingolstadt. In the background is the anatomy theater of the Faculty of Medicine, built between 1723 and 1736.

These were joined by leading academics from German-speaking countries who contributed to strengthening the sound reputation of the law faculty in Ingolstadt: The constitutional law specialist Christoph Besold (1577–1638), at Ingolstadt from 1638; Kaspar Manz, who was summoned at almost the same time; and later Christoph von Chlingensperg, who became respected for his extensive work as an expert is the field of law history.

FOUNDATION STONE FOR ANATOMY — MODERN IMPULSES IN MEDICINE

The situation in the Faculty of Medicine at Ingolstadt was less illustrious. The Faculty, which traditionally held health regulatory rights — the Apothecary Order of 1646 being created with its cooperation — suffered particularly in the turmoil of the Thirty Years' War. In the first half of the 17th

31

century, it was attended at times by less than ten students. The fact that the Faculty did not have its own medical building certainly also played a role. This and the utterly inadequate equipment did not make studying medicine at Ingolstadt particularly attractive.

Tuition under Franz Ignaz Thiermair (1626–1680), who was appointed in 1661 to carry out anatomical demonstations, intimated an improvement to the situation. After demands that went on for decades for improvements to teaching facilities, the foundation stone for a medical building with an anatomy theater was finally laid in 1723.

THE EARLY ENLIGHTENMENT PHASE

A complete change for the better came in the 1750s, when Johann Anton von Wolter, personal physician to the elector, was commissioned to reform the Faculty of Medicine — a task that he then tackled with great verve. First of all, Wolter composed a damning report on the Ingolstadt medics. The professors did not fufill their teaching duties sufficiently; moreover, they lectured from out-dated textbooks and neglected practicals. In short, doctors of medicine from Ingolstadt were murderers let loose on humanity.

Wolter immediately introduced a strict program of study that placed greater importance on practical medicine and pharmacology. In addition, he made sure that the financial basis was improved so that new medical instruments could be bought and the botanical garden and anatomy department could be expanded. As a result, Ingolstadt caught up with the standard of medical tuition considered modern at that time.

The transition from teaching from a lecturn to teaching by doing was just one sign of the shift to empirical science based on experiment and pre-

cise observation. The growing importance of natural science and experimental subjects in the Age of the Enlightenment and the interest of the state in their beneficial application generally confronted universities with an enormous challenge. On top of this, no small competitor was emerging in the form of research-oriented academies such as the Bayerische Akademie der Wissenschaften (Bavarian Academy of Sciences and Humanities), founded in 1759.

As such, for the Univesity of Ingolstadt, the 18th century was principally a period of greater control of the state in which curricula were modernized, and one which largely weighed on the Jesuit Order. In both respects, 1746 constituted a striking turning point. At that time Maximilian III Joseph, Elector of Bavaria, appointed Johann Adam von Ickstatt director of the university to turn the Ingolstadt Alma mater into an institution "of blossoming and standing."

Icksatt was one of the supporting pillars in the educational policy of Bavaria until his death in 1776. He studied in Marburg, among other places, under Christian Wolff, the leading proponent of the early Enlightenment in Germany. As law professor at the University of Würzburg, he gained prominence through his teaching of "jus publicum" — nowadays called public law. That was the discipline par excellence of modern universities in the Old Empire that were opening to the Enlightenment, as it aimed at overhauling the law of the land and the legal history of the empire.

Whoever was to deal later with state affairs in a legal capacity should be informed of the legal status and tradition of the empire and its territories. Based on the example of Protestant universities, this was first implemented in Catholic southern Germany at the University of Würzburg — through the appointment of Ickstatt. When he

Johann Anton von Wolter (1711–1789) radically reformed the Faculty of Medicine. He succeeded in bringing medical tuition up the modern standard of that time.

Johann Adam von Ickstatt (1702–1776), director of the university, turned it once more into an institution "of blossoming and standing."

was summoned to Ingolstadt by the Elector of Bavaria, this was an act of programmatic significance. This move was an expression of the decisiveness to open up the traditional Bavarian state university to modern movements.

Ickstatt certainly did not have an easy position in Ingolstadt, especially in the face of opposition from the Jesuits. He therefore chose to exclude those faculties dominated by the Jesuits during his reform process, contenting himself with a reorganization of the law faculty.

THE REFORMER'S SUCCESS AND THE DISSOLUTION OF THE JESUIT ORDER

Conflicts, such as the use of Protestant textbooks, did not fail to appear, but Ickstatt managed to assert himself in the face of his oponents with the elector's support. He not only succeeded in establishing new jurisprudence in the curriculum, but also in communicating the fundamentals of modern law to a wide circle of students in smaller private societies. In this light, it can be rightly considered that his work in Ingolstadt sent out

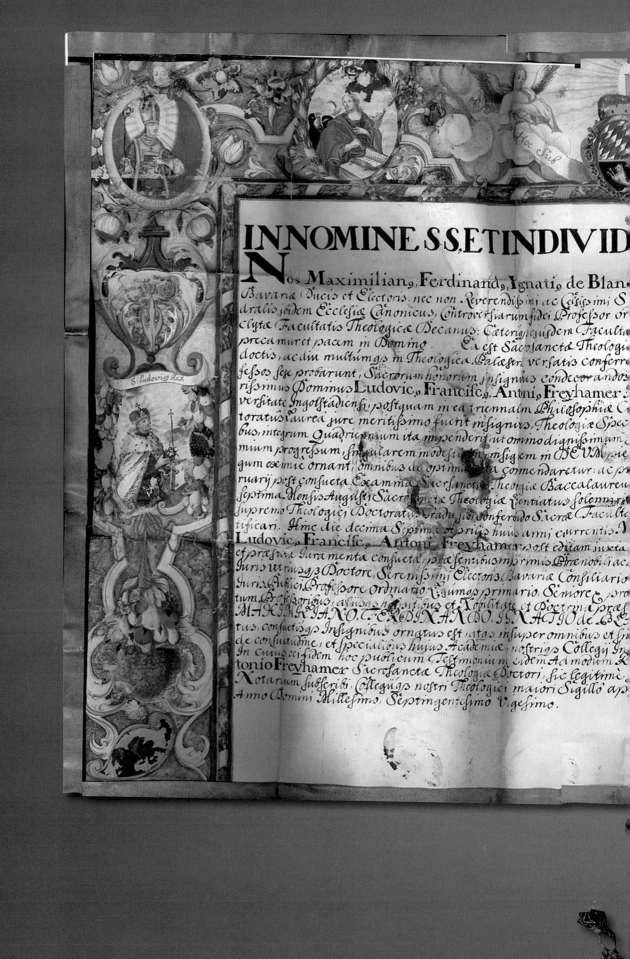

INNOMINE S.S. ET INDIVID

Nos Maximilian, Ferdinand, Ignati, de Blan
Bavariæ Ducis et Electoris: nec non Reverendiss.imi ac Celsiss.imi S
dralis ibidem Ecclesiæ Canonicus, Controversiarum fidei Professor or
Clytæ Facultatis Theologicæ Decanus: Cæteriqꝫ eiusdem Faculta
precamur et pacem in Domino. Ea est Sacrosanctæ Theologi
doctis, ac diu multumqꝫ in Theologica Palæstrᵃ versatis conferre
fessos sese probarunt, Sacrorum honorum insigniis condecorandos
rissimus Dominus Ludovic, Francisc, Antoni, Freyhamer
versitate Ingolstadiensi, postquam in ea triennalm Philosophiæ
toratus laureâ iure meritissimo fuerit insignitus, Theologiæ Spec
bus, integrum Quadriennium ita impenderit, ut omnino dignissimum
mium progressum, singularem modestiam insigem in DEum pie
qum eximie ornant, omnibus de optima ita commendaretur: ac pr
ruarij post consueta Examina Sacrosanctæ Theologiæ Baccalaureu
septima Mensis Augusti Sacrosanctæ Theologiæ Licentiatus solemni ri
supremo Theologiæ Doctoratus gradu sibi conferendo Sacræ Faculta
tificari. Hinc die decima Septima Aprilis huius anni currentis M
Ludovic, Francisc, Antoni, Freyhamer, post editam iuxta
et præfata Juramenta consueta, præsentibus imprimis Prænobili ac
Juris Utriusqꝫ Doctore, Serenissimi Electoris Bavariæ Consiliario
Juris Publici Professore Ordinario Linguamqꝫ primario, Seniore et pro
tum Professoribus, aliisqꝫ hᵒ.entibus et Nobilitate et Doctrina præ
MAXIMILIANO, FERDINANDO, IGNATIO de B
tus, consuetisqꝫ Insignibus ornatus est, atqꝫ insuper omnibus et si
de consuetudine, et specialibus huius Academiæ nostriqꝫ Collegij In
In cuius ei fidem hoc publicum Testimonium, eadem Ad modum R
tonio Freyhamer Sacrosanctæ Theologiæ Doctori, sic legitime
Notarium subscribi, Collegiusqꝫ nostri Theologici maiori Sigillo ap
Anno Domini Millesimo, Septingentesimo Vigesimo.

TRINITATIS, AMEN

...ofanctæ Theologiæ Doctor, Sereniffimi Utriufqs
...icipis et Epifcopi, Eyftettenfis Confiliarius Ecclefiafticus, Cathe...
...d Divam Virginem Speciofam hic Parochus, et pro tempore in...
...us et Profeffores omnibus præfentes litteras infpecturis Salutem
...tia et auctoritas, ut Facultatis fuæ Litterarios Gradus non nifi
...foleat. Econtra vero ad eos, qui in hoc ftadio impigres ac inde...
...fima eft. Quare cum Admodum Reverendus Nobilis ac Cla...
...gis, pro tempore Parochus Moerenghemij, in hac Electorali Uni...
...ta cum laude et fructu abfolvit, ut fupremi Philofophici Doc...
...tusqs Annexis Prælectionibus publicis et privatis Exercitationi...
...irit, qui ob præftans ingenium, conftantiffimam diligentiam,exi...
...ctam erga Majores Obfervantiam, aliasqs virtutes, quæ Theolo...
...ntiam pro meritis fuis Anno MDCCV, die undecima Menfis Feb...
...icus quam formatus: Jum vero Anno MDCCVI. die decima
...nfigni commendatione nunciatus fuerit. nunc autem cum pro
...caverit, non potuit ifta votis eius tam juftis non libentiffime gra...
...i præfatus Admodum Reverendus Nobilis ac Clariffimus Dominus
...onem CXXIV Pontificis Maximi, ... Catholicæ profeffionem
...o Viro, Domino **CHRISTOPHORO de CHINGENSPERG**
...ma Electorali et Catholica Univerfitate Ingolftadiana Codicis ac
...Rectore Magnifico, ceterisqs tum noftræ tam aliarum Faculta...
...is, à dicto Adm. Reverendo, Prænobili et Excellentiffimo Domino
...aerofanctæ Theologiæ Doctor, Solenni situ creatus, conftitu...
...ivilegiis, immunitatibus, ac Prærogativis, quæ vel de jure, vel
...petunt, aut quovis modo competere poffunt, donatus.
...Nobili, et Excellentiffimo Domino **Ludovico Francifco. An**
...gs creatode mire clari, pqs per juratum Univerfitatis huius
...mm uniri fecimis. Ingolftadij die decima feptima Aprilis

Joannes Georgius Agricola
Notarius Univerfitatis
Ingolftadienfis fubfcripfit

In 1594, Archduke Ferdinand of Austria (1578–1637) sent the famous "Golden Ship" — a magnificent cup of gold-plated silver — to his Alma mater as a token of his gratitude. The archduke, who was a fellow student of the later elector of Bavaria, Maximilian I, became Ferdinand II, Emperor of the Holy Roman Empire of the German Nation in 1619.
Not least of all due to the Jesuit education he had received in Ingolstadt, he was an ardent advocate of the Counter-Reformation.

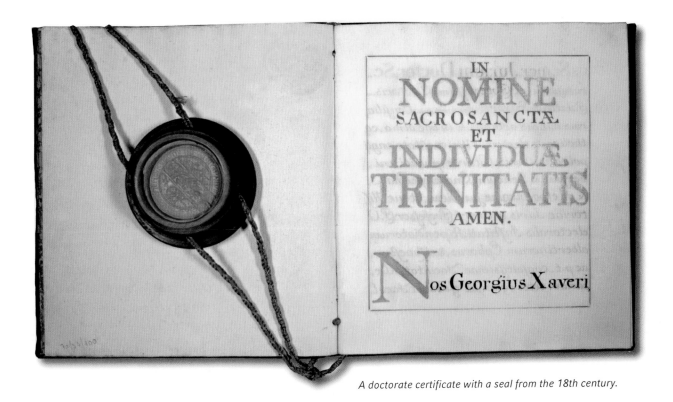

IN
NOMINE
SACROSANCTÆ
ET
INDIVIDUÆ
TRINITATIS
AMEN.

Nos Georgius Xaveri

A doctorate certificate with a seal from the 18th century.

impulses for the establishment of an efficient civil service that, two generations later, would be able to implement the reforms under Montgelas.

While first signs of the reform came to fruition in the Faculties of Law and Medicine in the 1740s and '50s, this was not the case in the Faculties of Philosophy and Theology until the '70s. The prerequisite for this was the abolition of the "Societas Jesu" through the papal brief "Dominus ac redemptor noster" of July 21, 1773, that opened up the way for reform.

In virtually all Catholic states, the Jesuit Order had long since been the target of hefty criticism. Generally speaking, a religious elite of the standing of the Jesuit Order might have appeared more dispensable with denominational differences becoming less pronounced in the 18th century than before. Most notably however, it was the dominant presence and autonomy of the "Societas Jesu" in the field of education that was found to be more and more of a hindrance by representatives of state educational reform policies.

The theology-based teaching under the Jesuits, that essentially still centered around the "ratio studorum" of 1599, was also considered increasingly outdated. It corresponded less and less with the utilitarian educational concept of the Enlightenment, at the center of which was the teaching of practical skills. For the state educational plan-

COLLEGIVM·STVDII·INGOLSTADIE·M·D·XXVII

GEORGIVS·IESSINGER·LL·DOCTOR·M·D·XXVI

COLLEGIVM·MEDICORVM·M·D·XXVII

ners, the dissolution of the Order came as a satisfying and liberating act.

"If ever there were an occasion for remedial changes and improvements to be introduced, then it is certainly this one, as — through the abolition of the Society with tutors in various sciences — a great revolution is taking place anyway." The academic reform was then tackled without delay. Based on a number of expertises, the *churfürstlich-Baierische hoher und niederer schulenordnung* (Bavarian electoral higher and lower school charter) of October 4, 1773, under Ickstatt's direction, was drafted.

TRENDS IN THEOLOGY AND PHILOSOPHY DURING THE ENLIGHTENMENT

Clearly intended to streamline the organization of the teaching system as a whole and strengthen the state's right of supervision in the field of education, the new study regulations placed particular emphasis on practice-oriented disciplines, as had been expected. In the Faculty of Theology, of theoretical, speculative subjects such as dogmatic theology were consequently cut. In its place, pastoral theology was introduced; a subject that

opposite page:
Glass roundels depicting coats of art of the "facultas artium" (bottom left), the university (top), the Faculty of Medicine (bottom right), and of Dr. Georg Tessinger (bottom center), from the workshop of Hans Wertinger, 1526/27.

played an important role in theological teaching in the Enlightenment as it served to intensify the degree of spiritual guidance. At the same time, from that moment onward oriental Biblical languages were to be given a permanent place in the study of theology that was shortened from four to three years, since it was regarded a prerequisite for an historically critical exegesis. In this connection, the subject History of Christianity also gained greater importance.

In the Faculty of Philosophy, it was mostly the math and natural science disciplines that were upgraded. In the other two faculties there were few changes due to the fact that these had already been reformed from 1773 onward. It is nevertheless interesting to note that so-called *maieutics* gained greater significance among medics. The creation of a professorship for "epizootic treatment" in 1777 marked the beginnings of vetinary medicine in Ingolstadt. From 1780, lectures in cameralism and economics were held.

SQUABBLES FILLING POSITIONS AND THE ORDER OF MALTA SCANDAL OF 1781

Ultimately the curricula reform also brought about a staff reshuffle. Ten of a total of twenty professorships with chairs had to be re-allocated. It soon became evident that Jesuits, who had been much rebuked before the Order was abolished, could not be dispensed with in one fell swoop after all. In addition to lay priests and members of other orders, they had to fall back on a not inconsiderable number of ex-Jesuits to fill chairs in the Faculties of Philosophy and Theology.

This co-existence of former Jesuits, under the leadership of the pugnacious dogmatic theologian Benedikt Stattler (1728–1797), and opponents of the Jesuits turned out to be a heavy burden for the teaching program. Feuds between professors were any everyday occurence until the problem solved itself as a result of a first-rate scandal related to educational policy in 1781.

After Maximilian III Joseph, Elector of Bavaria, declared that the assets of the defunct Jesuit Order should be used for teaching and cultural affairs, the elector Karl Theodor claimed the Jesuit funds to remunerate a Bavarian branch of the Order of Malta. This new foundation however was nothing less than an establishment to care for the illegitimate children and favorites of the aging elector. This re-allocation of Jesuit funds obviously left a gaping hole in the education budget. The prelate orders in Bavaria — Benedictine and Cistercian monks, Augustinian canons, and Premonstratensians — were saddled with having to stop this gap, and in return were charged with filling the chairs that, up to that time, had been paid for out of Jesuit funds. This led to the second major personnel shake-up after 1773, to which all ex-Jesuits fell victim.

At the same time however a similar situation was reached to the one before 1773, that had been so bitterly criticized. Parts of the university found themselves once again under the direction of a religious order. The teaching program though was no longer subject to an order's own study regulations but to a state curriculum. Moreover, with the university custos, the prelates were confronted with an effective state control mechanism. This constellation remained in force until 1799, and it must be said that the prelate orders always went to great lengths throughout this whole period to dispatch capable scholars to Ingolstadt. The theologian Stephan Wiest from Aldersbach, the cameralist Benedikt Holzinger from Raitenhaslach Monastery, the philologian Sebastian Seemiller from Polling, and the natural scientist Coelestin Steiglehner from the imperial St. Emmeram's Abbey are late representatives of the monastic culture in Old Bavaria.

The professor of canon law Adam Weishaupt (1748–1830) founded the radically progressive secret society of the Illuminati in Ingolstadt in 1776.

THE RISE OF A SECRET SOCIETY: THE BRIEF CAREER OF THE ILLUMINATI

In connection with the 1880s and '90s discussed above, one other organization has to be mentioned that caused a furor well beyond the borders of Bavaria. This was the radical, Enlightenment-era secret society of the Illuminati, founded by Adam Weishaupt, professor of canon law in 1776 in Ingolstadt. It combined moral rigorism with a strong political drive in equal measures. The Illuminati, who developed out of a sophisticated educational and supervisory system were to form a moral and intellectual elite, which — in modern terms — was to march through the institutions, i.e. they were to secure key positions in governmental administration and gradually render the authority of princely rulers dispensable.

Within the political landscape of the ancien régime, this was of course a concept of enormous explosive force that had a not inconsiderable appeal for young intellectuals. To begin with, the Bavarian Illuminati were particularly successful in infiltrating government bodies. However, the demise of the secret society came about after just a few years.

After it had come to a hypertrophic expansion into areas of northern and central Germany largely as a result of the activities of Baron Adolph von Knigge (1752–1796), the society of the Illuminati was uncovered in the middle of the 1780s. Weishaupt hastily abandoned his chair in Ingolstadt in February 1785 and subsequently several Illuminati at the university were dismissed or relegated.

The secret society was considered disbanded, at least in Bavaria. Despite this, the unreal fear of an Illuminati conspiracy flared up once more against the background of the French Revolution in the 1790s. At the University of Ingolstadt, all professors had to swear loyalty to the state by taking the so-called Illuminati oath. Student surveillance was increased under the cloak of persecuting the Illuminati, and even professors who were sympathizers of the Enlightenment were eliminated.

ADDITIONAL STRENGTHENING OF THE POSITION OF THE STATE DURING THE MONTGELAS ERA

Only after the change of government in 1799, which rang in the Montgelas era, did a new wind blow in Ingolstadt. The change of direction became immediately apparent in the personnel policy. Maximilian von Montgelas (1759–1838), the leading minister of the new elector Max IV Joseph, based his policy on

The rich plastered ceiling in the Illuminati room in Ingolstadt, gave meetings of the secret society a festive framework. It was originally in the building behind Theresienstrasse 23. The ceiling is now located in the former "Hohe Schule" in Goldknopfgasse 7.

the primacy of the state over the church. In doing so, he tried to oust the excessively religious among the prelate orders from their chairs and replace them with professors who really were or pretended to be allied with the Enlightenment.

Apart from former Illuminati such as Joseph Socher and Josef Milbiller, the so-called "three-leaf clover of Dillingen" — Johann Michael Sailer, Patriz Benedikt Zimmer, and Josef Weber — arrived in Ingol-

A letter from the elector Max IV Joseph to the Dominicans in Landshut, in which he ordered that the university be housed in rooms in the monastery. Officially, the move was justified by the acute military threat to Ingolstadt in the course of the Napoleonic Wars.

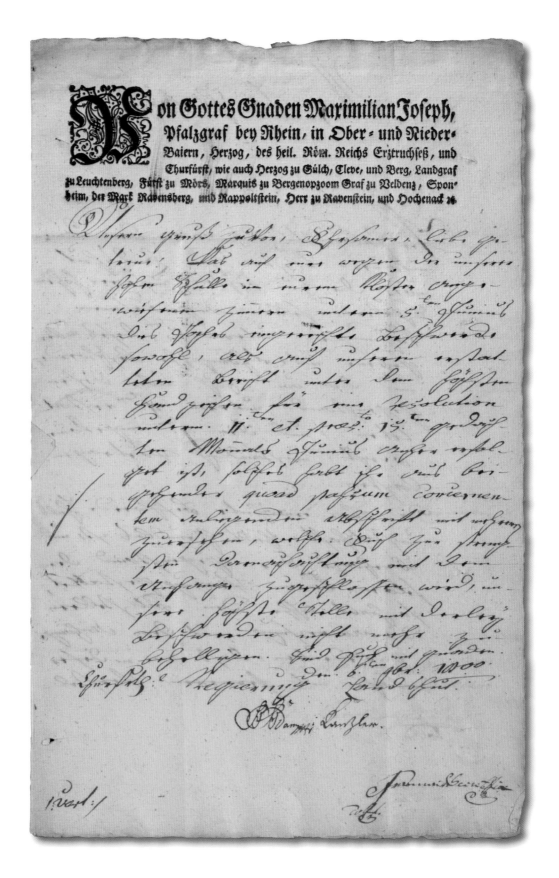

The so-called "three-leaf clover of Dillingen," comprising Johann Michael Sailer (1751–1832), Patriz Benedikt Zimmer (1752–1820) and Josef Weber (1723–1831), was supposed to introduce the Enlightenment into the university during the Montgelas era. However the path adopted by the three from Dillingen was different to that expected by the government.

stadt as a result. Turning their backs on the rationalistic utilitarian mentality of the Enlightenment, the path subsequently adopted by the three from Dillingen was certainly different than that expected by the government. The seeds for a conflict between "Enlightenment" and "Romanticism" that surfaced during the period Ludwig-Maximilians-Universität was in Landshut, had therefore already been sown.

PLANS TO MOVE TO LANDSHUT — THE END OF THE INGOLSTADT EPOCH

As such, the topic of moving the University of Ingolstadt to Landshut, as ordered in the rescript of May 17, 1800, and much discussed in the course of the 18th century, has just been addressed. It was officially justified by the acute military threat of being in the garrison town of Ingolstadt during the Napoleonic Wars.

It cannot however be overseen that this was a welcome opportunity for a considerable number of professors to turn their backs on Ingolstadt. All too

The minister Count Maximilian von Montgelas was one of the advocates of a central university in Munich.
Oil painting by Joseph Haubner, 1804.

often complaints had been raised due to the co-existence of garrison and university and the consequent tension between students and soldiers, not to mention the town's unwillingness to accept the needs of the university. Georg Friedrich von Zentner, one of Montgelas's leading members of staff, summed it up concisely: "In effect, everything speaks against Ingolstadt and nothing for it."

FAR-REACHING ACT
FOR THE HISTORY OF INGOLSTADT

The relocation of the university was a heavy blow for Ingolstadt as it lost its status as a university town. This has remained alive in the collective historical memory, demonstrated not least of all by the attempt to latch onto the university tradition with the opening of the economic science faculty of the University of Eichstätt in Ingolstadt in 1989.

While the year 1800 marked a turning point in the town's history, this had very little effect on the university itself. Efforts to reform the university undertaken during the final decades of the 18th century were of decisive importance with regard to its organizational structure and course legislation — and even more so during the changes introduced in the Landshut era that broke the bounds of a conventional university constitution.

The old university building in Ingolstadt as it would have been around 1571. The picture is taken from a book by Karl Emil Schafhaeutl from between 1855 and 1856 that depicts the "topical history of the University of Ingolstadt in floor plans, perspectives of buildings which belonged to the university or which were closely or distantly associated with it [...]."

Vue perspective de la ville de Landshut, de l'épanchoir et du pont à arche de 160 pieds d'ouverture. Cet épanchoir à été e...

Landshut 1800–1826

FROM THE ENLIGHTENMENT
TO THE ROMANTIC ERA

RAINER A. MÜLLER

1810 dans la rivière Isar, d'après le projet et sous la direction de Mr. Wiebeking. Le pont à arche est projeté et sera exécuté par le même

The new name that the prince-elector Maximilian IV Joseph gave the oldest Bavarian state university in 1802 was a symbolic expression for the end of the university's Ingolstadt epoch and its new beginnings in Landshut. It underlined both the continuity of its history as well as the move into the modern world associated with its new location on the Isar.

Ludovico Maximilianea was how the *Hohe Schule* was to be known from that time onward. This was not only to honor its founder, Louis the Rich, Duke of Bavaria (1417–1479), who resided in Landshut and later found his final resting place there in Seligenthal Abbey, but also its greatest benefactor and reformer, the later King Maximilian I Joseph (1756–1825). While still prince-elector he gave out a decree on November 25, 1799, that the university be moved from the threatened garrison town and, subsequently, supported the relocation energetically.

LANDSHUT BECOMES A UNIVERSITY TOWN

When Ingolstadt was besieged by the French army in 1800 and the Senate and "Translocation Committee" decided to evacuate the university — rather more hastily than after careful planning — the enlightened, anti-clerical, centralistically focused circle of reformers in Munich were given an opportunity that could not have been more fitting. The university was to be saved from the hands of its foes — and, while some may well have been thinking first and foremost of the waring enemy camped outside the town gates, others however will have had their minds set much more on breaking up the conservative, ex-Jesuit circle of academics, for whom Ingolstadt was still very much a bastion.

King Maximilian I Joseph (1756–1825). At the time the university was moved from Ingolstadt to Landshut, while still prince-elector, he gave the "Hohe Schule" the name it still bears today: Ludovico Maximilianea.
Lithograph after a painting by Karl Joseph Stieler from 1814.

opposite page
"Landshut from the west"
Etching from 1822 by Heinrich Adam (1787–1862).

previous double page
According to its inscription, this panorama of Landshut comes from a treatise on the erection of a huge weir, drafted by the architect and water engineer Carl Friedrich von Wiebeking (1762–1842), the planning and construction of which was carried out near Landshut under his supervision.

Maximilian Joseph
Pfalzgraf bei Rhein, in Ober- und Niederbaiern Herzog
des heil. röm. Reichs Erztruchseß und Churfürst.

Wir wollen den von Unserer Universität zu Landshut am 12.ten vorg: M: geführten Antrag genehmigen,
und hiernach diese hohe Schule von nun an Ludwigs-
Maximilians-Universität nennen lassen. Zugleich
bestättigen Wir ihren bisherigen Wohnsitz in
Unserer Hauptstadt Landshut hiemit für immer, und
erklären unwiderruflich, daß Wir sie für ihr Wohl das
nach reifer Rücksicht in jeder Hinsicht ununter-
brochen wachen werden.

Was das Fiskollationsrecht der hohen Schule in
obgenanntem Landshut betrifft, worauf in zwei
Berichten vom 21.ten dießes angetragen wird: so finden
Wir, daß solches schicklicher dann gesichert werden,
wenn alle Attribute derselben in ihrer Vollkom-
menheit auf den Staat hergestellt sehen werden,
der der Hauptzweck dieser Lehranstalt, und
Unserer höchsten Absicht erfordert. Einzig dahin
muß also die ganze Aufmerksamkeit des
akademischen Senats und der Hand-Deputation
vor allem gerichtet, und dazu alles Geld für
dieselben verwendet werden.

Aus diesen und anderen Uns bekannten
bewegenden Gründen finden Wir daher den
gegenwärtigen Zeitpunkt für die Restaura-

27 Mai 1802

München, den 27.ten Mai 1802.

Max Jos. Churfürst

The name Ludwig-Maximilians-Universität was given in honor of its founder, Louis the Rich, Duke of Bavaria (1417–1479) and its major benefactor, the later King Maximilian I Joseph (1756–1825). In this charter of May 27, 1802, the prince-elector sanctions the new name.

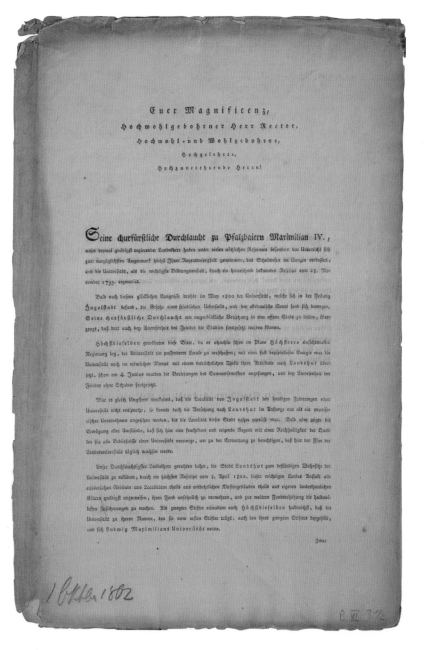

Translocation announcement of 1802: "Soon after this fortunate event, the university, located in the stronghold Ingolstadt, came under threat of an enemy attack in May 1800, and the academic Senate felt compelled to ask his electoral highness for its instant removal to an open town...." Due to impending danger from Napoleonic forces, the university was transferred to Landshut.

The move from Ingolstadt to Landshut, that was beset by obstacles and problems, took place between 1800 and 1804. Landshut had actually won the race to become the seat of the university against an equally determined Straubing — a contest whose outcome was decided by decree on April 8, 1802. From June 4 through 7 that year, the "inaugural festivities" were held, during which honorary doctorates were awarded to the well known philosopher Friedrich Wilhelm Joseph Schelling (1775–1854) and the no less famous educational reformer Cajetan Weiller (1762–1826). These tributes were made in full awareness and in line with the programmatically inspired motto used during the Enlightenment *Fiat Lux* ("let there be light"), under which the celebrations had been held.

Landshut was home to the university for only a short while, until 1826, but during this brief quarter century it gained considerably in profile and appeal. While around about, one major university after another was teetering on the brink with — in Bavaria alone — those in Altdorf, Aschaffenburg, Bamberg, Dillingen, and Salzburg either closing their doors completely or being degraded to lyceums, Ludovico Maximilianea survived the turbulence of the Napoleonic Wars together with the universities in Würzburg and Erlangen. And not only that: With its reformatory concepts it succeeded in setting new academic and sociopolitical accents in a "new Bavaria."

It was not Humboldt and the reformatory plans he initiated at Prussian universities that acted as a model, but France, whose university system exerted an increasing influence on the teaching and research structure that was still embroiled in its own strong — Jesuit — tradition.

The philosopher Friedrich Wilhelm Joseph Schelling (1775–1854) was awarded an honorary doctorate in 1802 during the inaugural celebrations of Ludovico Maximilianea in Landshut.
Pastel drawing by Christian Friedrich Tieck, c. 1801/02.

STEPS TOWARD THE ORDERLY PROVISION OF ACCOMMODATION

The decision to release the Alma mater from "its iron cage" (Ingolstadt) and to set it in such a "delightful idyll on the Isar" (Landshut), as it was described during the inaugural celebrations in 1802, gave rise to the acute question of accommodating and equipping the future university. Bearing the lack of money and time in mind, this might have presented a serious problem, but in fact it was one that could well be solved as the secularization of church and monasterial property

— that had been thoroughly planned and was simply waiting to be put into effect — was just around the corner.

Initially in provisional quarters, the university found its first permanent home in the Dominican monastery dissolved during the secularization. As a result of this change of use, lectures were resumed on June 9, 1802. "This is where Wisdom is erecting a temple to itself under the auspices of Maximilian. This monastical building will be transformed into a nursery in which the future servants of the church and the state will be educated and blessed with all the knowledge to be had that their professions have ever demanded," the rector of the university, Georg Alois Dietl, expressed optimistically in his inaugural speech in 1802 in the university church. At the same time, he euphorically praised the advance of scholarship, which he believed to be founded on the harmony of reason and revelation.

Following secularization in 1803, that provided the university with funds of 10,000 guilders a year from the property of former Seligenthal Abbey and the Convent of St. Cross, thoughts could reasonably be turned to expanding and optimizing the buildings, with the auditorium of the old Jesuit college being incorporated into the university complex. Larger tracts of the Franciscan monastery were added, and from then on used as an anatomy theater and chemistry laboratories, among other purposes. The Georgianum found a home in the Convent of St. Cross, while medicine and surgery were housed in the hospital. A wing of Trausnitz Castle above the town served as an observatory; the *Kapuzinergraben* as a riding track.

The rather imprecise legal status of the university as a corporation, foundation, and state-run institution as well as its complex financing from a

Trausnitz Castle above Landshut was home to the university observatory.

combination of interest on capital, rent, and income from real estate and state funds, that always brought difficulties with it, led almost automatically to an increase in the influence of the state. This development seemed virtually inevitable considering the massive social upheaval and humongous financial transactions carried out by the public authorities.

ACUTE PROBLEM WITH NO CONVINCING SOLUTION: THE FINANCIAL MISERY

On top of this, the university's continuously growing budgetary deficit was a trump card in the hands of the authorities who knew only too well when to play it.

In 1813/14, for example, salaries at Ludovico Maximilianea ran to around 46,000 guilders, with professors earning between 500 and 2,500 guilders, depending on the faculty and years of service. Return on investment from liquid university assets, however, amounted to 40,000 guilders for the same period. If material costs of around 15,000 guilders are included in this calculation, the deficit approached an estimated 20,000 guilders. Several years later, in the fiscal period 1820/21, this figure had almost trebled to around 55,000 guilders.

Das Universitätsgebäude in Landshut.

Landshut bei Ant. Weber.

The Dominican monastery, dissolved in 1802, provided space for the university in Landshut: "This monastical building will be transformed into a nursery in which the future servants of the church and the state will be educated and blessed with all the knowledge to be had that their profession have ever demanded," the rector of the university, Georg Alois Dietl, announced in his speech at the university's inauguration.

Only for a brief period in Landshut: Paul Johann Anselm Ritter von Feuerbach (1775–1833), the founder of modern criminal law and father of the modern Bavarian penal code of 1813. He later adopted the role of legal guardian and sponsor to the foundling Kaspar Hauser.
Steel engraving by Johann Leonhard Raab after a work by J. Kreul, c. 1830.

The university was on the verge of financial ruin and all proposals aimed at offsetting the deficit, even the further appropriation of ecclesiastical funds or the closure of other universities in Bavaria, were carefully examined.

While the right of the university to manage its own finances had been removed in 1806, by 1815 the old administrative rights *(Verwaltungsausschuss)* had, to a large extent, been restored once again. A solution to the financial problem that could be considered even remotely satisfactory to both the state and the university was, however, never reached in the time Ludovico Maximilianea was in Landshut.

INTELLECTUAL FIGURES AND ACADEMIC IMPULSES DURING THE LANDSHUT EPOCH

During Ludovico Maximilianea's Landshut period the academic staff comprised 73 professors in total: 22 philosophers, 10 theologians, 17 medics, 17 lawyers, and 7 cameralists. Looking at their social backgrounds, the sons of academics and clerks held sway in the faculties of jurisprudence and medicine, whereas it was largely the offspring of craftspeople and farmers in the faculties of philosophy and theology (40 to 50 percent). This contemporary trend could also be seen elsewhere.

Some of the chairs, partially given to supporters of the Enlightenment and other well-known figures by Montgelas as a clear signal, were acknowledged experts in their field. They enjoyed a reputation as scholars that extended beyond Bavaria, and — as far as one can talk of a university professor's importance being honored at all in a provincial town — a certain popularity as well.

These included the renowned constitutional lawyer Nikolaus Thaddäus Gönner (1764–1827), head of the *Landshuter Kränzchen* and *Illuminati*

Club. From an academic point of view, he stood in opposition to the criminal lawyer Paul Johann Anselm Ritter von Feuerbach (1775–1833), who admittedly only taught in Landshut for a brief period. Friedrich Carl von Savigny (1779–1861), the founder of the historical school of law, also only lectured at the Bavarian State University for two years. The Brentano siblings were frequent guests in his house. Savigny, used to an extravagant lifestyle and social manner, found the town on the Isar too patriarchic and empoverished. The lawyers Leonhard Dresch (1786–1836), Johann Nepomuk Wening-Ingenheim (1790–1831), and Carl Joseph Anton Mittermaier (1787–1867), on the other hand, dealt more easi-

The founder of the historical school of law, Friedrich Carl von Savigny (1779–1861), shown in an etching by Ludwig Emil Grimm, c. 1808, taught in Landshut for two years. He cultivated an extravagant lifestyle and found Landshut too patriarchic and empoverished.

The medic Andreas Röschlaub (1768–1835), a representative of Landhut's "Romantic Medical School" propagated integral medicine as opposed to traditional teachings. For him, a fever was not an illness but a symptom of an anomaly in the usually well-balanced relation between an organism and the environment.
Lithograph by Ferdinand Piloty the Elder.

ly with their modest urban and cultural environment and did not complain of either intellectual or social shortcomings.

The Faculty of Medicine gained the epithet "Romantic Medical School" as it went to lengths to investigate new trends and contemporary fashions in addition to traditionally taught medicine. A precursor of medical teaching with a pronounced emphasis on psychology — that today would be called integral medicine — was Andreas Röschlaub (1768–1835), a follower of Schellings's natural philosophy and founder of the "excitability theory." He was joined by Philipp Franz von Walther (1782–1849), later King Louis I's personal physician, and the physiologist Friedrich Tiedemann (1781–1861). The research carried out by the pharmacologists Georg August Bertele (1767–1818) and Johann Andreas Buchner (1783–1852), among the best known representatives in their field, was in keeping with the work of this triumvirate.

Johann Michael Sailer (1751–1832), professor of liturgical and pastoral theology and educational science, later bishop of Regensburg, was a charismatic teacher who influenced a whole generation of clergy thanks to his irenicist theological approach. The dogmatic theorist and anti-Kantian proponent Patriz Benedikt Zimmer (1752–1820), the reformative liturgist Vitus Anton Winter (1754–1814), and the pastoral theologian Peter Roider (1776–1820) managed to free the theology of that time from its intellectual torpidity despite their differing academic intentions. They stand for successfully surmounting the orthodox teaching that dominated the final years of the Ingolstadt epoch and its opposition to the Enlightenment.

Lecturers in the Faculty of Philosophy or, as it has been known since 1804, in the division of general science, included the classical philologist and modern humanist Georg Anton Friedrich Ast

(1778–1841), the philosopher Friedrich Köppen (1775–1858), the former Jesuit and esthetics professor Alois Dietl (1752–1809), who was also the priest of St. Martin's at the same time, and the rationalist Jakob Salat (1766–1851), a passionate opponent of the fashionable philosopher Schelling.

The disputes fought out between Schelling and Salat, which often caused a furor on a national level, were unknown to the mathematicians. A sound representative of this subject in Landshut was, among others, Maurus Magold (1761–1837), who was highly regarded by others in this field.

The historian Konrad Mannert (1756–1834), and the state economists and cameralists Konrad Frohn (1752–1829) and Franz Xaver Moshammer (1756–1826), also achieved fame outside Bavaria.

THE MEASURE OF THE UNIVERSITY'S ACCLAIM: THE NUMBER OF STUDENTS

During Ludovico Maximilianea's Landshut era, some 5,700 students matriculated. Approximately one fifth of these were enrolled in the Faculty of Philosophy, a quarter in the Faculty of Theology, a third in the Faculty of Law, and about a tenth in the Faculty of Medicine.

The rate of new enrollments over the whole period was around 200 a year, although the number rose to more than 340 in the final two years. Assuming an average study period of two-and-a-half years, between 500 and 600 students were generally to be found living within the town's walls. In 1825/26, at the time of the final move, the number of students was almost 1,000, making the university in Landshut one of the largest in Germany after Leipzig, Göttingen, Halle, and Berlin. With a population approaching 7,500, the proportion of students to local residents remained constant for a long period, only tilting in favor of the students in the 1820s.

PROVENANCE OF THE STUDENTS AND THEIR SOCIAL BACKGROUND

Due to its Catholicism and competition from other universities and lyceums, Landshut remained a traditional Bavarian seat of learning. A fifth of all students came from just ten different places in Bavaria, each of which sent more than 50 young people to study on the Isar: Munich 340, Landshut 166, Amberg 117, Straubing 105, Regensburg 91, Augsburg 90, Passau 82. One third came from medium-sized to small towns; the vast majority coming from market towns and villages.

Social status was also determined by the region a student came from. Around 40 percent of all scholars came from families of academics or clerks, a further 40 percent from the skilled working class, 15 from farming families. This was reflected in both the student population and the professional careers followed. Farmers's sons were primarily drawn to theology or to philosophy; the sons of clerks and academics however were much more strongly represented in the subjects of jurisprudence, cameralistic, and medicine.

PROFESSOR/STUDENT RATIO IN FIGURES

What was only worth a brief mention in "Eos" in 1824 — a light-hearted, high-brow journal published in Munich — namely that "the number of teachers in all public universities in Germany together, with its total population of 30 million, now reaches 800, and that of students, 12,800, making it not quite fifteen students to one teacher," was extraordinarily significant from the point of view of educational policy. With a ratio of 1:15, there was hardly a question of a disparity between teachers and pupils, unlike the much bemoaned situation today.

For students, the ratio in Landshut was slightly worse, but the 400 to 600 scholars must have felt they were in good hands with between 20 to 30 professors. The author of the article in "Eos" went on to criticise that, when compared to other regions, "only one student for every 2,300 inhabitants attends university." According to this calculation, for every one million inhabitants there were around 425 students. Research sets the ratio even quite a bit lower at 300–350 per million inhabitants, as regards the university landscape in the northern region of the Old Empire in the first quarter of the 19th century. With 1,500 to 1,800 university students, Bavaria, with its state universities and five supplementary lyceums, lay way above average and, at least quantitatively, belied the popular notion of a "north/south educational divide."

A total of 362 doctorates were awarded from Landshut University: 15 in theology, 61 in jurisprudence, 263 in medicine, 18 in philosophy, and five in cameralistic. As such, 6.4% of all students gained a doctorate.

Without a doubt, Landshut was not an elitist university that would have launched professional careers or optimized individual vitae without personal commitment. But it cultivated talented pupils, who then went on to climb to political or academic heights on their own. Of those who studied in Landshut — including the prince-elector and later king Louis I, a pupil of Savigny's — a number of major figures emerged, who made their mark on the academic and political face of Bavaria and of Germany in the first half of the 19th century: the medic Johann Nepomuk Ringseis (1785–1880), the lawyers Carl Joseph Anton Mittermaier (1787–1867) and Johann Nepomuk Wening-Ingenheim (1790–1831), the ministers Count Joseph Ludwig Armansperg (1787–1853), Eduard von Schenk (1788–1841), and Prince Louis of Oettingen-Wallerstein (1791–1870), the orientalist Jakob Philipp Fallmerayer (1790–1861), the bishops Georg von Oettl (1794–1866), Melchior von Die-

penbrock (1798–1853), and Count Karl August Reisach (1800–69), the natural scientist Franz von Kobell (1803–82), the writer Count Franz Pocci (1807–76), and the Lord Mayor of Munich Josef von Teng (1786–1837).

SOCIOLOGICAL ASPECTS IN UNIVERSITY LIFE DURING THE ROMANTIC ERA

Despite the town's rather tranquil atmosphere — from today's perspective — and the lack of any noteworthy cultural or academic life, they knew how to entertain themselves in Landshut. Both at student and professorial levels, a lively social and academic network was cultivated. The group of "Romantics," to which Johann Nepomuk Ringseis, Eduard von Schenk, Anton von Salvotti, Karl von Gumppenberg, Max Prokop von Freyberg, and various others former and active students belonged, used to meet at Savigny's residence; a youth movement with literary ambitions, committed to the spirit of Romanticism and mockingly called "Juvenism," formed around the Ringseis brothers, Joseph Löw, Johann Nepomuk Vanino, Josef Teng, and Karl Loe. Despite an official governmental prohibition in 1807 and the restrictions imposed by the Carlsbad Decrees of 1819, student fraternities blossomed on the Isar; in fact they entered Bavarian university life via Landshut. The regional "Landsmannschaft" fraternities Suevia, Franconia, and Bavaria were formed, and their ritualized feasts, "commercia," drinking bouts, occassional brawls, and academic fencing known as "mensur," were — for the better or the worse — notable, and in any case, sensational events.

LANDSHUT BECOMES A "REFORM UNIVERSITY"

As an educational establishment for future civil servants, Ludovico Maximilianea played a central role in Bavaria's reorganizational concept that was

The medic Johann Nepomuk Ringseis (1785–1880) received his academic training at the University of Landshut. He was the confidant and personal physician to Crown-Prince Louis, later King Louis I of Bavaria, and was appointed professor in 1826, the same year that the university was moved to Munich. Drawing by Moritz von Schwind.

The mineralogist Franz von Kobell, a graduate from the University of Landshut, took a keen interest in photography early on, even taking a picture of the Church of Our Lady in Munich back in 1839. In 1834, Kobell became professor at his Alma mater, which by then had moved to Munich.

dominated in particular by the desire to increase the influence of the state. The aim behind structuring the curricula for public servants more thoroughly and tying them more closely to professional requirements was emphatically pursued. The result of this concerted effort was the far-reaching restructuing of universities in Bavaria, in the course of which Landshut mutated into a "reform university."

Reforms took place on several levels and in several phases. The traditional faculty structure and the usual formalities that had been observed up until that time for electing the rector, were radically changed in 1804 in an organizational edict, drawn up by the constitutional lawyer and later attorney general of Bavaria, Georg Friedrich von Zentner (1752–1835). From then on, the rector would be elected through a state-run ministerial channel and proclaimed by the king and, instead of the previous four faculties, there were to be two principle divisions, one for "general" and one for "special sciences," which in turn were subdivided into four categories. From then on, philosophy, mathematics/physics, history, and the fine arts came under "general sciences"; religious education (for the teaching profession), law, economics (of the state) and medicine under "special sciences." A "select Senate," some of whose members were appointed by the state, was annexed to the plenary meeting of professors, the central, self-administrative, academic organ.

The lawyer Carl Joseph Anton Mittermaier is welcomed on Klausenberg near Landshut on May 15, 1817, by a gathering of the Bavarian "Corpsbursche" fraternity. This painting is by Carl Schultheiß and hangs in the hall of the Corps Bavaria in Munich.

The office of chancellor, previously held by the Bishop of Eichstätt, was dissolved in 1807. From then onward, doctorates were no longer awarded "sub auctoritate pontificia," i.e. with papal authorization, but *sub potestate regia*, in the name of the king. The centuries-old university lost virtually all attributes of its corporative autonomy: The seals used by the rector and the faculties were broken and replaced by a state seal, and professors had to wear a uniform in future instead of their traditional academic robes. This new outward appearance was to signal that they were no longer the subjects of a privileged body but served the university and the community as citizens of the state. The powers of academic jurisdiction that had once formed the heart of the university's privileges were radically curbed. What remained was merely limited to the rector's disciplinary authority within the university buildings.

INTEGRATION OF EDUCATIONAL ASPECTS INTO THE BAVARIAN HIGHER EDUCATION SYSTEM

A number of government regulations ensured the integration of Landshut University in the higher education system of Bavaria that was no longer under the control of the church but of state-run authorities. The "Wismayer Educational Proposal" of 1804 and the "Niethmann Normative" of 1808 stand out as exceptionally far-reaching laws in the spirit of the philanthropism of the Enlightenment and the humanist revival.

Both decrees once again underline that the structural reorganization of Ludovico Maximilianea into a "seat of learning" and "state-run institution" was by no means piecemeal, but flanked by supportive measures. These ranged from disciplinary regulations for students (statutes from 1814), shorter study periods, and the precision of course material, through to a restructuring of the system for profes-

Academic fencing, or "mensur," in the fencing hall.

View of the university town of Landshut with St. Martin's Church.

sional qualifications (the first examinations for the teaching profession were held in 1808) and for university attendance through the introduction of the *Abitur* in 1809.

Despite these measures, Landshut University slipped into mediocrity in the 1820s, not least of all due to its desolate financial situation. Vacant chairs were the rule, the elite among the professors having left the town. Many had taken up positions in the Bayerische Akademie der Wissenschaften (Bavarian Academy of Sciences and Humanities) in Munich. The stream of students however did not run dry, and this in spite of increasing competition from better known university towns such as Göttingen and Berlin. The unfolding dilemma of the Bavarian temple of wisdom being doomed forever in a country town provoked King Louis I to abort the "Landshut reform experiment" and to relocate Ludovico Maximilianea in Munich, his "Athens on the Isar," in 1826.

The structural reorganization of the university to a "seat of learning" and "state-run institution" was flanked by numerous supportive measures, such as disciplinary regulations for students, the observance of which was assured, among other means, by the university's own uniformed police officers.

An expression of the all-encompassing influence exerted by the state and the reforms made in favor of corporative autonomy: Instead of the old faculty seals, new ones with the state's coat-of-arms appeared in the early 19th century. The old seal of the Faculty of Theology— with saw marks — and the new seal of the theology division from 1805/06.

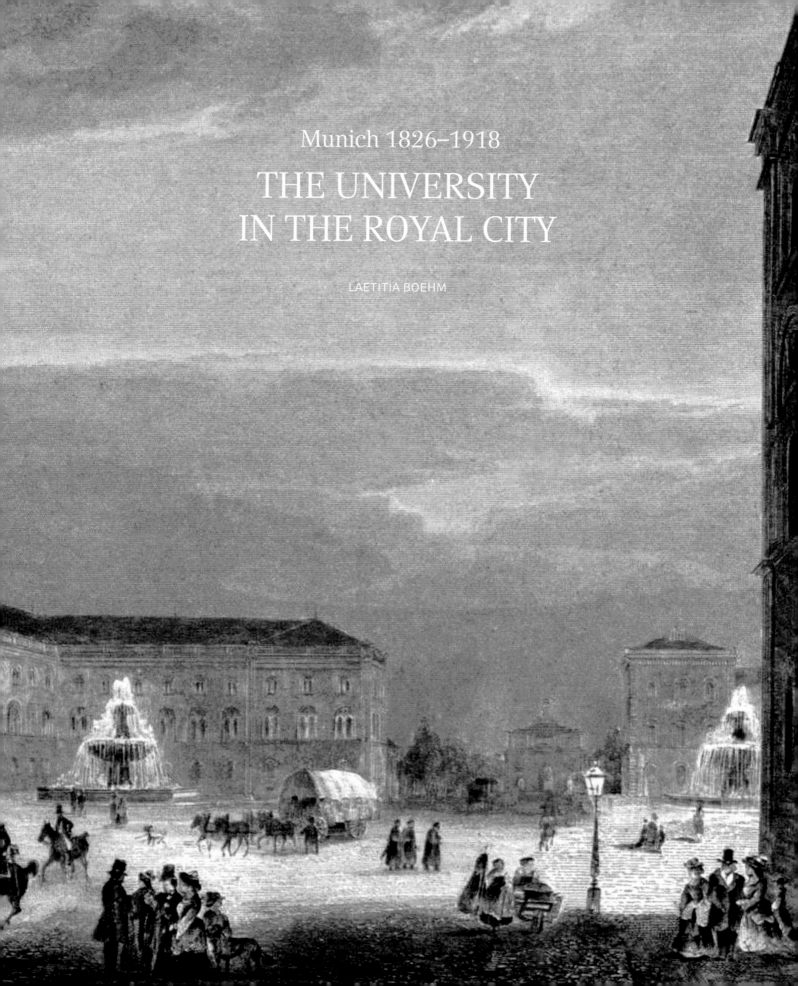

Munich 1826–1918

THE UNIVERSITY
IN THE ROYAL CITY

LAETITIA BOEHM

Crown-prince Louis in an Old German costume. Even in his abdication proclamation of March 1848, he professed his German sentiments: "Bavaria's king is proud to be a German." Painting in oil by Joseph Stieler (1781–1858), c. 1816.

opposite page:
Louis I in his coronation robes. His son and heir to the throne recalled the personal traits and opinions of his father: "[...] a great lover of art; nobody should be able to claim to have seen Germany without having visited Munich. Of liberal views at first [but] a strict adherent to the rights of the crown [...], autocratic rule under constitutional forms of government." Painting in oil by Joseph Stieler, 1826.

previous double page:
The main building at LMU. Engraving by Johann Poppel (1807–82) after a drawing by Gustav Seeberger (1812–88).

I belong to the old and new age and to two centuries," was how King Louis I (1786–1868, reigned 1825–48) saw himself. While monarch, he introduced a combination of heterogenous restorative and modernizing measures. Coupled with Louis's creative benefactory energy, the city and the University of Munich made impressive progress without renouncing their traditional Bavarian roots. The experience that Prince Louis had made — his year studying in Landshut (1803), the dynamics of a political shift away from the Napoleonic system, right through to the constitutional debate — formed the basis of his principles: The renunciation of a French-style centralized government with associated political consequences, ecclesiastically and educationally; Bavaria's sovereignty within the German Confederation while upholding an unchanging commitment to the politics of the nation as a whole; and a commitment to Bavaria's proclamation of the first state constitution in 1818 beyond the dismissal of his minister, Count Maximilian von Montgelas (1759–1838) in 1817. From 1819 onward, the constitutional monarchy granted one elected representative from each of the three universities the right to vote in the chamber of deputies in the first state assembly, which after 1848 evolved into the *Landtag* parliament.

EPOCHAL CHANGES WITHIN THE UNIVERSITY LANDSCAPE

Similar to Wilhelm von Humboldt's founding of the university in Berlin in 1810 as the crowning glory of Prussian reforms, the concentration of all cultural institutes important to the state in the regional capital lay at the heart of this reorientation. Seeing that the most important names in the field of research and teaching had left Landshut after 1814 for other universities and government organizations, the oldest state university now had to be integrated with the Bavarian Academy of Sciences and Humanities, founded in 1759 in Munich as the "brain of the state," with the young Academy of Fine Arts, with the art collections, and with the Court Library, that had profitted from the holdings of monasterial libraries dissolved during secularization. The rising status of the royal city since 1806, as well as the pluralization of the university landscape in Bavaria, triggered an urban expansion in the monarchical seat that also reflected the future status of the kingdom of Bavaria within the triad of the restructured central states.

For a quarter of a century the University of Landshut had contributed directly to epochal changes within the university landscape in Germany since the end of the Old Empire. Apart from the Old Bavarian state university, only the modern Bavarian sister institutes in Würzburg and Erlangen retained full university status out of the eight universities in Bavaria gained as a result of mediatisation. Others, such as Altdorf, were dissolved, or as in the case of Dillingen, downgraded to colleges of philosophy and theology (lyceums).

EDUCATION POLICY AS THE CORNER STONE OF THE KING'S GOVERNMENT LEGISLATION

Plans to move the university from Landshut to Munich had already been mooted around 1750 by advocates of a reform who were opposed to the military and to the Jesuit order. The most prominent among them was the lawyer Johann Georg Lori (1723–87), the high-profile founder of the Bavarian Academy of Sciences and Humanities in Munich and militant opponent of the Jesuit "kings" at Ingolstadt University. These plans were not neglected even after re-establishing the university in Landshut, all the more since the minister Montgelas strove to set up a centralized university in Munich for fiscal reasons. King Maximilian I Joseph, on the other hand, reinforced his aversion

to an unruly hoard of students so close to the Residence in Munich right up until his death. However, he did favor the "Teaching Institute for Applied Medicine," established in 1824 at the general hospital in Munich, by passing a decree on October 6, 1825, granting it doctoral rights and thus elevating it to a "central institute" within the academy with teaching courses — a provocation in the eyes of the University of Landshut. The renowned doctor Johann Nepomuk Ringseis, who worked at the teaching hospital, was one of the most outspoken advocates of the move. He attested to the crown-prince, whom he had accompanied on journeys on numerous occasions since 1817, that "our university could be on a par with Vienna, Göttingen, and Berlin if, but only if, it were transferred to Munich." Louis was not unfamiliar with this notion, having pursued his policies for turning the city into a "German Athens" for years. As early as 1814, he had set the foundation stone for his bold cultural policies by holding a competition to design the Glyptothek, the first museum of sculptures from Antiquity of its type in Europe, and by summoning the best contemporary artists to Munich.

CHANGE OF GOVERNMENT — A NEW BEGINNING FOR THE UNIVERSITY IN MUNICH

The death of King Maximilian I on October 13, 1825, opened up the possibility for decisive action to be taken. "Forward, forward, that's where to look / Never should thou cast a gaze back" — Louis composed a poem of seven verses "to myself as king" on November 5, according to his own notes, "the first since my ascension to the throne." In December 1825, the king had already called for the formation of a separate section of the "supreme council of the church and schools" and summoned Eduard von Schenk (1788–1841), a capable cultural advisor, to chair it and commissioned him with preparing the move. Proposals for this were finalized by April 1826, signed by Schenk and the new Minister of the Interior and Finance Minister Count Joseph Ludwig Armansperg (1787–1853); the approval of the king soon followed. Both ministers were familiar with the material, being former students at Landshut, albeit of differing persuasions. Schenk, a university friend of Louis's, showed talent as a poet and upheld the religious views propagated by Sailer and his circle of followers, and the Romantic era. The situation with Armansperg, also known as *Sparmansperg* — the cost cutter — during his time as minister, was different. He had extensive administrative experience in the Montgelas tradition and had demonstrated his unadulterated liberalism as a former benefactor of the student fraternity "Bavaria" (1806), for which he was "relegated" under the police state only to be "rehabilitated" by the king.

The Decree of the Highest Order of October 3, 1826, ruled that "Ludwig-Maximilians-Universität, located up until now in Landshut, shall be transferred to Munich, our capital and royal seat," while retaining its institutional identity. Louis had previously pledged his continued solidarity to the mayor of Landshut, explaining: "only more exalted considerations moved me to take this step; it had to be!"

CEREMONIAL ACT IN 1826 AND THE PRELUDE IN MUNICH

The *Wilhelminum*, named after its benefactor Duke William V (1548–1626), was earmarked as provisional accommodation. The church of the former Carmelite monastery on Promenadeplatz, allocated to the ducal Georgianum as the first base in Munich, acted as the university auditorium. Some 800 students moved with the university from Landshut to Munich, many of them from the

King Louis I commissioned Eduard von Schenk, who chaired the "Supreme Council of the Church and Schools" with preparing the move. A talented writer, Schenk's play "Belisar" was performed in 1827 in Vienna.

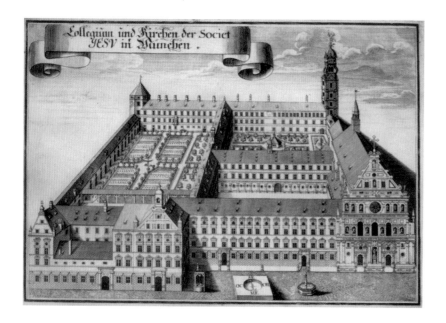

LMU's first seat in Munich: St. Michael's Jesuit college, founded in 1559 near the palace, on what is today Neuhauser Strasse. The building complex extended in 1597/98 with the Maxburg accommodated the Bavarian Academy of Sciences and Humanities from around 1780 until the mid 20th century. For this reason, it is still known as the "Old Academy."
Engraving by Michael Wening, 1645–1718.

oldest *Landsmannschaft* fraternities. The program of lectures for the winter term 1826/27 included a total of 132 courses in five faculties.

The tone of the inaugural festivities on November 15, 1826, in the presence of the king, was set by the first rector magnificus of Munich, Georg Leonhard von Dresch (1786–1836) in his official speech, a courageous one bearing the Metternich system of demagogical persecution in mind. The lawyer, who had relocated from Landshut, spoke of the dignity of scholarship and emphasized the importance of upholding the "freedom of the word" and the "unrestricted impartation of thoughts" necessary for them to blossom.

His majesty rewarded the students, who made a torchlight procession to the Residence, with words that were soon to become familiar to all: "A former student of Ludwig-Maximilians-Universität offers his sincere gratitude. Religion must form a basis and be a guide through life — I tolerate neither bigots nor the obscure, nor those who hang their heads — young people should be allowed to be joyful."

INITIAL PERIOD OF RULE MARKED BY THE KING'S LIBERALITY

Louis's liberal gestures through his recognition of university traditions found a noticeable echo: The restitution of voting rights for the rector and Senate, albeit with the proviso of royal approval, the restoration of the faculty system, which amounted to a negation of French university policy, still the subject of discussion at that time, the donation of new robes of office for the now five faculties, and the presentation of a golden ceremonial chain for the rector combined with the right to attend court. "I am well disposed to the freedom of the university," the king said, "as long as it does not endanger others."

King Louis` liberal views were also reflected in his acknowledgement of academic traditions. The rector's golden chain of office is still in use today. The designs for new gowns to be worn by the professors in the colors of the faculties — black (theologians), red (lawyers, cameralists), green (medics), blue (philosophers) (not illus.) — were made by the court painter Peter von Cornelius (1783–1867).

A feeling for history is demonstrated by the approval given in December 1829 to a motion presented twice to the Senate under the rector Friedrich Wilhelm von Thiersch (1784–1860), that called for the restoration of the university seal, destroyed in 1802, to be used by the institute as its "House and family coat-of-arms." He was able to announce that the decree had been passed at the founder's day festivities on July 26, 1830. Since then, this celebration has been traditionally held annually at Ludovico Maximilianea — with the exception of politically incurred interruptions. In 1858, Louis also honored Landshut, the town where he had studied, by erecting a memorial to Louis the Rich, the founder of the university opened in Ingolstadt on June 26, 1472, thus documenting continuity in the dynasty of benefactors.

ALLOWANCES WITHIN THE FRAMEWORK OF AUTOCRATIC RULE

The invalidated university seals were restored under the rector Friedrich Wilhelm von Thiersch in 1802 and used once again. The saw marks can still be seen.

Legislation introduced in November 1827 — so-called "free study regulations" — marks the most liberal phase of the royal educational policy, replacing the statutes of 1814. Contrary to the spirit of the Carlsbad Decrees of 1819, student associations were conditionally permitted once again. Despite conservative reservations, the monarch granted greater freedom both in the "general sciences" (Faculty of Philosophy) and in the "special sciences" (specialist or professional studies) — a first within the Bavarian university landscape. Motivating forces behind this innovative impetus were the experience Louis had gained studying in Göttingen as well as the representatives of Idealism and humanist teaching, Friedrich (von) Schelling and Friedrich von Thiersch, with their "instructions" — guidelines that were to replace the syllabus as a means of orientation.

ELATED DEMAND:
APPOINTMENTS IN THE HUMANITIES

The reorganization of the university emanated from paradox presuppositions. On the one hand, "as regards the number and constellation of teachers," it should "far exceed the two other universities in Bavaria without academically impoverishing the latter" (Schenk); its fundamental character should be Christian/Catholic and not denominational, according to the king's wishes, but directed against the dominance of pure Rationalim. On the other hand, the state's impending bankruptcy forced radical cost-cutting.

Academic political perspectives were primarily focused on the Faculty of philosophy propaedeutic responsibility, considering that the study of philosophy and history was to form the "basis of all positive sciences." The five luminaries, Thiersch, Schelling, Baader, Schubert, and Görres, were the embodiment of a conceptually rich spectrum for the new start in Munich. Thiersch, a passionate advocate of modern humanism and the first "northerner" from the Göttingen school of thought, had been working on the development of a philological seminar since 1810 as a model school at the lyceum in Munich that was then incorporated into the university. Although he hardly fulfilled any of the conditions with regard to religious positivity, he was considered an expert ancient historian and emerged as the "praeceptor bavariae" due to his reforms to the Gymnasium secondary school system. Like the brilliant Neoclassicist architect Leo von Klenze (1784–1864), Thiersch — as a chief proponent of Philhellenism — supported Louis I's political ambitions, in line with European protectorate policies, to proclaim his son Otto (1815–67) as the first "free" king of Greece in 1832/33 after the end of Ottoman rule. Both of them also contributed to the educational reform in Hellas itself. The experienced lawyer Georg Ludwig (von) Maurer (1790–1872), a civil servant in Bavaria, member of the Bavarian Academy and the University of Munich, established the modern Greek judiciary system. Despite the commitment of such culturally versed luminaries, the government in Greece — also referred to as the Bavarian "adventure" or "dream" by analysts — collapsed in 1862 with the deposition of Otto, following a national uprising by the Greeks.

How different from the practitioner Thiersch was the philosopher Schelling with his exceptional mind. Along with Georg Wilhelm Friedrich Hegel (1770–1831) he was the chief proponent of German speculative philosophy. The prophet for the philosophy of nature was awarded a doctorate (Dr. med. h. c.) at the University of Landshut in absentia in 1802, when he was still teaching in Jena, and while professor in Würzburg he was elected a member of the Bavarian Academy of Sciences and Humanities in Munich. In 1820 he moved to Erlangen, and ultimately to Munich in 1827, where he held his inaugural lecture on November 26. Schelling was moving toward a Christian philosophy, motivated not least of all by colleagues of the Late Romantic Era, including the profound Franz von Baader (1765–1841) and Gotthilf Heinrich von Schubert (1780–1860), who had pietistic leanings, and of whom Thiersch's son related that he

Despite doubts from Prussia, Louis I recalled Joseph Görres, accused of being a Jacobin and ultramodern public enemy and ridiculed as a dilettante publisher, from exile in Strasbourg. This bronze bust by Theodor Georgii (1883–1963) in the atrium at LMU was unveiled in 1926 during a celebration to commemorate the 150th anniversary of his birth.

"really reached the highest ethical level possible for a Christian" in his lectures on natural history and psychology.

The summoning of the philosophical visionary Joseph (von) Görres (1776–1848), a contemporary, rhetorically powerful critic, caused a furor. The *Rheinischer Merkur* that he had founded in 1814/15 (a medium of the constitutional movement) was reputedly even described by Napoleon as the "fifth major European power." Görres fled to Alsace to escape the threat of being arrested by the Prussian police in 1819. Even more so than with Schelling, Baader, and Schubert, the professor for "general literary history" cannot be placed in any one specific academic category; he shirked examination and official duties — "mere mechanical operations" — and only begrudgingly accepted the honorary doctor title he was awarded in 1831.

The politcal upheaval in the 1830s, accompanied by the renewed consolidation of Catholicism, especially after 1838 under the administration of Karl von Abel, forced Görres onto the faculty stage. In 1838/40 he could not elude the post of ephorus for the students of "general sciences" — a position linked to the deanery. And all the less so after making a mark for himself as the moral authority of political Catholicism through his polemic writing *Athanasius* (1838), followed by his editing of the *Historisch-Politischen Blätter* together with this son, Guido. Today, this publication, that ran until 1923 (totalling 171 volumes), is one of the most valuable sources for research on the history of Bavaria. His residence on Schönfeldstrasse (now the Josephinum private clinic), was the meeting place of the "Görres circle" at that time, to which like minds from France such as Charles Forbes René de Montalambert (1810–70) and Hugues Robert de Lamennais (1782–1854) also belonged.

The multiplicity of new directions being pursued in Munich were reflected thoughout the whole teaching staff and the beginnings of subject-specific specialization. The refined philologian and Platonist Friedrich Ast (1778–1841), a close follower of Schelling, stood in Thiersch's shadow. His hermeneutic theory of art, however, paved the way for musicology that became established much later. In Landshut he looked after the neglected collection of copperplate engravings and paintings that was then transferred to Munich. The Sanskrit expert Othmar Frank (1770–1840) established the specialist foundations for Oriental studies, and on an interdisciplinary level complemented the theologian and important translator of the

Johann Andreas Schmeller, with his "Bavarian Dictionary," was an ingenious autodidact whose tireless research of manuscripts paved the way for today's "Commission for Research into Dialects" at the Bavarian Academy of Sciences and Humanities.

*The ecclesiastical historian Johann Ignaz von Döllinger,
a central figure in the renewal of the Catholic church as
advocated by the Görres Circle, left his mark on the faculty
through his critical research expertise and apologetic
eloquence (with parliamentary experience in 1845–49),
propagating theology as a free science, as well as through
a commitment to the apostolical tradition of Catholicism
based on universal history.*
Historical photograph by Franz Hanfstaengl

bible, Joseph Franz Allioli (1793–1873), perfectly. In 1833, they were joined by the Jewish/Protestant Sinologist Karl Friedrich Neumann (1793–1870), to whom the Bayerische Staatsbibliothek (Bavarian State Library) owes its valuable East Asian holdings. Now highly renowned, Johann Andreas Schmeller (1785–1852) remained unrecognized during his lifetime. As the "Bavarian Grimm" he became one of the co-creators of comparative linguistics and founder of the chair for German Philology at the University of Munich.

THEOLOGIANS, NATURAL SCIENTISTS, MEDICS, LAWYERS, AND ECONOMISTS

The traditionally close relationship between the Faculties of Philosophy and Theology faculties was maintained. Alongside Allioli, theology was represented by the pastoral theologian Georg Friedrich Wiedemann (1787–1864), who also held the post of director of the Georgianum. The Faculty was enduringly shaped by Johann Ignaz (von) Döllinger (1799–1890). An accomplished teacher of ecclesiastical history, dogmatic theology, and the philosophy of religion, he grew to become one of the most prominent figures at the university of Munich due to his impressive criticism of established teachings as well as his unflinching commitment to the politics of the church, and was elected to become rector on three occasions (1844/45, 1866/67, and 1871/72).

In the natural sciences, Lorenz Oken (Okenfuß, 1779–1851) was appointed physiologist, having resigned his post in Jena in 1819. The "political natural philosopher" had become well-known through the founding of the *Gesellschaft deutscher Naturforscher und Ärzte* (society of German natural scientists and doctors) in 1822, aimed at serving to "promote a national science culture." However, he was forced to resign once again in 1832. Thaddäus Siber (1774–1854), a pupil of the Benedictine monks, who experienced the university's transfer from Ingolstadt to Landshut while a student, lectured in mathematics and physics in Munich over a period of many decades. He also taught the royal princes and was curator of the *Physikalische Akademiesammlung*. Carl Friedrich Philipp von Martius (1794–1868) made a name for himself in the field of botany as an enthusiastic researcher and an inspiring teacher, as the successor of Franz von Paula Schrank (1747–1835), the creator of the botanical garden at the University of Landshut and, from 1809 onward, chief curator of the same in Munich. After 1832, Martius became head of the *Hortus botanicus R. Academiae Monacensis*, founded in 1809. In 1854 he handed in his resignation prematurely, his protests against sacrificing the Old Botanic Garden near Karlstor to make way for the construction of the Crystal Palace having fallen on deaf ears.

Carl Friedrich Philipp von Martius gained fame through the expedition to Brazil in 1817–20, funded by Maximilian I, that he undertook together with the zoologist Johann Baptist von Spix (1781–1826). Their widely documented scientific findings are today considered to be on a par at least with those of Alexander von Humboldt.
Photo: Franz Hanfstaengl

Cartoon by Count Franz von Pocci (1807–76) on the expedition to Brazil.
The verse reads: "Martius journeyed to Brazil,
In search of parsley, herbs, and dill;
Thank God, he wasn't, by mistake,
Eaten by a mammoth snake!"

The Crystal Palace in Munich, erected for the First German Industrial Exhibition in 1854;
burned down in 1931.

In the Faculty of Medicine, it was a good move placing the anatomist Ignaz Döllinger (1770–1841), the father of the theologian Johann Ignaz Döllinger from the Franconian family of court physicians, at the side of Friedrich Karl von Loé (1786–1838), director at the institute of applied medine, and his colleague, Ringseis. And it was a stroke of good fortune being able to persuade the internationally famous surgeon and ophthalmologist Philipp Franz von Walther (1782–1849) to return to Bavaria, having been summoned to Bonn from Landshut in 1818.

The Faculty of Law excelled in the person of the legal historian Konrad von Maurer (1823–1902) — an expert on Scandinavian law and an authority in research on the agricultural law of the Germanic cultures. As Maurer's career soon led him to the higher echelons of the civil service, the teaching, committee, and parliamentary work of the legal scholar Hieronymus J. P. Bayer (1792–1876) was, in contrast, to have a lasting influence on law students over several generations.

The early days of the fifth faculty, that of economics, represented to start with by the long-serving cameralist, agricultural and forestry expert Ludwig Wallrad Medicus (1771–1850), were initially caught up in the struggle to establish its own profile and graduation rights. The statistician Friedrich Benedikt Wilhelm Hermann (1795–1868), who was summoned from Erlangen, demonstrated his forward-looking expertise in political economics, financial and commercial science during a brief experiment in Munich in the form of a "technical university" within the faculty.

NATIONAL AUSTERITY POLICY AND SCHOLARLY ORGANIZATION

Since the number of lecturers was to be more than doubled following the university's move, allowances had to be made for the state of emergency

The refractor made by the brilliant optician and inventor Joseph Fraunhofer (1787–1826), is still in the possession of the observa-
tory built in Bogenhausen in 1816–18 and structurally overhauled in the 1960s. The best large telescope in the world at the time,
it enabled an early series of measurements to be made on Halley's comet that are still considered important today. Through the re-
organization of the "Staatliche Wissenschaftlichen Sammlungen," the observatory was affiliated to the Faculty of Natural Science,
thus becoming the "university observatory."

The Scot Johann (von) Lamont, a pupil at the academy and an adjunct, was recommended as director of the observatory in Bogenhausen in Munich, a post he held in 1833/35. In 1852, he was appointed professor ordinarius for astronomy at the university. His research as an astronomer, as well as his findings on the earth's magnetic field, in geophysics and meteorology earned him many honors, including the unique distinction of having a crater on the Moon and another on Mars named after him by astronomers.
Photography by Karl Rexhäuser, 1896.

with regard to the national budget. From 1825 onward, a ministerial "cost-saving commission" worked on creating a tariff structure to lower the excessive staff and salary increases that had resulted from Montgelas's civil service pragmatism of 1805. The "simplification of public authorities" started by slashing ministers' salaries. Modernization could only be achieved without incurring additional costs by reallocating funds. As a result, professors at universities and lyceums in Bavaria were moved to other posts and use made of the civil service status of members of the Bavarian Academy of Sciences and Humanities. The decree of May 1807 had changed the academy from being an association of scholars to a royal "central institute," with designated members in full-time salaried positions as civil servants, who were obliged to look after the collections, archives, and libraries, as well as — something completely new — to train pupils and assistants or "apprentices." The new system however did not prove successful. Schelling in particular criticized that the research academy had become an "administrative authority" and advocated the freedom of scholarship that would necessitate the academy and university in Munich being merged.

AFFILIATION TO THE UNIVERSITY, AND TEACHING AND SALARY STRUCTURES DEFINED

The culturally and politically pivotal royal decree of March 21, 1827 compensated for repercussions incurred through relocating the university. The academy was changed back into a free association of scholars but linked to the university along the lines of the Göttingen model, in the sense that salaried academics at the university were obliged to act as "honorary professors" for little or no payment. This organizational model accounts for the complex network of nominal and secondary subjects at that time.

The March decree relaxed the bond between the academy's "attributes" and its administration. It turned central institutes (the court and central library, together with the mineralogical, zoological, ethnographical, polytechnical collections, the cabinet of instruments for physics and mathematic, the Mint Cabinet, the Antiquarium, the observatory in Bogenhausen, as well as the chemistry and anatomy theater) into "state and national property." Attributes acquired from Landshut (library, collections, apparatus, and cabinets) were to be left as part of the university. This implied an organizational division of the state and university library in Munich. From then on, both state and university collections were also to be used for teaching purposes. The observatory "near Bogenhausen," erected in 1816–18, was initially excluded from this regulation. According to a ministerial expertise it was "not entirely suitable for the purpose of academic teaching [...] due to its distance from Munich." However, Johann (von) Lamont (1805–79), as its director (appointed in 1833/35), was made lecturer at the university from 1837 alongside his existing nominal subject professorship for astronomy.

To manage the state collections that were partly under the care of chairholders at the university from 1827 onward, an umbrella authority — the "General Conservatorium" — was created, a new organization that also had a positive ad hoc benefit on state finances. Through his appointment to the position of director general, Schelling stayed in Munich for the time being while simultaneously retaining his well-paid post as president of the Academy, responsible for both institutions — the university and the academy.

The situation regarding private lecturers remained precarious. While faculties and the state both valued nurturing habilitation candidates in the "nursery for university lecturers," private lecturers on the other hand were neither civil servants nor corporate members.

IN THE FACE OF REVOLUTIONARY UNREST

When the French Revolution of 1830 threw Europe into political turmoil, the university in Munich — selected to become Bavaria's role academic hub — had to face its first real test in the face of competition from the major cities of Berlin and Vienna.

During this time of political crisis a new form of solidarity evolved between students and local residents, while the relationship between the king and parliament had to face a buffeting. Radically liberal members of the *Landtag*, primarily from regions in Bavaria that had recently been annexed, were severely reprimanded by the king. Schenk was ousted from his ministerial position.

The monarch replied to the unrest in Munich in December 1830, which was harmless by comparison, by temporarily closing the university, as he felt that his trust in the younger generation had been abused. Louis I kept a distrustful eye on the growing number of signs that pointed to a radicalization among groups of students and teachers, such as at the Hambacher Fest on annexed territory in 1832, and later at the *Frankfurter Wachensturm* (Charge of the Frankfurt Guard House) in 1834. *Germania*, a fraternity in Munich that had been banned, propagated students and citizens forming revolutionary clubs.

LUDWIGS-MAXIMILIANS-HOCHSCHULE.

Verlag von R. Sauer in München.

The foundation stone for the university and the Georgianum clerical seminary was laid on August 25, 1835, Louis I's birthday; that for the "School for Daughters of the Gentry" (now the Faculty of Law) on Queen Theresa's birthday in 1837, as proven when the foundation stone was rediscovered after the end of the war.

The reactionary change in the style of Louis's rule, had ambivalent repercussions on university policies. Disciplinary measures for students were in force by 1832: The monitoring system was expanded and the pressure to produce results increased by introducing interim and "detention" exams. The decision to reduce the duration of courses from five to four years, had already been reversed however by 1838, as this placed an additional burden on the "general sciences" (the biennium).

Changes in the educational policy were also felt among the staff at Ludovico Maximilianea, and although Louis I still saw himself as the "protector and upholder of true religiosity," in particular, and as a "staunch opponent to both Protestant and Catholic fanaticism," he appointed professors of both denominations and even of different political persuasions in the 1830s.

ARCHITECTURAL PROJECT OF AN AUDACIOUS MAGNITUDE: LUDWIGSTRASSE

Uneffected by the changing political climate, Louis I's ongoing passion for building benefitted the university, despite being up against the constant restraints of cost-cutting policies that primarily hit civil servants. Opening up the ring around the old city to the north by constructing the boulevard named Ludwigstrasse in 1822, was the king's most audacious and at the same time most controversial plan. It was to serve as an axis for the new royal buildings — St. Ludwig's Church and the educational institutes of the State Library, the National Institute of the Blind, the "School for Daughters of the Gentry," and the university. Unperturbed by criticism, also voiced by professors, the king pressed ahead with the costly building project, supported by Thiersch as his consultant.

Plans for an auditorium to seat between 600 and 1,000, lecture theaters for 50 to 300 students, and

Not Klenze, court director of building works to the king, was commissioned to design Ludwigstrasse and the university buildings, but his "rival," Friedrich von Gärtner (above).

various "cabinets" (institutes) were to provide much more space than in the university's provisional location in the Wilhelminum. It was not however planned to move the clinics, the botanical garden or the collections.

The foundation stone for the university building and the Georgianum clerical seminary was laid on the king's birthday, August 25, 1835; that of the "Royal School for Daughters of the Gentry" in July 1837 on the birthday of Queen Theresa of Bavaria, Louis I's wife. The oldest, state-run boarding school for girls of its kind in Bavaria (founded in 1813 by King Maximilian I in Oberanger and renamed the Max-Joseph-Stift in 1851) was located right next to the university from 1840 onward for almost a century, despite reservations by the headmistress at the time as regards the "dangerous" proximity of seminarists and students. Later, the slogan "Faith (Georgianum), Hope (students) and Love (Max-Joseph-Stift)" for the tripartite constellation on Ludwigstrasse entered the local venacular. In 1938 it had to make way for the site of the *Akademie für Deutsches Recht* founded in 1933, and for the *Haus des Deutschen Rechts* built in 1936–39. Today, the site of the building destroyed in the war is occupied by LMU's Faculty of Law.

Louis I did not commission his court director of building works, Leo von Klenze, to design the royal boulevard, but his younger rival, Friedrich (von) Gärtner (1792–1847), a pupil of Carl von Fischer (1782–1820), the architect of the National Theater and the Prince Carl Palais in Munich. Gärtner's architectural language, borrowed from the Early Renaissance, seemed to the king to be more modern. The completion of the Triumphal Arch a few years after Gärtner's death, in 1852, took place under the supervision of the king, who had in the meantime abdicated.

Lola Montez, an Irish woman by birth and King Louis I's mistress, was raised to the nobility by him. The schism this provoked led to professors being discharged from the university.

1847/48: REVOLUTION IN MUNICH AND THE ABDICATION OF LOUIS I

In Munich, the revolution in the German States found its peculiar beginnings in a chain of events surrounding the scandalous appearance of the beautiful "stranger" Lola Montez (1818–61). An Irish woman by birth, who masqueraded as a Spanish dancer, she arrived in Munich in 1846. Louis I soon fell under her spell and the state, city, and university were captivated by her. On August 25, 1847, she was raised to the nobility and given the title Countess Landsfeld. The schism that this provoked resulted in changes within virtually all government offices and also led to professors being discharged from the university. Following

the fall of the minister Karl von Abel, almost all members of the Görres circle were forced into retirement.

The closure of the university ordered by Louis on February 9, 1848, and the immediate expulsion of students from other areas, marked the beginning of the rebellion in Munich. Although he listened to the citizens's protests, he was not able to prevent news of the deposition of the King of France in Paris (February 24, 1848) from turning the "family dispute" in Munich into a political revolution. Louis's "March Proclamations," the dismissal of ministers, the revocation of the citizenship given to Lola in the face of public opposition one year previously, who had by this time now vanished, led to the monarch abdicating on March 19, 1848, his self-esteem having taken a blow: "I could no longer rule, I did not want just to give my signature. So as not to become a slave, I became a free man."

And this was how the crown fell to Maximilian II (1811–64), Louis I's son, right in the middle of the German revolution. He felt it was a "crown of thorns," as the reputation of the government seemed to be weakened, the monarchical principle shattered, the burden of responsibility heavy.

THE REVOLUTION IN THE GERMAN STATES AND POLITICAL TRENDS AT THE UNIVERSITY

The wringing for liberal teaching and studying continued throughout 1848, the year of the revolution, on various levels within the university. Progressive student groups set up "conventions of representatives" with the aim of fighting for the political representation of students in university bodies — that was not achieved until 1920. The Jena student fraternity "Germania" pleaded for a more radical approach at the Second Wartburg Festival student assemblies in Eisenach.

The *Pfingststudentenparlament* (Whitsun Student Parliament) under the learned Arnold Ruge (1802–80), a follower of Hegel from northern Germany, and the president of the law students's committee in Munich Elias Lang — called "Little Gagern," with reference to the popular Pauluskirche politician Heinrich von Gagern (1799–1880) — passed a programmatic petition to the National Assembly.

In fall 1848, an "organizational draft for German universities" was made. The demand for the transformation of universities into national institutes, for abolishing the *Länder* (states) principle and special courts, as well as faculty, examination, and collegiate fees, etc., revealed a train of thought

In his memoirs, King Maximilian II described the difficult situation at the time of his ascension to the throne: "… and thus I have to face the violent storm that is gathering strength by the day; an inexperienced helmsman in a leaky ship on a choppy sea."
Historical photograph by Franz Hanfstaengl.

"It is in science that I see a beacon for mankind and a pillar of strength for the well-being of the state. Munich, December 28, 1858, Maximilian" — thus reads the dedication accompanying the elaborately chased silver cup. King Maximilian II donated the cup to LMU Munich in 1858 as an expression of his recognition of scholarship. The cup depicts the four "masters of the time-honored faculties": "Theologia," "Iurisprudentia," "Medicina," and "Philosophia." Below are three banderoles with drinking ditties.

close to the statements of far-left wing lecturers, who were working toward the founding of a central university.

Five delegates from each of the three Bavarian state universities were sent to the convention of German university teachers in September 1848 on the order of King Maximilian II. After the politically divided National Assembly in Frankfurt voted against an hereditary Prussian empire on March 28, 1849, triggering the fall of parliament, students in Munich once again called for the adjuration of the imperial constitution under the black, red, and gold flag, even though the politicization of the university had already passed its peak.

The legacy from the years of the revolution was the reciprocal assimilation of German universities with greater allowance being given to the freedom of teachers and students under the protection of the monarchistic state constitutions. As a consequence, scholarship developed into the nucleus of the royal triumvirate policy, according to which Bavaria was to rank as the third power within the German Confederation alongside Austria and Prussia.

AN "ACADEMIC ON THE THRONE": ROYAL EDUCATION POLICY

Maximilian II found his own style for furthering culture without breaking with the Ludovician tradition. As different as the mentalities of father and son were, cultural policy remained a dominant feature. Louis I's impulsive passion for art was replaced by the heir to the throne's enthusiasm for science. The objectives Maximilian II formulated in his government program included the following: "[…] to do everything within our power to nourish the sciences and to continue to provide support to the arts, […] to take on a role in southern Germany similar to that of Prussia in the north. […] to uphold the positive relationship between Catholics and Protestants."

Interested in history ever since he was a child, he widened his knowledge as a "full student and not just a studying crown-prince" in Göttingen and Berlin in 1829–31 under Arnold Heeren (1760–1842), Friedrich Christoph Dahlmann (1785–1860), Friedrich von Raumer (1781–1873) and particularly under Leopold von Ranke (1795–1886). From 1835 he immersed himself more deeply in philosophy with his private tutor Schelling. His manner as sovereign was conditioned by a belief in the objectivity of the sciences; he continuously informed himself of innovations in all areas. He always based his decisions on balanced assessments, backed up by advice and reports by experts. Nevertheless, such an academic policy could never be without its contradictions.

RECRUITING "NORTHERNERS": NATIONAL IMPACT OF CONFLICTS IN MUNICH ON THE UNIVERSITY'S IMAGE

Despite his defensive attitude towards the hegemonic cravings of the Prussians, the king went to lengths to raise Bavaria's importance nationally by appointing academics of northern German provenance. This recruiting method, that spared no expenses, sometimes triggered hefty controversies not only among "patriots," since local aspirants — at least in the early days — were at a disadvantage compared to "foreign" luminaries.

As a result, of the some 135 university lecturers employed — up until 1856, 55 new appointments to posts in Munich had been made — there were such illustrious names as that of the Swiss lawyer Johann Caspar Bluntschli (1808–81), the chemist Justus Liebig (1803–73), the cultural historian from the Rhineland, founder of ethnology, and the first director of the National Museum of Bavaria in Munich Wilhelm Heinrich von Riehl (1823–97), the latter's friends from the university in Giessen, the philosopher Moriz Philipp Carrière (1817–15), or

Summoned back in 1848, the politically engaged expert in constitutional law Johann Caspar Bluntschli from Zurich was able act as an advisor to the new king in the face of revolutionary pressure. In 1861, Bluntschli accepted a call to Heidelberg, where he was also active as a member of parliament.

In 1853, the king introduced the "Maximilian order for science and art" to be given in recognition of exceptional performance, while reserving the nomination of recipients for himself as the grand master. The statute (of Nov. 28, art. III) determined that it should be awarded "preferably to German academics and artists." This photograph shows an order from 1980, a new award respecting traditional obligations, the design of which however does not have the head of the benefactor as found on earlier orders.

Liebig's friend Theodor Ludwig Wilhelm Bischoff (1807–82), an anatomist and physiologist from Hanover. Academics from the south of Germany, however, also played a decisive role, such as the physician Georg Simon Ohm (1789–1854) from Erlangen, the surgeon Carl Theodor von Siebold (1804–85) from the Würzburg family of physicians, the hygienist Max von Pettenkofer (1818–1901), or the anti-clerical philosophy historian Carl von Prantl (1820–88), who came from Upper Bavaria. Even followers of Görres who had been forced into retirement in 1847, were rehabilitated. These included Döllinger and the philologist Ernst von Lasaulx (1805–61), who had gained the sympathy of students demonstrating against Lola Montez.

The confrontation between locals and "outsiders" that had been growing since the restructuring of the state of Bavaria around 1800, intensified in the

1850s and '60s. Debates enflamed by questions of denomination and educational patriotism concerning "northerners" or "ultramontanes" became woven into the potential political conflict associated with a (Prussian) "Smaller German Solution" or a "Greater German Solution" within the Imperial Constitution, ever since the National Assembly in Frankfurt in 1848/49.

The policy behind the awarding of the Maximilian order for science and art, founded in 1853, also fuelled the conflict. The order, that gave its bearer the right of presentation at court, was intended to demonstrate the presence of "German intellectuals" in the south in Bavaria. Of those honored the first time it was awarded, it was the Northerners who gained clearly in number. Of a total of 34 recipients for science, 13 were from Munich (including Döllinger, Bluntschli, Martius, Thiersch,

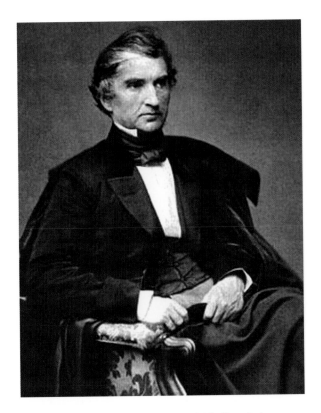

Maximilian II appointed Justus von Liebig first chairman of the order, originally restricted to nine members, that reviewed future bearers of the Maximilian order (see p. 90) for science and art.

Franz von Pocci created a caricature of the chemist Justus von Liebig for posterity: It depicts Liebig mixing magical potions in his laboratory in which he also held lectures on popular science for the interested general public.
Historical photograph by Franz Hanfstaengl.

and Liebig), 12 from Berlin, others from Göttingen and Vienna; of a total of 29 artists honored, 13 were from Munich and three from Berlin.

New members of the "intellectual aristrocracy" were also given intransparent key positions. These included literary figures and scholars invited every week to the "round table" by King Maximilian that had been held in the Residence since 1854, so that the king could be kept informed of contemporary advances and trends.

Events held in the large chemistry lecture hall — built for Justus von Liebig next to his private residence — where he and his colleagues held lectures on popular science, enabled locals and outsiders to meet publically. It was a stage for those recently appointed to present themselves and for the interested educated middle classes to amuse themselves. Liebig's own lectures were considered sensational due to the experiments he carried out, and even the auditorium acted as a strong magnet thanks to the presence of members of the royal fami-

The lyricist Emanuel Geibel was appointed professor at the university with no lecturing obligation and moved to Munich. Count Franz von Pocci was inspired to make this caricature, adding the verse:
"Geibel came at our behest,
Upon his steed, so that all
Of us in Munich could, at last,
Be inspired, both big and small."
Historical photograph
by Franz Hanfstaengl;
caricature by Franz von Pocci.

The highly esteemed mineralogist Franz von Kobell (1802–1882) at the academy and university was a passionate deer hunter. His hunting book "Wildanger" (1859) became a standard reference; his brilliance writing in dialect continues to live on in the "Tale of Brandner Kaspar" (1871), popular today thanks to a modern interpretation for the stage.
Historical photograph
by Franz Hanfstaengl;
caricature by Franz von Pocci.

"As prof of mineralogy
What other place would I but seek,
Than right up high above the trees
A'top a craggy mountain peak?!"

ly. Ladies were also among those listening, as the satirical magazine *Punsch* remarked on February 13, 1853: "The rush to my colleagues is huge; the ladies have moved a step forward, they don't just talk but also listen. When [...] the subject is an important male, the refined lady no longer says 'I spoke to him,' [or] 'I danced with him', but 'I listened to him.'"

No less prominent social events were appearances by leading figures of the Munich school of poets such as Emanuel Geibel (1815–84), who was appointed professor for literature and esthetics

(with no lecturing obligation) in 1852, or the productive writer Paul Heyse (1830–1914), who was awarded the Nobel Prize for literature in 1910. Other notable names were Friedrich Bodenstedt (1819–92), the mediator of Russian and Oriental poetry, the director of the court theater Franz von Dingelstedt (1814–81), the art benefactor Adolf Friedrich von Schack (1815–94), and, for a brief time, also Felix Dahn, (1834–1912), who started to work on his magnum opus "A Struggle for Rome" (4 vols., 1876) in 1857 while a private lecturer in the Faculty of Law.

MUNICH AS A CENTER OF HISTORICAL SCHOLARSHIP

Promoting historical scholarship was of central concern to the monarch in the course of his elitist policy. After the vain attempt to persuade Leopold von Ranke (1795–1886), a highly esteemed teacher from his student days in Berlin and a leading figure of the time for his methodology based on critical source classification and as a universal historiograph, to come to Munich, Maximilian II summoned two of Ranke's pupils with different profiles in 1856: Heinrich von Sybel (1817–95) and the Catholic Carl Adolf von Cornelius (1819–1903). The epochal innovation that turned Munich into the center of historical scholarship was the *Commission für deutsche Geschichts- und Quellenforschung* (commission for German historical and source-related research) within the Bavarian Academy of Sciences and Humanities. The pan-German research facility was to serve 15 to 20 selected members working on the publication of comprehensive, national source material. The first presidents, who were external as stipulated in the statutes, were the foundation's initiator Ranke (Berlin), followed by Sybel (Bonn) from 1886. Up until 1861 he had held the position of first executive secretary (local, as per the statutes). Apart from Sybel, Professor Georg Thomas von Rudhart (1792–1860), director of the Royal Bavarian Imperial Archive, was also a co-founder. In 2008, the Historical Commission celebrated its 150th anniversary.

EDUCATION IN THE SERVICE OF THE STATE

That Maximilian II's pragmatism discerned the need at that time to raise the level of academic vocational training is reflected in his founding of the Maximilianeum (1852). The importance the royal household attributed to the academic foundation with its secure financial backing from private means, transferred to the university's administra-

Heinrich von Sybel, a prominent representative of the Ranke School, who was called to LMU Munich in 1856, demonstrated the Protestant Prussian direction, also within the history of science, under medieval imperial rule. Under pressure as a "northerner," he followed a call to Bonn in 1861. Drawing by C.L. Sandberg.

For King Maximilan II it would have been particularly satisfying to know that the Historical Commission initiated an innovative form of endowment in 1980 to support a personalized fellowship for top-level historical research, headed by a board of trustees. The "Historisches Kolleg München," housed in Kaulbach's former city residence.

As a "nursery" for the upper echelons of the civil service, the Maximilianeum Foundation is aimed at promoting highly talented Gymnasium graduates in Bavaria. Today, the Bavarian parliament is also housed in the same building.

left
The foundation deeds of the Maximilianeum.

tion, is manifested in the Maximilianeum, completed in 1872. Seen from Maximilianstrasse, the monumental building forms the crowning glory that catches the eye, soaring above the far bank of the Isar. Today, it is occupied by the Bavarian parliament. During the Wittelsbach anniversary in 1980, Albrecht, Duke of Bavaria (1905–96) confirmed the allocation of funds to support female students, who are not housed in the historical building but in the Biederstein hall of residence.

The tightening clasp of the state on many areas of public life and their use for civil purposes also had ramifications on the university and its organizational structure. Innovations included establishing seminars at the university, an idea that had its roots in the classical disciplines at Halle and Göttingen universities. Based on the experience he had made in Königsberg, the mathematician Philipp Ludwig (von) Seidel (1821–96) introduced the mathematics and physics seminar in Munich. The historical seminar, instituted by von Sybel in 1857 and continued by his successor to the chair Wilhelm von Giesebrecht (1814–89), was a revolutionary success. A new organizational model with two branches — one providing instruction in crucial research methodology, the other preparation for ongoing Gymnasium teachers.

INTERNATIONAL GLAMOR AT JUBILEE CELEBRATIONS IN 1872

In 1872, Ludovico Maximilianea celebrated its 400th anniversary as the first German university within the complex ecclesiastical and political landscape that followed the First Vatican Council, convoked in 1869/70, and the "Smaller German Solution" within the Imperial Constitution (Imperial Proclamation of 1871). The quatrocentennial jubilee that was held amidst a conflicting environment of national enthusiasm, cultural struggles, ecclesiopolitical liberalism, and patriotic Bavarian conservatism, became an impressive demonstration of how self-assured the Alma mater had become. It was represented by the 73-year-old rector Ignaz von Döllinger, who was among the most high-profile, German theologians, as a result of his distancing himself from the dogma of papal infallibility and despite his excommunication. At 3,377, the official number of participants testifies to the magnitude of the four-day celebration attended by deputies from ten countries and 38 universities. The history of LMU by Carl von Prantl, commissioned by the Senate, appeared punctually in 1872.

"Jubilee celebrations for LMU`s 400th anniversary: Ovation from the students for Ignaz von Döllinger on August 1, 1872."
Drawing by L. Bechstein in the "Illustrirte Zeitung" of August 24, 1872.

In the course of the celebrations, some 30 honorary doctorates were awarded by the four worldy faculties. They were given to prominent figures in Germany and abroad from the fields of science, the arts, and economics. Apart from the Bavarian Minister of Cultural Affairs Johann Lutz (jurisprudence), recipients included the English reformist statesman and four-times Prime Minister William Ewart Gladstone (1809–98), his fellow countryman, the social reformer Anthony Ashley-Cooper, Earl of Shaftesbury (1801–85), the American mineralogist James Dwight Dana (1813–95), and Lord John Acton (1834–1902), a pupil and likeminded friend of Döllinger, all of whom turned up in person. The photo shows Döllinger (2nd from the right), Acton (right) and Gladstone (2nd from the left) at Villa Arco-Valley on Tegernsee in 1885.

The two-volumed standard work based on sourced archival material by the philosopher Carl von Prantl — who was not a historian — is still considered fundamental reading on the university's history, despite the polemic of certain eras.

Heinrich von Sybel, by this time in Bonn, gave the address on behalf of all German universities. The performance of Wagner's opera *Lohengrin* during the celebrations was a reflection of the king's interest in the arts, who was greeted by a "deafening applause" in the National Theater. A resounding echo to the university's anniversary came in 1873 in the form of the "Louis II Grant," with the stipulation to further an awareness of history among students.

INCREASING STABILITY
TO THE FINANCING OF THE UNIVERSITY

The ascension of the new king to the throne in 1864 marked a new era for the university and how it was perceived by the public, although parallels to the time under Maximilian were inevitably drawn at the outset. The benefactory disposition of the House of Wittelsbach did not suffer under the rule of Louis II (1845–86, reigned from 1864) or the prince-regent Luitpold (1821–1912, reigned from 1886), although Louis's personal aptitude was more strongly focussed on the arts.

The prestige that science enjoyed as a factor governing civilization grew steadily and was accompanied by the interest of the general public. As a result, the promotion of science no longer required any particular legitimization: The state and parliament had the moral obligation to adapt to dynamic developments.

To meet the university's needs, this necessitated — in concrete terms — the successive increase of state funding. This had to be included in the budget report, as specified by government legislation that superseded a similar method formerly used for the financing of trusts. The self-administrative rights over corporate assets through its own administrative body — "with full responsibility" — that were returned to the university in 1815, nevertheless remained unchanged (until 1970 — in Munich — when it was replaced by the budget committee). With the exception of those from the ruling house, initiatives from private benefactors stagnated to such an extent that the university's assets melted away, apart from the low income generated by real estate (such as from the *Universitätswald* forested areas around Landshut). From the middle of the century onward, private endowments, which actually provided genuine help in times of need, such as tuition grants or start-up capital for clinics, individual institutes, and seminars, could be registered once again. The gap between state finances to those of the university, however, became ever wider and increased the depedancy of the university on the state.

The immatriculation card of crown-prince Louis, later King Louis II of Bavaria, for the winter term 1864/65 at LMU.

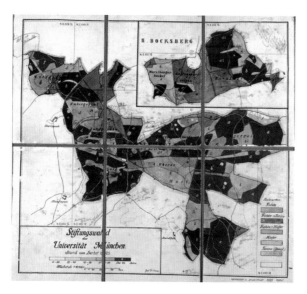

The Universitätswald (University Forest) around Landshut still belongs to LMU's assets, even though forestry engineering, formerly part of the Faculty of Economics (and an independent department since 1974) was transferred to the Technische Universität München in 1999.

ACADEMIC DISCIPLINES AND THEIR "FOUNDING YEARS" DURING THE EXPANSION OF THE UNIVERSITY

The number of students, which had dropped dramatically after 1851/52 due to wars and cholera epidemics, rose sharply after 1876 to approximately 4,000 around 1900 and some 7,000 by the outbreak of war in 1914. In the course of the 19th century, a swift process of specialization within academic disciplines took place. Symptomatic of this was the division of the Faculty of Philosophy into two sections under one dean in 1865 (later to become two faculties in 1937).

Partially as a result of examinations being recognized across Germany, students of law and medicine soon gained the upper hand. Differentiating between new disciplines, the founding of chairs, clinics, institutes, and seminars brought a radical structural change to the university on its way to

becoming a "large concern." This was reflected in the increase in the number of professors without chairs and associate professors, as well as academic staff (assistants, demonstrators), although responsibility was still monopolized by the professor ordinarius in each case. The rapid advances in research and teaching molded the fields of medicine and natural science in particular, as well as the humanities.

Progress in medicine and experimental subjects made a permanent and also visible mark on life in Munich and the cityscape itself. Trailblazing developments in diagnostic and therapeutic methods, combined with the invention of medical and technical instruments, resulted in a revolution of humongous dimensions in everyday society and in public health care.

With the old municipal hospital *Links der Isar* at its core, the university clinic district spread out around Sendlinger Tor. In 1855, an extension and new-build was erected for the physiological institute, in 1853–56 the maternity clinic in Sonnenstrasse (with the nursing school added in 1900), in 1874 the pathological, in 1878 the clinical medicine, and in 1879 the hygiene institutes, in 1891 the surgical clinic, in 1893 the pharmacological institute, followed by the construction of other major clinics around the turn of the century, such as that for psychiatry, opthalmology, and dentistry, the latter as the first dedicated new building of its kind in Germany. The new anatomy building with its imposing dome dates from 1905–08, the new structure for the first gynecological hospital from 1914. In 1908, a new building for the previously private orthopedic clinic was opened some distance from the "clinic district" in Harlaching. For a long time the parallel existence and intertwining of municipal and state institutes resulted in an overlapping of specialist areas; its disentanglement lasted until well into the 1950s.

The Clinic for Gynecology and Maternity Care with chapel, c. 1928.

The Outpatient Clinic on Pettenkoferstrasse, c. 1910.

Exterior view of the Surgical Clinic …

… and a view of the operating theater.

The new physiological institute of 1855.

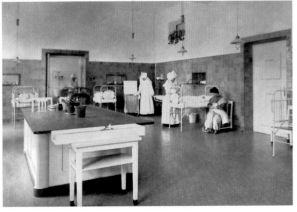

Infants' ward in the Dr. von Hauner childrens' hospital.

Munich's Institute of Anatomy on Pettenkoferstrasse with its characteristic domed rotunda is the first reinforced concrete building in Germany. In a strictly conformative Jugendstil design, it was conceived as a "Gesamtkunstwerk." This did not only refer to the exterior of the building itself, but the whole of the interior fittings as well. In 2008, it celebrated his 100th jubilee.

PIONEERING WORK IN MODERN MEDICINE

The "Munich Medical School" radiated brilliance thanks to the personalities mentioned here, whose names are representative of the extensive specialist areas and success attained in research in the field of medicine: Karl von Pfeufer (1806–69), whose "rational medicine" superseded the Ringseis era; his pupil Josef Lindwurm (1824–74), a specialist for typhus and syphilis and a pioneer of dermatology in Munich; Max von Pettenkofer (1818–1901), a genius in experimental hygiene in Germany, whose fight against epidemics led to the construction of the sewage system in the city of Munich. Other figures worthy of mention include the multitalented zoologist and phyiologist Carl

Theodor Ernst von Siebold (1804–85) and Carl von Voit (1831–1908), teacher and friend of Pettenkofer's and the founder of nutritional science that led to physiology developing a mementum of its own; the pathologist Ludwig von Buhl (1816–80) who made a name for himself researching tuberculosis; Hugo von Ziemssen (1829–1902), a pupil of Virchow's, whose modern clinical research institute set new standards in the field of diagnostics; and the surgeon Johann Nepomuk von Nußbaum (1829–90), whose antiseptic treatment of wounds launched a new era in abdominal surgery. Franz Christoph von Rothmund (1801–91) is considered the inventor of inhalational anesthesia using ether and chloroform (c. 1850), an innovation that rapidly raised the number of operations; his son,

Munich owes its sewage system to Max von Pettenkofer. Thanks to his initiative, the city was one of the cleanest in Europe at the turn of the 20th century. Today, the Institute for Hygiene and Medical Microbiology at LMU is named after him.
Photograph by Friedrich Müller.

August von Rothmund (1830–1906), lectured on opthalmology at Munich University. Emil Kraepelin (1856–1926), the initiator of the *Deutsche Forschungsanstalt für Psychiatrie* (German Institute for Psychiatric Research, later the Max Planck Institute) established in 1917, is not to be omitted from the list of success stories in Munich. Psychiatry had evolved since the 1860s from the regional lunatic asylum into a university subject; one of its early professors was the neuroanatomist Bernhard von Gudden (1824–86), whose name remains inextricably linked to the death of his royal patient, Louis II. Apart from Kraeplin, the circle of Gudden's pupils included the specialist in internal medicine Friedrich von Müller (1858–1941), who taught generations of clinicians and gained fame at a later date. His *Taschenbuch der medizinisch-klinischen Diagnostik* reached its 50th edition in the year of his death.

PRIVATE BEQUESTS FOR CLINICS

The polyclinic deserves a special mention. Teaching at the polyclinic, introduced back in 1843 (for the fields of medicine, surgery, pediatrics, etc.), owes its advancement to the legacy of a medic — and latterly doctor in Augsburg — Franz Reisinger (1787–1855). The bequest of the former professor of surgery in Landshut was earmarked for the establishment of an "educational institute for doctors," whose tuition was to be based on "practical application." Thanks to the dedication of the internist Franz Paul Seitz (1811–92), a property on Sonnenstrasse was acquired and a clinic opened. It included, among other facilities, two sick rooms each with three beds, a postmortem room, and even a stall for laboratory animals. By 1910, the Reisingerianum that had since been expanded and which treated more than 40,000 patients a year, had grown to accommodate eight polyclinical divisions thanks to donations.

The Dr. von Hauner children's hospital was an entirely private initiative. It was set by the general practitioner August Hauner (1811–84), who trained in Munich, with a certain private capital and through donations. The sanitorium for children upto six years of age, opened in 1846 and modelled on St. Annen Hospital in Vienna, came under the patronage of Queen Theresa. With help from the city of Munich, a new building was erected for the clinic on Goetheplatz, that had more than 300 in-patients around 1860. It was incorporated into the university in 1886, where Hauner had held the position of honorary professor since 1853.

RAPID PROGESS IN THE NATURAL SCIENCES

There were many reciprocal effects generated between the disciplines of medicine and natural science. From a legal point of view, the latter was largely tied to the state collections and institutes. It evolved from the "attributes" of the Bavarian Academy of Sciences and Humanities and came under the direction of professors whose standing increasingly resulted from their tenured professorships. It was in this way that subjects such as minerology,

paleontology, geology, prehistory, botany, and zoology were gradually incorporated into the university syllabus.

Important representatives of this subject who succeeded Martius as director of the old and new botanic garden were Carl Wilhelm Nägeli (1817–91) and Karl von Goebel (1855–1932). The latter, appointed in 1891, is associated with the final move from the site in the city center to Nymphenburg. Together with his zoology colleague Richard von Hertwig (1850–1937), who taught for a period of many decades, Goebel — a highly

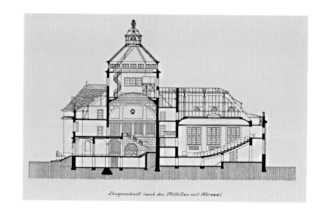

The south front of the institute building at the Royal Botanical Garden in Nymphenburg and as longitudinal section.

regarded botanist — turned Munich into an international center for experimental biological research.

Following a spectacular initial period, the chemistry laboratory on Sophienstrasse led a quiet existence for some time. It was not until Liebig's successor Adolf von Baeyer (1835–1917) was appointed in 1873 that the institute developed into a world-famous center for research and teaching with departments for organic and inorganic chemistry, from which more than 50 university lecturers emerged. His discoveries in the synthetic manufacture of dyes brought the "Titan of chemistry" into contact with major industrial enterprises (BASF). As a point of interest, he was able to help the "fairytale king" Louis II obtain the blue suited to the light filter in the Venus Grotto at Linderhof Palace. Baeyer and his no less famous successor Richard Willstätter (1873–1942) were awarded the Nobel Prize for chemistry in 1905 and 1915 respectively.

Physiological chemistry was also practiced in the older pharmaceutical institute that belonged to the university. Pharmaceutics, a nominal subject within the Faculty of Medicine under the auspices of the professors Johann Andreas Buchner (1783–1852) and his son, Ludwig Andreas Buchner (1813–97), entered a new phase under Albert Hilger (1839–1905). Like his predecessors, Hilger was a pharmacist. In 1896/97 the institute — that by then belonged to the Second Philosophical Division — moved from rooms in the Ludovician university building, which it had been allocated in 1840, into an extension added to the Botanical Museum, before taking over the whole building at Karlstrasse 29 in 1915. In connection with Imperial and Bavarian legislation governing foodstuffs (including the introduction of an examination for nutritional biochemists in 1894), the affiliated, state-run research institute for foodstuffs, drinks and tobacco gained importance in the public's eye when Hilger was director.

The chemistry laboratory became a center of research and teaching of world renown under Adolf von Baeyer. In 1937 it legally became part of LMU.

INDIVIDUAL ASPECTS OF HIGHLY SPECIALIZED METHODS

The "physical cabinet" founded in 1753 moved into the university building on Ludwigstrasse in 1840, where Philipp Jolly (1809–84) together with the mathematician Philipp Ludwig von Seidel established what was already known as the mathematics and physics seminar in 1856 (institutional division: 1922). He used the purpose built auditorium tower for gravitation measurements to determine the earth's density. Despite its disadvantageous location — the magnetic field being effected by the nearby tramlines — the seminar subsequently retained its old site to which an extension was added in 1892–94. It was here where Wilhelm Conrad Röntgen (1845–1923) worked between 1900 and 1920. The discovery of x-rays that he had made while still in Würzburg earned him the Nobel Prize for physics in 1901.

A stroke of good fortune for the continuation of Röntgen's research on the electrical conductivity of crystals was the appointment of Arnold Sommerfeld (1868–1951) in 1906. With the help of endowments, including that made by Hermann Anschütz-

Kaempfe († 1931), the inventor of the gyrocompass, Sommerfeld founded the Institute of Theoretical Physics in 1909, kept adding equipment and forged a way for nuclear physics while in contact with the Dane Nils Bohr. His colleague, the private lecturer Max (von) Laue (1879–1960), made his discovery of the diffraction of x-rays by crystals in 1912 (the Laue interference equation), which led to his being called to Zurich and to his receiving the Nobel Prize for physics in 1914.

THEOLOGY AND JURISPRUDENCE IN THE EXTENDED MAIN BUILDING COMPLEX

While medicine and natural science continued to expand on several sites in different areas, the advancement of the humanities was initially limited to around the main university building in the Maxvorstadt district, which could not even remotely provide adequate accommodation. The physics building extension already mentioned was followed in 1897–98 by an addition to the north wing on Adalbertstrasse, and in 1905–09 the architectural masterpiece, adjoining Gärtner's building, comprising the new block with the atrium and *Auditorium Maximum* extending as far as Amalienstrasse. The expansion of the university building now provided space for 41 lecture halls instead of 15, and 60 rooms for seminars.

New specialist subjects were organized into "seminars" (in the sense of both instruction and premises, similar to the "institute" structure in experimental disciplines), each being provided with its own reference library, work room, own specific budget from the state, and within a short time with their own assistants. Ministerial approval did not always mark a seminar's beginnings; sometimes professors's apartments and private book collections were used, with the donation of libraries forming the basis of a seminar.

Faculty seminars dominated in theology and law. In 1864 the ministry of education approved a homiletic seminar under the director of the Georgianum as a professor ordinarius in pastoral theology. The government funding of the ecclesiastical history seminar under Alois Knöpfler (1874–1921), that had existed since 1886 and that he himself supported in the form of annual grants for his students, admittedly took a considerable effort. It was only in 1912 that it was given the necessary financial basis. Meanwhile, the Faculty of Theology was able to open the Biblical exegetical and the canonistic seminars with ministerial approval as early as in 1905.

The first law seminar owed its establishment in 1881 to the foundation bequest of councilor Dr. Heinrich Hofmann, who died in 1877. The "strictly academic practices" were initially criminal law and the history of law, the German branch of which was represented from 1892 onward by Karl von Amira (1848–1930), a commanding and illustrious authority.

In addition, following the appointment of Leopold Wenger (1874–1953), a pupil of the legal historian Ludwig Mitteis (1859–1921), the seminar for papyrology — that at that time was unique in Germany — was founded in 1909 as a center for comparative ancient legal history. Turned into an "institute" in 1923, it now bears Wenger's name. In 1916, the institute for comparative law followed, under the direction of the Mitteis pupil Ernst Rabel (1874–1955). The state science seminar goes back to Lujo Brentano (1844–1931), the founder of the historical German school of national economics in 1892.

FACULTY OF PHILOSOPHY: DIFFERENTIATION IN THE HISTORY CURRICULUM

A wave of newly founded seminars conditioned Division I of the Faculty of Philosophy that had been independent since 1865. Disciplines, includ-

The atrium at LMU was built in 1905–09 as an extension to the main building. The picture shows monuments made by two sculptors, Bernhard Bleeker (1881–1968) and Knut Åkerberg (1864–1955) of the benefactors, Prince-Regent Luitpold and Louis I, respectively.

The west façade on Amalienstrasse, flanked by two monolithic allegories to "Truth" and "The Victory of Science," brought the building assessor German Bestelmeyer (1874–1942) a certain fame, as did his designs for the Deutsches Museum and the Technische Universität München.

Karl von Amira, professor for constitutional law from 1892 onward, was the father of legal archeology.

The "lecturn socialist" Lujo Brentano, one of the most prominent sociopolitical advocates of the German Empire, was a brilliant speaker and teacher. The crowds of listeners to his lectures, around 570 students, initiated the building of an extension to the university building with the Auditorium Maximum, that had already been on the books since the rectorship of 1901/02.

ing history, in which students were prepared for the teaching profession, set a standard in the move toward greater professionalization. The history seminar, founded in 1858, however, focussed on "general history" as a collective subject. As part of a national political and cultural idealism, this was to reinforce that Bavaria's status as a center of learning was on a par with Prussia's, something that — despite King Maximilian II's popular gestures — relegated the history of Bavaria to the wings.

Sporadic, approved moves during the Ludovician period — in Görres's time and later — to teach Bavarian history and "historical auxiliary subjects" propagated by the theologian Andreas Buchner (1778–1854) and the archivist Michael Söltl (1797–1888), were neglected for centuries. Those who thirsted for information were dependent on other faculties which touched on historical aspects in Bavaria (such as ecclesiastical or legal history). Only after the university's celebrations in 1872 did public debates in parliament, which were also in the spirit of a cultural struggle, once again call to mind the urgent need for a professor of Bavarian history. It was however to take a few more years until an independent chair for Bavarian history was finally created in 1898, held by Sigmund von Riezler (1843–1927), and followed in 1917 by Michael Doeberl (1861–1928). Doeberl also worked to found a commission for the regional history of Bavaria at the Bavarian Academy of Sciences and Humanities, that was established in 1927.

Dividing history into epochs was also a method introduced in nominal subjects. In light of this cultural struggle and as a result of the history seminar's denominational equality, Theodor von Heigel (1842–1915) was appointed Giesebrecht Professor for modern history in 1885, while Cornelius was succeeded by Hermann (von) Grauert (1850–1924) as the "Catholic" *ordinarius* for medieval history. Both historians are associated with the reorganization of the university archive following their appointment to the governing body (1892, 1905) as, with a view to the year 1906 — a royal jubilee and the 80th anniversary of the university's move to Munich — the academic Senate had decided on the publication of the Ingolstadt register.

At around the turn of the century, ancient history was also institutionalized as an independent subject. Robert (von) Pöhlmann (1852–1914) was appointed its first representative at LMU in 1901. That he was not a genuine ancient historian of the Mommsen school but a medievalist, constitutional historian and pupil of Giesebrech as well as an accomplished economist, drew criticism at the time from historian colleagues, not least of all with regard to the "antiquated state" of Bavarian examination rules, which are not aimed at the "expert" but an accumulation of knowledge in all subjects.

Hermann von Grauert (1850–1924) did not live to see the secular jubilee in 1926 that he had helped organize. The board of directors of the provisionally equipped university archive decided on a new professional indexing of the repertorium, made possible financially by taking on an "assistant": Karl Alexander von Müller (1882–1964), doctorate candidate (1906), then assistant professor for Bavarian history. The chronic of the academic institutes at LMU compiled in 1926, marked so to speak the beginning of a successful career (1928: university, 1935: academy), that however due to the history of the times, moved into a politically dubious area. H. v. Grauert as Rector; painting in oil by Gebhard Fugel, 1916.

The byzantinist August Heisenberg. His son, Werner Heisenberg, was awarded the Nobel Prize for physics in 1932.

The Medieval Latin philologist Ludwig Traube liked to hold his lectures in his apartment — where it was not such a squeeze — and with international participants. The institutionalization of the medieval latin seminar in Munich was the first in this subject at a German university.

PHILOLOGY AS A MAJOR SUBJECT AND FRINGE DISCIPLINES

The Faculty of Philosophy, structured to provide training for Gymnasium teachers, was modelled on the Thiersch philological seminar. From 1863 onward, the Greek scholar Wilhelm Christ (1831–1906) was its head. He was succeeded in 1880 by the Latin scholar Eduard Wölfflin (1831–1908), the principal initiator of the *Thesaurus Linguae Latinae*, a daunting, lexicographical research undertaking, anchored in the Bavarian Academy, that was spread over several institutes.

In the wake of the pan-German petition by the Weimar "German Shakespeare Society" from 1865 for the introduction of chairs for English and French, as well as in the course of the Bavarian

school reform, the seminar for modern languages and literature was established in 1876. Konrad Hofmann (1819–90), as a German philologist, was appointed successor to his teacher, Schmeller, in 1856. At the same time he was a representative of Ancient Romance Studies, whereas Hermann Wilhelm Breymann (1843–1910) stood for the modern language branch. Through the appointment of Hermann Paul (1846–1921) and Franz Muncker (1855–1926) in 1893 and 1896 respectively, the seminar for German philology became institutionalized. In 1912, the study of English language and literature became a subject in its own right. Thanks to Karl Vossler (1872–1949), Romance Studies evolved into a discipline in the field of cultural and scientific history from 1911 onward through positivistic and philological methodology.

Bread-and-butter courses aside, it was the highly specialized "minor subjects" that gave the faculties in Munich their unmistakable profile rather than academic disciplines attended by the "masses." One example of the considerable personal effort that had to be mustered up at times for innovative research in the face of political and official short-sightedness, is Byzantine Studies. It was called to life by Karl Krumbacher (1856–1909), a pupil of Christ. Due to the low frequency that this seemingly foreign subject was taught, the Bavarian parliament denied to give its support; university funds conceded a paltry annual allowance of 100 German Marks. It was only with the help of funds donated by, among others, the Greek government and the city of Trieste that the seminar for medieval and modern Greek philology was given ministerial approval in 1898. Krumbacher bequeathed his specialist library to it in 1909, thus ensuring that the seminar under his successor August Heisenberg (1869–1930) could develop into a meeting-place for scholars from around the world and a nursery for the next generation of experts in Byzantine Studies.

Medieval Latin Philology, officially established in 1906, had de facto already gained a lasting presence in the field of research since the habilitation of its founder Ludwig Traube (1861–1907) in 1888. Today it is a research discipline of world renown.

Other philological seminars followed: In 1905, that of oriental languages with an Aryan and Semitic department; in 1909, the seminar for Indo-European languages; in 1911, that of Slavic Studies.

CULTURAL STUDIES, PHILOSOPHY, AND PEDAGOGY

Disciplines in the field of cultural studies became established, centered on classical philology. Archeology and the history of art were already rooted in the "art museum" at Landshut University (antiquities chamber with collections of copperplate engravings, casts, and paintings), that had been installed by the history painter Simon Klotz (1776–1824) under the elector Maximilian IV Joseph. Klotz was appointed professor of "fine arts" in 1804, thus becoming the first professor ordinarius for the history of art at a university in Germany. After his dismissal in 1817, the chair remained unoccupied; the "Klotz Inventory" kept in the archives is now being analyzed.

The archeology seminar was founded with the help of a donation from the historian Carl Adolf von Cornelius in 1887 and accommodated in the gallery in the Court Garden. It enjoyed a considerable boost after 1894 under the direction of Adolf Furtwängler (1853–1907) — the father of the famous conductor — thanks to the use of modern methods of critical anaysis using replicas and research into the work of the great masters, as well as the expansion of teaching material to include a photographic collection. This took place in close association with the art history seminar that was not officially recognized until 1909, although its earlier existence had been acknowledged. Under Heinrich Wölfflin (1864–1945), the son of the classical philologist Eduard Wölfflin, it gained a position of world renown from 1912 onward.

After protracted negotiations, a chair and seminar for musicology was created in 1909/10, the suitability of the subject as a university discipline being contentious. It was pioneered by Adolf Sandberger (1864–1943) of Würzburg, who had been teaching the history of music in Munich ever since his habilitation in 1894, for which he was supported by Wilhelm von Riehl, and deepened through his curatorial position for hand-written music scores at the state library. In 1899, he founded the *Gesellschaft zur Herausgabe von Denkmälern der Tonkunst in Bayern*, issuing its first "monuments of art music in Bavaria" in 1900. Sandberger's pupils include the composer Werner Egk (1901–83).

Martin Grabmann, an exceptional scholar of medieval philosophy and theology (standard work on the history of scholastic methodology, 1909/10), gave his name to the Grabmann Research Institute founded at LMU in 1954, that was based on the library he bequeathed.

The educationalist and pacifist Wilhelm Foerster polarized public opinion at the university.

The seminar organization also set the signal for the methodological independence of psychology within the philosophy division. Steps undertaken by the philosopher Carl Stumpf (1848–1936) led to a psychology seminar being established in 1894. The philosophy seminar, that the Munich philosophy professor Georg von Hertling (1843–1919) — a member of the Center Party, Prime Minister of Bavaria from 1912 through 1917, and Chancellor of the German Empire in 1917/18 — had fought for since his appointment in 1882, was first established under his successor Clemens Baeumker (1853–1924) in 1912. Baeumker, known in particular for his studies in the history of medieval philosophy, was also the teacher of Martin Grabmann (1875–1949).

The institutionalization of pedagogy as a "philosophical" discipline and its positioning between classical philology, experimental psychology, and its school-oriented application was accompanied by hefty controversy. The founding of the seminar in 1914 had not just been delayed because of the war but also as a result of the contentious appointment of Friedrich Wilhelm Foerster (1869–1966) as professor of pedagogy in 1913/14. His fundamental concept linking pedagogy with politics was based on a radical ethical and pacifistic stance that was critical of the Empire. Student demonstrations for and against him fuelled the "Foerster case" all the more as the war drew on, resulting in the ministry ordering his suspension, followed by his resignation in 1920. For the time being, pedagogy remained a methodological political issue. The highly esteemed successor to the chair, Aloys Fischer (1880–1937), could do nothing to change this either.

GEOSCIENCES

The geosciences evolved more or less between the different divisions in the Faculty of Philosophy. Like zoology, botany, and mineralogy, they were the offspring of natural science, for which Louis I had given Gotthilf Heinrich von Schubert — the curator of the zoological and paleontological collection — a teaching position, which also encompassed anthropology. This branch proved itself to be a Munich specialty. The medic and private lecturer Johannes Ranke (1836–1916), the nephew of the Berlin historian and Schubert's grandson, was granted the post of professor extraordinarius in 1869 for the subject that by then had been separated from general natural science. This was upgraded to the first full professorship for anthropology in Germany in 1886. Ranke established a prehistoric collection, initially as part of the large state-owned paleontological collection, run since 1865 by Karl Alfred von Zittel (1839–1904). In 1902, he founded an anthropological, prehistoric collection in its own right with skulls from finds in Bavaria and Europe. These were supplemented by gifts from Princess Theresa of Bavaria (1850–1925) from former German colonies. In 1912, a seminar (institute) was allocated to the tenured professorship, to which Ranke bequeathed his private library.

Geography, taught by an adjunct professor as "the study of the regions of the world" for a long time, became an independent subject after the creation of a professor extraordinarius post in 1892. In 1899, ministerial approval was given for a geography seminar to be established, but the "institute" did not start to flourish until the appointment of the renowned explorer of the South Pole, Erich von Drygalski (1865–1949) in 1906 to the new chair for geography.

ACADEMIZATION OF VOCATIONAL COURSES

Is it surprising that the staggering development within the faculties acted as a catalyst for the practical profession branch? In the search for greater social prestige, an increasing academization of vocational courses followed. In appeals and at congresses across Germany, engineers, foresters, and vets fought increasingly volubly for the "scientification" of their professional studies and for them to be put on an equal footing with a university education. This led on the one hand to the establishment of the "Fachhochschule" (such as the Technische Universität München, the Academy of Fine Arts, and the University of Music and Performing Arts in Munich). On the other, it led to other branches of education being integrated into the university curriculum. Forestry engineers and veterinary surgeons decided in favor of the latter.

FORESTRY

Although forestry engineering came under cameralism at Ingolstadt University, the teaching of aspirants to the state forestry department took place from 1790 onward in the school of forestry founded in Munich that same year. In 1802, it was moved to Weihenstephan, and since 1819 has been at the Royal Central College of Forestry in Aschaffenburg. The Faculty of Economics at Munich University, however, offered a supplementary course for those wishing to pursue a career at a higher level under the honorary doctor Professor Karl Friedrich Roth (1810–91).

From 1870 onward, the re-organization of forestry engineering could be delayed no longer. Support came in the form of an appeal for a reform published under the pseudonym "Silvius" by the forester August Ganghofer (1827–1900), later to become director of the Bavarian state forest authority. From his son, Ludwig Ganghofer, he was even turned into a literary monument as the fictional character *Forstmeister Ehrenreich*. In 1878, the main course for forestry engineers was transferred to LMU, initially while still retaining the foundation course in Aschaffenburg (until 1911), which prolonged the length of the subject as a whole. The

The new building erected in 1899 on Amalienstrasse served forestry engineering until its move to Weihenstephan in 1992. It now forms part of the historicum.

Karl Gayer was one of the pioneers of modern forestry. His publications "Die Forstbenutzung" (The Use of the Forest) and "Der Waldbau" (Silviculture) were among standard works of literature in this field.

faculty was given several chairs, to which five acknowledged forestry experts were called. These included Karl Gayer (1822–1907), the most famous pioneer in this subject at that time.

Initiated by the *Verein deutscher Versuchsanstalten*, the state research institute for forestry was created in the garden to the south of the university building with several departments (from 1924: "institutes") for pedology, forest botany, applied zoology, etc., that were under the direction of faculty professors.

VETINARY MEDICINE: PROMOTION TO A UNIVERSITY FACULTY WITH DOCTORAL RIGHTS

Vetinary medicine, that also developed out of cameralism, had its first educational institution in the *Thier-Arzney-Schule* (Animal School of Medicine) on the edge of the English Garden. Founded in 1790 by the Ingolstadt professor Anton J. Will

The entrance arch into the courtyard at the veterinary clinic on Veterinärstrasse, designed by the landscape architect and former director of the state gardens and parks Ludwig von Sckell (1750–1823), also reflects the history of the English Garden around 1800.

The new surgical clinic of veterinary science in Königin-strasse (above) and the operating theater (below).

(1752–1821), its status was raised to that of the central vetinary college in the kingdom of Bavaria in 1810. The core of the animal clinic building was the secularized so-called *Jesuiterwasch* (Jesuit bathhouse) on the bleaching fields in what was then the suburban district of Schwabing, that was revamped and fitted out with 37 stalls for horses. Since the middle of the century, the struggle by the association of vetinary surgeons to raise the status of their profession led to a re-organization of the school. The clinical methods used were modernized and brought up to the level of human medicine at that time, the professors initially coming from that discipline of medicine themselves. In this respect, only the pathologist Otto (von) Bollinger (1843–1909), who achieved international fame for his work on epizootics, and Johann Feser (1841–96), who set up a therapeutic research station, the first of its kind in a vetinary teaching institute, are worth a special mention.

At the time of the secularization celebrations in 1890, the academization process in veterinary medicine had initially been concluded with university status being officially conferred on the vetinary college. A decree pronounced by the prince-regent in 1892, raised the rank and uniform of professors at the vetinary college to those of university professors. The new self-confidence within the discipline is reflected in the construction of the proud new clinic complex on Königinstrasse in 1896–1902.

From 1902 onward, the *Abitur* became a prerequisite for studying vetinary science. The granting of doctoral and habilitation rights was given by decree in 1910. The first holder of an honorary degree in vetinary medicine (Dr. med. vet. h. c.) was Crown-Prince Louis (1845–1921), later to become Louis III, Bavaria's last king (1913–18), in recognition of his work to confer doctoral rights on the subject within Bavaria. Modelled on Swiss vetinary colleges (Bern, Zurich 1900/01), the royal Bavarian university of vetinary science was incorporated into the University of Munich in 1914. It was as such the first faculty for vetinary medicine in the German Empire.

THE UNIVERSITY ENTERS THE 20TH CENTURY

At the turn of the century, the inner-political conflicts at the university to do with corporate autonomy and the representation of the interests of specific groups that had been smoldering since 1848, surfaced once again. Initially a free student movement, based on the *Finkenschaft* fraternity in Leipzig emerged, whose idealistic aims soon became mixed with Socialist ideas. It primarily championed an improvement in the legal and social situation of non-corporate students. Its petitions to the academic Senate in 1900/02 sparked debates about the student regulations from 1891, and in 1913 effected first of all the much delayed revision of association rights and the right of assembly. Only in 1918 did the

Senate approve the provisional draft of a bylaw on the formation of a "General Students' Committee" (AStA), the prerequisite for a representation of the constituted student body in the Senate. The revolutionary change from a monarchy to a republic lay between the first AStA elections in December 1918 and it being legally recognized.

The will among students for reform was also behind the "student workers's further education courses" established in 1906/07 in Munich, and the "Academic Social Committee" founded in 1914. Headed by Fritz Beck (1889–1934), later initiator of the *Studentenhaus München e.V.* association to "alleviate the hardship of young students" (1920), these set a precedent for student self-help organizations in the post-war period.

The need for a solution to the extraordinarius problem, that had grown as a result of the number of habilitations, was voiced once again. While the founding of the German Professors's Day in 1907, largely through the involvement of Lujo Brentano, was primarily aimed at defending academic freedom from party and ecclesiopolitical constrictions, so the interests of professional groups, that found their continuation in regional organizations of lecturers and professors without chairs, were awakened at the same time as a result. The Ministry of Education and Cultural Affairs's reaction to this in 1913 led to untenured professors being accepted from then on in "other faculties."

THE SITUATION DURING WORLD WAR I

Leading up to and during World War I, in which more than two thirds of the generation of students at that time fought on the front, German universities professed their loyalty to the empire. An expression of this national patriotism was the introduction of official festivities at universities in 1914 to celebrate the founding of the empire. The party political climate in Bavaria, however, suffered under the burden of constitutional debates concerning the change of government following the death of the prince-regent, Luitpold, on December 12, 1912, and the accession to the throne of Louis III, the last king of Bavaria.

LMU Munich, whose professors held the most varied of views regarding the debate on the objective of the war, had to face a particular challenge due to the "Foerster case," that came to a head in 1914. Demonstrations against the pacifist professor had once again called the principle of academic freedom into question, especially in the light of his public attacks on the empire's foreign policy and national conservatism. Despite attempts by the rector in 1915/16, Hermann von Grauert, to mediate, disturbances escalated and Foerster was forced to take involuntary leave.

OPENING UP UNIVERSITY EDUCATION TO WOMEN

Up until World War I, the female student had become a conspicuous factor in Germany too. Although somewhat hesitantly, universities had started to accept female students in the 1890s, albeit only on a guest visitor basis that was approved in each individual case. Officially, women were only allowed to matriculate after the turn of the century (Baden in 1900, Bavaria in 1903, ultimately Prussia and Mecklenburg in 1908/09). For Bavaria, the Prince-Regent, Luitpold, signed the ministerial petition in September 1903, that permitted "women, who possess the matura certificate from a humanist Gymnasium or Realgymnasium in Germany, to matriculate at universities in Bavaria." 15 female students enrolled in the Faculty of Medicine for the winter term in 1903/04.

The reform in girls's education — traditionally in convent schools in Bavaria — however, limped far behind modern developments. It was only in 1911

Kühne Begründung

Student: "Schau mal, Fritz, welch ein netter Käfer!"
Professor: "Wie sind Sie denn auf die unglückliche Idee gekommen, Naturwissenschaft zu studieren? Auf diesem Gebiete werden Sie's nie zu eTwas bringen, nachdem Sie im vierten Semester noch eine Gans für einen Käfer halten."
[Eugen Kirchner 1922]

The university very hesitantly opened itself up to female students. That they were not seldom subject to mockery and discrimination is shown in the drawing of 1922 made by the Munich caricaturist Eugen Kirchner (1865–1938). The text, entitled "Bold Reasoning" reads as follows:
Student: "Look, Fritz. What a nice bird."
Professor: "Where on earth did you get the unfortunate idea from to study natural science? You'll never make it very far in this field if — in your fourth term — you still can't tell the difference between a nice bird and a silly goose."

K. Ludwig-Maximilians-Universität München.

DEKANAT
der medizinischen Fakultät.

EINLADUNG

zur

Antrittsvorlesung des Fräulein Dr. med. Adele Hartmann

am

**Freitag, den 20. Dezember 1918, abends 6 Uhr punkt
in der Poliklinik, Pettenkoferstr. 8a, mediz. Hörsaal Nr.235 (I. Stock)**

Vortrag:

Ueber die bisherigen Erklärungsversuche der Zellteilung.

The first woman to gain a position as a private lecturer in Germany was the Bavarian officer's daughter Adele Hartmann (1881–1937). Her schooling and studying lasted a long time before she was able to hold her inaugural lecture in anatomy in Munich in December 1918. She went to school in the Max-Joseph-Stift and took her teaching exams in 1898, followed by a two-year stay in England as a governess. From 1903 she attended an Abitur class which she successfully completed in 1906 as an external pupil at the Ludwig Gymnasium, before beginning to study.

that schools for daughters of the gentry were allowed to teach up to *Abitur*. Alternatives were to be found in private Gymnasium courses for girls, evidence for which can be found from 1900 onward, as well as taking the *Abitur* as an external pupil at a boys's Gymnasium.

The first female postgraduates at the university, Agnes Kelly from Australia and Maria Ogilvie-Gordon from Scotland, were educated in England and took their doctoral vivas in 1900 in Division II of the Faculty of Philosophy. Both were pupils of the zoologist Richard von Hertwig, among others, who penned the following opening sentence to his dissertation assessment, which is frequently quoted even today: "We are dealing here with something entirely novel."

Before this, two honorary doctorates in philosophy had been given: In 1897 in Division II, to Princess Theresa of Bavaria, for her services to natural history; in 1898 in Division I, to Lady Charlotte Blennerhasset, née Countess Leyden (1843–1917), for services to literary history. Up until 1993, they were to remain the only women to receive this honor from the Faculty of Philosophy. To commemorate the 100th year since the first honorary doctorate was given to a woman, the "Theresa of Bavaria Foundation for Women in Sciences" was founded. Princess Theresa, who undertook long research expeditions abroad, is to be remembered by her membership to the Bavarian Academy of Sciences and Humanities that she was granted in 1892 — albeit "only" on an honorary basis — after proposals that were first mooted in 1890 to elect Lady Blennerhasset and Theresa failed legally due to the traditional statutes. Only since 1995 have ordinary Academy members also included women.

When, in article 109 of the Imperial Constitution of 1919, it was laid down that "men and women have

Princess Theresa of Bavaria, the first woman to be given an honorary doctorate from LMU. (certificate on page 118)

the same fundamental civil rights and obligations," female students were already increasingly contributing to the "quantum leap" in the number of students at universities in Germany, including Munich. While out of a total of 4,855 students there were only 47 women in the winter term 1903/04, their number had risen to 699 out of 6,213 (11.3 percent) by the winter term 1919/1920, and ten years later was at 1,506 out of 8,583, which corresponds to 17.5 percent. Up until 1918, the university could count 174 female doctorates in a wide variety of

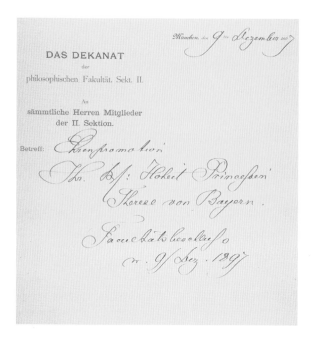

subjects. The first doctorate in law was awarded in 1927; the first in vetinary science in 1928. The face of academic professions began to change radically due to the emancipation of women in education — just at the time when the work "On the Physiological Deficiency of Women" by the neurologist and endocrinologist Paul Möbius (1853–1907) of Leipzig, completed in 1900, became a bestseller. Its tenth edition was printed in 1912.

CENTENARY CELEBRATION OF THE UNIVERSITY'S MOVE IN 1926 — A WARNING SIGNAL FOR ACADEMIC FREEDOM

University foundation celebrations — sensitive social events — were and still are indicators of their contemporary and historical situation, and signalize the direction of future developments, especially in critical political and social times or reform periods concentrated around the turn of a century.

11826 — a time still effected by the censorship of the press within the police state that was intensified in a new law in 1819, and demagogical perse-

cution, based on the feared radicalization of fraternities — conditioned the beginnings of LMU in Munich under the rector Georg Leonhard von Dresch, who pleaded for the dignity of knowledge, the "freedom of the word and the unrestricted impartation of thoughts" necessary for them to blossom; i.e. for the freedom to teach and to learn, in principle the focus of the debate on fundamental rights held at the National Assembly in the Paulskirche in 1848/49.

In 1926, during the difficult post-war years and after the revolutionary transition of the German empire and its individual states, including the Bavarian monarchy, to democratic forms of government, the celebration of the university's move to Munich was held in the midst of tense party political threats — partly also due to student groups — to the guarantees given for the freedom of art and science laid down in the constitutional law in August 1919 (Weimar Constitution, article 152, Constitution of the Free State of Bavaria § 20). The jubilee celebration in Munich, held between two extreme political visions of the future, gained an historic and epochal importance through the "dignified and shrewd" speech by Karl Vossler, who was elected rector in the centenary year. His "Swabian candor" met with the admiration of Thomas Mann, and in addition found an unusually far-reaching public echo in the press and literature.

Under the black-red-gold political symbol Vossler spoke of the relationship between politics and academic life. He called for "illiberal sentiments" of all kinds to be overcome; German culture would have to bear the brunt "if academic life, in Bavaria for instance, were to be kept in place and debased to a satelite of political will from one side or the other!" That was also directed at the extreme right-wing, nationalist, anti-Semitic tendencies, which at that time were coming to the fore and which had brought about Richard Willstätter's expulsion a little while

The ceremony to mark the 100th anniversary of the relocation of the university from Landshut to Munich, on November 27, 1926, in the National Theater. Heinrich Held (1868–1938), Prime Minister of Bavaria from 1924–33 is speaking; left: the rector Vossler; right: Professor Michael Doeberl — the programmatic contents of his official speech caused King Louis I to honor him as the "second founder" of the university.

earlier. The centennial celebrations were framed by religious services by both Christian denominations, as well as in the Jewish and Old Catholic communities, in four churches. The Free State of Bavaria and the city of Munich made magnanimous endowments.

In the same year, in 1926, a celebration to commemorate the 150th anniversary of Joseph Görres's birth paid tribute to the daring Ludovician exploit in summoning someone outlawed at that time as

Prussian. The speech was held by the legal historian Konrad Beyerle (1872–1933), who helped draft the Weimar Constitution. A bust of Görres in bronze by the sculptor Theodor von Georgii (1883–1963) was then placed in the atrium.

1918–1945

STUDYING
BETWEEN THE WARS

HELMUT BÖHM

After being approved by the Board of University Representatives, the first General Students' Committee was elected in December 1918, creating one lobby to represent the interest of students.

previous double page:
In June 1935, Hitler visited LMU on the anniversary of the "Akademie für Deutsches Recht." The Faculty of Law is now housed in the building on Ludwigstrasse. The academy's objective was to remodel German law in keeping with National Socialist ideology and to bring the study of jurisprudence into line with it.

Allgemeiner Studenten=Ausschuß der Universität München

Geschäftsstelle Zimmer 144 und 152. Eingang Ludwigstr. Tel. 23470.

Der Allgemeine Studenten=Ausschuß vertritt die reichs= deutsche und deutsch=österreichische Studentenschaft der Münchener Universität in ihrer Gesamtheit. Zu seinem Aufgabenkreis gehören rechtliche, wirtschaftliche und Studien=Angelegenheiten der Studierenden. Die Mitarbeit in Studienfragen erfolgt vor allem in den Fakultätsausschüssen. Der wirtschaftlichen Fürsorge dienen:

Das Amt für heimkehrende kriegsgefang= ene Studierende will allen heimkehrenden kriegs= gefangenen Studierenden Berater und Helfer sein und ist vor allem bestrebt, die wirtschaftliche Notlage derselben zu lindern.

Das Amt für Leibesübungen ist bemüht, das studentische Turn= und Spielwesen zu heben und billige und gute Gelegenheit zur Ausübung desselben zu ver= mitteln.

Das Arbeitsamt verschafft Studierenden geeigne= ten Nebenverdienst, wie Instruktionsstunden, Hauslehrer= stellen, wissenschaftliche Hilfsarbeiten usw. an Studierende.

Das Lehrmittelamt vermittelt den Ankauf und Ver= kauf gebrauchter Bücher unter Studierenden durch Über= nahme der Bücher in Kommission. Die Schätzung ob= liegt einem Ausschuß, dem der Oberbibliothekar der Universität mit angehört.

Das Nachrichtenamt erteilt mündlich und schrift= lich Auskunft über alle in das Arbeitsgebiet des A. St. A. einschlägigen Fragen und sammelt das diesbezügliche Druckschriftenmaterial für das Archiv.

Das Soziale Amt, welches die praktisch=sozial arbei= tenden studentischen Organisationen: die Akademischen Arbeiterkurse, die sozial=studentische Zentrale und die studentische Gruppe für Jugendfürsorge und Jugend= gerichtshilfe in München umfaßt, vertritt unter voller Wahrung der Sonderinteressen jeder zugehörigen Gruppe die gemeinsamen Interessen derselben und sucht die Studentenschaft zu ernster sozialer Arbeit anzuregen und entsprechende Arbeitsgelegenheit zu schaffen und zu vermitteln.

Das Vergünstigungsamt vermittelt bedeutende Ermäßigungen zum Besuche der Sammlungen, Theater, Konzerte und erwirkt auch in verschiedenen anderen Fällen wie Schülerfahrkarten, Rauchwarenbezug usw. Vergün= stigungen.

Das Wirtschaftsamt stellt sich die Aufgabe, die wirtschaftliche Notlage der Studierenden nach Möglichkeit zu lindern, indem es zunächst die von der Universität unterhaltenen Einrichtungen der Studentenküchen und des Wohnungsamtes fördern hilft, kleinere Darlehen, sowie gute und billige Bekleidung für minderbemittelte Studierende zu beschaffen sucht. Seine Hauptaufgabe sieht es in der Schaffung einer großzügigen studentischen Krankenversicherung, Darlehenskasse und einer genos= senschaftlichen Versorgung der Studenten mit den nötigen Nahrungs= und Bekleidungsmitteln.

Der A. St. A. der Universität München ist für 1919/20 zugleich Geschäftsstelle des Kreises Bayern der Ver= tretung der Deutschen Studentenschaft.

Die Sprechstunden des Vorstandes und der Ämter des A. St. A. werden bis zur Neuwahl des A. St. A. in folgender Weise abgehalten:

1. Sprechstunden des Vorstandes: Mo., Di., Mi., Do., Frei., vormittags 12–1 Uhr, Zimmer 144, Eingang Ludwigstraße linker Seitenflügel.
2. Sprechstunden der Ämter: Mo., Di., Mi., Do., Frei. 11–1 Uhr, Zimmer 152, Eingang Ludwigstraße, rechter Seitenflügel.

Kommilitonen und Kommilitoninnen!

Der Allgemeine Studentenausschuß ist mit ganzer Kraft bestrebt, die von Euch in ihn gesetzten Erwartungen zu erfüllen, soweit es die jetzigen außerordentlich ungün= stigen Verhältnisse ermöglichen. **Vergeßt aber nicht, daß ohne Eure tatkräftigste Mitarbeit und ohne Euer verständnisvolles Rücksicht= nehmen auf die gegenwärtig sich uns in den Weg stellenden Schwierigkeiten der von Euch gewählte Ausschuß ein Körper ohne Mark und Seele ist. In Eure Hand ist Euer Wohl und Wehe nun gegeben.**

Alle jene Kommilitonen und Kommilitoninnen, welche bereits an anderen Hochschulen in Allgemeinen Studen= ten=Ausschüssen tätig waren, werden herzlich gebeten, ihre Erfahrungen und ihre Mitarbeit uns zur Verfügung zu stellen! Auch junge Mitarbeiter, die ernsthaft in dem einen oder anderen Amte für das Wohl ihrer Kom= militonen mindestens ein Semester tätig sein wollen, sind uns herzlich willkommen!

Die Anmeldung zur Mitarbeit in den Ämtern wird in den Sprechstunden des Vorstandes und der Amter entgegengenommen.

Mit studentischem Gruß!

Der Vorstand.

The aftermath of World War I and political turbulence during the Weimar Republic both effected teaching and studying. The far-reaching social upheaval between the wars was also mirrored in the structural changes at LMU Munich. Nevertheless, the appeal of Germany's second largest university remained undiminished.

Even from as early as 1926, provocation, propaganda, and targetted attacks by the National Socialist German Students' League were harbingers of the Nazi dictatorship to come that led to repression, expulsion, murder, and war. Freedom in the field of teaching and learning became radically restricted after 1933. Opposition could result in death — as epitomized by the "White Rose."

Caught in a grey zone between conformity and resistance, the university embarked upon a treacherous route. The entanglement with the Nazi system was complex and not merely manifest in individual incidents. The end of the "Third Reich" also led to the temporary closure of the university. There was no summer term in 1945.

RE-ORIENTATION PHASE:
THE FIRST FEW MONTHS AFTER WORLD WAR I

The early days as a republic were marked by massive intellectual, political, and organizational challenges for the university as well. First of all, students returning from the war — some of whom had joined forces to create associations — had to be re-integrated, accommodated, and supported on a material level. Through the introduction of interim regulations, LMU Munich was able to continue teaching during the turbulent months following the war.

The General Students' Movement gained a further boost during the revolutionary period. After the Board of University Representatives had approved the organization's provisional statutes on November 11, 1918, the first General Students' Committee (AStA) was elected in December that same year. The AStA — as the 30-seat student parliament was called — appointed a board of five members. It was financed by a compulsory fee for students. In 1919, local interest groups became integrated under the umbrella German student association.

CAMPAIGNS AND COUNTER-CAMPAIGNS:
THE UNIVERSITY CAUGHT BETWEEN
DIVERGING OPINIONS

At the university, the revolution was fiercely opposed by the students, the majority of whom were nationalistically oriented. On February 10, 1919, a leaflet threatening the Bavarian prime

Armed workers from the Krauss factory on Ludwigstrasse during the Bavarian Soviet Republic (with the main university building in the background).

The Bavarian prime minister Kurt Eisner was not popular among the largely nationalist students. On February 21, 1919, he was shot by the student Count Anton Arco-Valley in the street. After the news of Eisner's death became known, the university was closed to prevent clashes between revolutionaries and students.

minister Kurt Eisner (1867–1919) with the words "Make haste, bailiff, your time is up!" had already caused a considerable uproar. Just a few days later, on February 21, Eisner was shot on his way to the Bavarian parliament by the student Count Anton Arco-Valley (1897–1945). News of the assassination was received enthusiastically by the bulk of students. The Board of University Representatives, that deeply deplored the "heinous crime," felt compelled to close the university as clashes between armed revolutionaries and students were feared.

With the proclamation of the Bavarian Soviet Republic on April 7, 1919, the university finally became embroiled in the revolution. Earlier, on April 5, the General Students' Committee had convened a "Preliminary Student Council," that was recognized by the Board of University Representatives while simultanously appointing three professors to it. This was ousted by the so-called "Revolutionary University Council," authorized by the Commissioner of Enlightenment and Public Instruction, Gustav Landauer (1870–1919). He propagated changing the "university of the better classes" into an "educational institution for the people," ordering the university to be closed and the red flag hoisted.

So as not to lose the initiative, the Board — headed by the medic Friedrich von Müller (1858–1941) which had appointed him prorector — assembled a "committee to reform the university" during this "diarchical" phase, in which assistant professors, civil servants, and students enjoyed a large majoritiy. Despite favoring a radical reform and while threatening to strike, members at a general convention of lecturers committed themselves to the principle of a liberal form of teaching not influenced by politics. On April 12, the Board was replaced by the "Revolutionary University Council," and the university declared a "proletarian transitional school." The entry of the *Freikorps Epp* and the crushing of the Bavarian Soviet Republic marked the end of this revolutionary episode in early May 1919, during which time — despite considerable pressure — the Board never completely let go of the reins.

CONFLICT LEADS TO CHANGES TO ESTABLISHED STRUCTURES

In the years that followed, the student scene was dominated by a fundamental, German nationalistic mood, which was cultivated in particular by the *Allgemeiner deutsche Waffenring* — an affiliation of duelling fraternities. Armed student organizations took part in 1920 in suppressing uprisings in central Germany and — as part of the *Freikorps Oberland* — in clashes in Upper Silesia. After its dissolution they evolved into regional paramilitary groups.

The student demonstrations unleashed by the trial of Eisner's murderer, Arco, in January 1920, showed that sympathy was predominantly not with the victim but with his murderer. He had become

Max Weber criticized the mild treatment of Eisner's assassin Arco-Valley and incurred the anger of a great number of students as a result.

the personification of the protest against the revolution and the republic. Several professors also affirmed their support for the assassin. The anatomist Siegfried Mollier (1866–1954), for example, honored Arco's "supreme benevolence" in a minute's silence. The sociologist Max Weber (1864–1920), on the other hand, had the courage to criticize the mild treatment shown toward the assassin. As a consequence, he incurred the anger of a great number of students who repeatedly disrupted his lectures.

The campaign committee continued to hold reform-related consultations under Professor Karl Rothenbücher (1880–1932). The new university constitution brought into force by the Minister for Cultural Affairs, Franz Matt (1860–1929), however, was largely based on that drawn up by the Board of University Representatives. As such, the responsibilities of academic bodies remained unchanged, and the Board and the rectorial election committee were enlarged through the participation of elected representatives of assistant professors, civil servants, and students. The AStA had now gained statutory recognition in the Board as the "overall representative" of student interests. This was followed by ministerial confirmation in 1922, and in 1923 detailed regulations governing students at universities in Bavaria came into force.

NATIONALISTIC FORCES RE-GROUP

The Board of University Representatives that consequentially rejected official Constitution Day celebrations on August 11, a national holiday during the Weimar Republic, showed on the other hand considerable sympathy for academic demonstations in favor of South Tyrol and the annexation of Austria, and against the dictates of the Treaty of Versailles. There were very few "rational" Republicans among the professors, such as Max Weber, the lawyers Karl Rothenbücher and Konrad Beyerle (1872–1933), who made a substantial contribution to the Weimar Constitution, and the modern historian Hermann Oncken (1869–1945). A staunch opponent of the Republic was the Egyptologist Baron Friedrich Wilhelm von Bissing (1873–1956), who together with the forestry engineer Karl Leopold von Escherich (1871–1951) and the historial Karl Alexander von Müller (1882–1962) were among the earliest sympathizers of the Hitler movement.

The activities of the nationalistic forces also reached a preliminary climax at the university in November 1923. Both the Munich branch of the SA and the *Freikorps Oberland*, under the university assistant Friedrich Weber (1892–1955), counted many students among their followers. Just like these, the *völkisch Hochschulring für Deutsche Art*, supported by "armed students" — in other words by members of duelling fraternities — also joined Hitler's "March on the *Feldherrnhalle*" on November 9, 1923. The violent suppression of Hitler's putsch resulted in riotous demonstrations at the university on November 10, and to a second protest march that was stopped by the police and the *Reichswehr*.

On November 12, 1923, there was a tumultuous student assembly in the university atrium followed by a clash with national defence troups outside the entrance. For a second time, the university was closed. To take some heat out of the situation, the participants at the "thoroughly patriotic rally" were — with the Board of University Representatives' approval — promised immunity from prosecution by the rector Carl von Kraus (1868–1952).

RISING STUDENT NUMBERS AND THE EASING OF THE WORST HARDSHIP

Irrespective of the political upheaval, student self-help institutions continued to develop. In Munich, these were structured in an exemplary fashion by Fritz Beck (1889–1934), who emerged from the "Free Student Organization" — which represented the interests of students not in fraternities. These groups were dependent on the financial support of the student community. Organized on a national level in 1922, they joined forces in 1928 to form the *Deutschens Studentenwerk e.V.*, and aimed to ease immediate hardships by distributing goods, clothes, and food, bought with donations.

Under the direction of Beck, who is presumed to have been murdered during the "Night of the Long Knives" in 1934, the *Verein Studentenhaus e.V.*, student association — founded in Munich in 1920 — coordinated most support measures. Beck set up canteens, which even in 1921 were providing 2,500 students with a cheap meal every day, and ran places where student papers could be attested as well as writing rooms for exam students. Health care was provided from 1924 onward. The association achieved its greatest goal at the end of 1926: By revamping the municipal *Luisenbad*, a student building was created with a canteen for 2,000 and a number of different offices.

In the post-war years, organized university sport was also introduced which corresponded very closely to the military-political endeavors of nationalist groups. The sportsground in Freimann, for example, dates from this period, c. 1926–28.

Goods being issued to needy students: Student self-help institutions contributed toward easing post-war hardship.

The "Verein Studentenhaus e.V." student association, founded in Munich in 1920, actively collected funds to help increase the support given to students. It achieved its greatest goal in 1926: The conversion of the municipal "Luisenbad" into a student building with a canteen seating 2,000.

After the Great War, the appeal of what was then — next to Berlin — the second largest university in Germany, remained undiminished. The number of matriculated students rose from 6,600 in 1914 to more than 9,000 in the winter term of 1921. This fell slightly before showing a gradual upward trend to level off to between 7,000 and 8,000. What was particularly noticeable is the disproportionate rise in the number of female students, especially in the Faculty of Philosophy.

ACADEMICS OF INTERNATIONAL IMPORTANCE

Renowned and internationally recognized academics safeguarded the university's first-class reputation and contributed to Munich's global importance. The two Nobel Prize winners Richard Willstätter (1872–1942) and Heinrich Wieland (1877–1957), who taught in Munich between 1916 and 1925, and from 1926 to 1952 respectively, continued the tradition of famous chemists from Munich. In 1920, Wilhelm Wien (1864–1928) followed on from Wilhelm Röntgen as the Nobel Prize winner for physics. From 1906, Arnold Sommerfeld (1868–1951) was a prominent theoretical physicist over a

Heinrich Wieland, in charge of the chemistry laboratories at LMU. During the Nazi era, he allowed many so-called "half-Jews" to study under him and to take exams. He even went to Donauwörth in 1943 to speak in defence of his students Hans Leipelt and Marie-Luise Jahn.

period of some three decades, his institute becoming one of the major international centers in the field of atomic physics.

Max Weber, who died in 1920, the heart and lung surgeon Ferdinand Sauerbruch (1875–1951), and the art historian Heinrich Wölfflin (1864–1945) are among the outstanding figures of the post-war period. The specialist for internal medicine Friedrich von Müller, the educationalist and pedagog Georg Kerschensteiner (1854–1932), the German studies scholar Carl von Kraus (1868 –1952), the Romanist Karl Vossler (1872–1949), the Classical philologist Eduard Schwartz (1858–1940), the "theater professor" Artur Kutscher (1878–1960), and the theologian and dogma historian Martin

Grabmann (1875–1949) were well-known outside Munich too. The large Faculty of Law with more than 2,000 students, included a number of important scholars such as the legal historian (for German law) Konrad Beyerle, the legal historian (for Roman law) Leopold Wenger (1874–1953), and the professor for civil law Wilhelm Kisch (1874–1952).

THE SCHOLARSHIP OF TOMORROW AND THE POLITICS OF YESTERDAY

The increase in specialized scholarship led to the establishment of several new chairs and institutes, even if financial constraints left much to be desired. The Faculty of Theology gained seminars for dogmatic theology, patrology, and missiology. In the

Artur Kutscher is considered the founder of Theater Studies.
Photo: Felicitas Timpe (1923–2006).

emerging field of economics, a seminar for economic history was set up under Jakob Strieder (1877–1936). Journalism emerged as a subject in its own right in 1924 under Professor Karl d'Ester (1881–1960), and one year earlier, in 1923, a chair and institute of meteorology were created.

The majority of — nationalistically oriented — professors, however, did not develop a positive relationship to the Weimar state in Munich either. With one exception, the university avoided any clear acknowledgment of the republic or propagating the cause. The celebration of the founding of the empire, on the other hand, commemorating the imperial proclamation of 1871, was a permanent fixture in the academic festival calendar. This

was staged as a powerful demonstration of patriotism with generally melodramatic speeches — as, for example, that given by Eduard Schwartz in 1925 — in which the woefully depicted present was compared to the splendor of the past.

LIBERAL SENTIMENTS AND A MOVE TOWARD MODERATION

A spectacular exception to this was Vossler's rectorship in 1926/27. The renowned Romanist had the black-red-gold flag hoisted as early as in 1926 during the magnificent centenary celebrations, held along traditional lines, to mark the university's move from Landshut to Munich. At the celebration of the founding of the empire in 1927, he also

The Romanist and democrat Karl Vossler was rector of the university twice — in 1926/27 and again in 1946.

terms, the *Hochschulring deutscher Art* and later the *Kampfbund für deutsche Kultur* were favored for example when allocating times to use lecture theaters. In this respect, the university administration — that gained in importance during the process of expansion anyway — did not play an unimportant role. Its director, the long-standing syndic Robert Einhauser (1871–1931), succeeded in building up a central and exceedingly influential position within the university in this manner.

The case of the highly esteemed Jewish chemist Richard Willstätter, who handed in his resignation as he felt that anti-Semitism had begun to play a role even when new appointments were made, caused quite a sensation in 1925. For the mostly conservative professors in Munich, the majority of whom were close to the nationalist German People's Party as well as the Bavarian People's Party, National Socialist ideology remained unappealing despite certain points of similarity. Only a few were members of the Party before 1933, and none of these held a professorship for life.

insisted on the participation of the Jewish fraternities, in the face of student societies but with the support of the majority of the Board of University Representatives. As a consequence, couleur-bearing fraternities and a number of professors did not attend the celebrations. The guest speaker canceled; Vossler himself then held a speech in which he took a stance against the political fantasies of the students.

FUNDAMENTAL CONSERVATIVE TENDENCIES AND NATIONALISTIC IMPULSES

The university supported "patriotic" student rallies, even tolerating certain lapses in the interests of an academic truce, and sought to react with moderation. Based on an understanding of politics that did not regard nationalistic factions in party political

THE STUDENT BODY IN MUNICH AND ITS RELATION TO THE NAZI MOVEMENT

The situation for students was completely different. Between 1924 and 1928 they saw themselves best represented by the nationalistic *Großdeutsche Studentenschaft* (Greater German Student Body), until they became increasingly receptive to Nazi paroles. The advancement of the "National Socialist German League of Students," founded in 1926, saw the beginnings of a new phase of radicalization from 1927/28 onward at LMU as well, with political fights at the university taking on new dimensions.

The university group, headed by Baldur von Schirach (1907–74) from 1928, who later became Reich Youth Leader in the NSDAP, operated with

The chemist and Nobel Prize winner Richard Willstätter resigned his position at LMU in 1925 due to increasing anti-Semitism.

the following year and, as the most powerful group from December 1930 onward, also appointed the chairman of the AStA board, it still did not achieve the breakthrough it had hoped for in Munich. However, through its ceaseless actionism, aggressive propaganda, and systematic provocation and disruptions it conditioned student politics and largely the picture the rest of the world had of the university, forcing the university board to adopt a defensive position.

TARGETED POLITICAL AGITATION BY THE NATIONAL SOCIALISTS

These attacks came to a head in 1931 in a carefully staged attack known as the "Nawiasky Scandal" that caught the attention of the media, and was aimed against the respected expert in constitutional law of Jewish extraction, who ventured to draw a comparision between the peace treaties of Versailles and Brest-Litovsk in one of his lectures.

maximum propaganda effort from then onward, distributing for example 40,000 leaflets in the summer term in 1930, and was able to call upon Party leaders, including Hitler on several occasions, in the run up to AStA elections. Despite this, the result did not meet expectations and was below that in other universities. While the National Socialists were able to reach the 30 percent mark in Würzburg, even 51 percent in Erlangen, and a third of the votes in many other universities in AStA elections in the winter term in 1929/30, they only managed 18 percent at LMU.

Although the National Socialist Student League succeeded in virtually doubling its share of votes

In the run up to AStA elections, the National Socialist German League of Students was able to call upon the support of high-ranking Party leaders, including Hitler, in 1931.

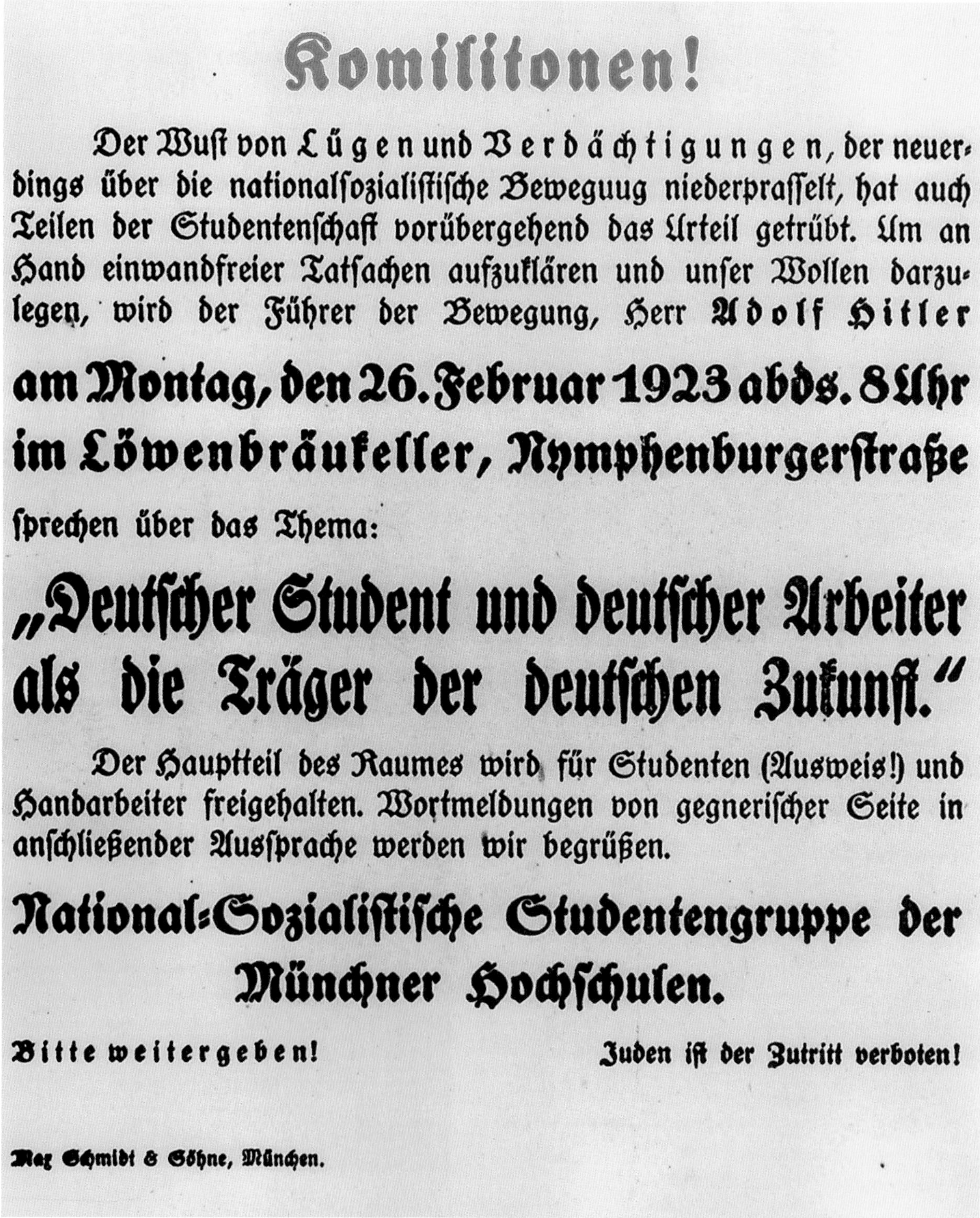

Komilitonen!

Der Wust von Lügen und Verdächtigungen, der neuerdings über die nationalsozialistische Bewegung niederprasselt, hat auch Teilen der Studentenschaft vorübergehend das Urteil getrübt. Um an Hand einwandfreier Tatsachen aufzuklären und unser Wollen darzulegen, wird der Führer der Bewegung, Herr Adolf Hitler

am Montag, den 26. Februar 1923 abds. 8 Uhr im Löwenbräukeller, Nymphenburgerstraße

sprechen über das Thema:

„Deutscher Student und deutscher Arbeiter als die Träger der deutschen Zukunft."

Der Hauptteil des Raumes wird für Studenten (Ausweis!) und Handarbeiter freigehalten. Wortmeldungen von gegnerischer Seite in anschließender Aussprache werden wir begrüßen.

National-Sozialistische Studentengruppe der Münchner Hochschulen.

Bitte weitergeben!   Juden ist der Zutritt verboten!

Reg Schmidt & Söhne, München.

One of the National Socialist Student Group's leaflets. Extreme right-wing propaganda forced its way into university life, radicalizing political discussions within the institution.

In the course of the so-called "Nawiasky Scandal" cheap propaganda was aimed against the constitutional lawyer in 1931. It led to riotous scenes and to the closure of the university for a week.

It unleashed pandemonium and led to the clearance and closure of the university for a week. The ringleader was merely reprimanded, as the court of inquiry convened felt it was not in a position to agree in full to the opinion propagated by Professor Hans Nawiasky (1880–1961).

The university tried to gain control of the situation by implementing disciplinary law. This resulted in the sporadic prohibition of the student league and in a freeze on compulsory fees for students. These belated measures however were only enacted in small doses for fear of an escalation in the politicization and solidarity among students with the National Socialist Student League, and the anticipated impact could not be reached in the face of the general political development.

Professor Hans Nawiasky emigrated to Switzerland after the National Socialists seized power. He returned to Bavaria in 1946 to help draw up the new Bavarian constitution. That same year he was appointed professor at LMU once again and granted the privileges of a civil servant for life.

Call by the NSDAP to female students to go to the AStA election on November 24, 1927, and to vote for the National Socialists.

main picture:
The Görres commemorative celebration in the university atrium (1927). A memorial to the "White Rose" is now be found where the Görres bust is shown here in the center of this picture.

THE KEY YEAR 1933: FIRST REACTIONS AT LMU MUNICH UNIVERSITY

There was no exceptional response at first at the university to the National Socialists's seizure of power on January 30, 1933, with just a student demonstration for the Reich chancellor on January 31 being reported. In the weeks that followed, the university officially continued to keep a low profile.

When, for example, signatures were collected in a call by university lecturers for an election on March 5, the rector Leo von Zumbusch (1874–1940) did not undertake anything and reacted hesitantly, as he did to the petition to confer Hitler with an honor-

With considerable pomp and an official speech held by the Bavarian Minister for Cultural Affairs and Gauleiter of the "Bayerische Ostmark," Hans Schemm, the university "celebrated" the introduction of the National Socialist "student law."

ary doctorate. This shows that there was no race to change sides even if the number of Party members among lecturers and assistants rose from around 20 to some 90 between March and May 1933 — without, however, this being visibly manifested at any way.

After the Association of German Universities, with the Munich psychiatry professor Oswald Bumke (1877–1950) as a member of its board, had meanwhile also started along the path to assimilation and self-imposed *Gleichschaltung* or "forcible coordination," the Board of University Representatives officially declared its willingness to help promote a National Socialist state on July 11, 1933.

A "new era" for students began in the summer term of 1933 with the presentation of the new "student law," which was celebrated in Munich on May 10 in the university atrium, with the new Minister for Cultural Affairs Hans Schemm (1891–1935) holding the official speech. Without being accompanied by any official representatives from the university, the students then moved off to Königsplatz, where books by authors defamed as being "non-German" were burnt as part of a campaign organized on a national scale.

Members of student fraternities took up their positions on May 10, 1933, on the steps to the Neue Staatsgalerie (now the State Collections of Antiques) on Königsplatz for the book burning.

Burning bonfire of books on Königsplatz.

SWIFT CHANGES
WITHIN THE UNIVERSITY ADMINISTRATION

By July 1933, regularly held elections had already
been stopped. In Bavaria, measures to restructure
the university constitution were introduced on
August 28, 1933, in the form of "preliminary regulations for simplifying the university administration." Seemingly without any protest from within
the university, this saw the abolition of collegiate
bodies, the removal of self-administrative rights,
and the introduction of the *Führerprinzip*. Karl
Leopold von Escherich, no longer elected democratically but appointed rector by the ministry, did
however still enjoy the trust of the university, and
his position was confirmed by the ministry at the
request of the majority of professors in 1935.

The lecturing body was originally the source of
academic recruits, and from 1935 it was seen as a
representative for all lecturers and assistants, and
acted as an instrumental and supervisory authority
on a political level, especially with regard to personnel matters. It was closely affiliated with the
Nazi Lecturers's League within the NSDAP. Young,
active National Socialists such as Dr. Wilhelm
Führer (1904–74), assistant at the university observatory, let their political clout be felt here in no
uncertain terms.

OSTRACIZED, BANNED, EXPELLED:
THE NAZI DOCTRINE AND ACADEMIC
TEACHING

The National Socialists's "cleansing measures"
severely effected LMU Munich too. The so-called
"Law for the Restoration of the Professional Civil
Service" of April 7, 1933, had immediate repercussions on several assistants and 20 professors, who
being Jews, were not politcally "acceptable." Those
who were dismissed or forced into early retirement
included the expert in constitutional and adminis-

*The mathematician Alfred Pringsheim, Thomas Mann's
father-in-law, just managed to escape to Switzerland in
1939. He was among the many professors and private
lecturers who were forced to give up their academic work
on account of the anti-Semitic laws.*

trative law Hans Nawiasky, the astronomer Alexander Wilkens (1881–1968), the philosopher Richard
Hönigswald (1875–1947), the lawyer Karl Neu-
meyer (1869–1941), the ethnologist Lucian Scher-
man (1864–1946), and the mathematic professor
emeritus Alfred Pringsheim (1850–1941).

IN INCLYTA

UNIVERSITATE LUDOVICO=MAXIMILIANEA MONACENSI

RECTORE MAGNIFICO

MARIANO SAN NICOLÒ

UTRIUSQUE IURIS ET RERUM POLITICARUM DOCTORE · DOCTORE PHILOSOPHIAE HONORIS CAUSA · ROMANI ET
CIVILIS GERMANICI IURIS SCIENTIAE PROFESSORE PUBLICO ORDINARIO · INSTITUTI PAPYROLOGICI PRAESIDE
ACADEMIAE LITTERARUM MONACENSIS VINDOBONENSIS ET MOGUNTINAE SOCIO ORDINARIO VEL EXTERNO

ERVINUS KOSCHMIEDER

PHILOSOPHIAE DOCTOR · PHILOLOGIAE SLAVICAE ET BALTICAE QUAM DICUNT PROFESSOR PUBLICUS ORDINARIUS ·
SEMINARII PHILOLOGICI PRAESES · ACADEMIAE LITTERARUM MONACENSIS SOCIUS ORDINARIUS
ORDINIS PHILOSOPHORUM HOC TEMPORE DECANUS · DIPLOMA PUBLICUM INFRA SCRIPTUM

QUO VIRO SUMME VENERANDO ET PIA MEMORIA SEMPER RECOLENDO

CURTIO HUBER

DOCTORIS PHILOSOPHIAE GRADUS CONLATUS ERAT INFAUSTIS TEMPORIBUS CONTRA IUS ET FAS RESCISSUM
EX UNANIMI ORDINIS PHILOSOPHORUM DECRETO RENOVAVIT RATUMQUE ESSE EDIXIT

SUB AUSPICIIS GLORIOSISSIMIS AUGUSTISSIMI AC POTENTISSIMI DOMINI DOMINI

LUDOVICI III BAVARIAE REGIS

COMITIS PALATINI AD RHENUM · BAVARIAE · FRANCONIAE ET IN SUEVIA DUCIS · CET. IN INCLYTA UNIVERSITATE
LUDOVICO-MAXIMILIANEA MONACENSI

RECTORE MAGNIFICO PLURIMUM REVERENDO AC DOCTISSIMO ET ILLUSTRISSIMO VIRO

CAROLO DE GOEBEL

PHILOSOPHIAE NATURALIS DOCTORE · SCIENTIAE DOCTORE H. C. · IURIS UTRIUSQUE DOCTORE H. C. · BOTANICES
PROFESSORE PUBLICO ORDINARIO · HORTI BOTANICI ET INSTITUTI PHYTOPHYSIOLOGICI REG. DIRECTORE ·
ACADEMIARUM LITTERARUM MONAC. BEROL. CHRISTIAN. KOPENHAG. ROM. UPSAL. VIENN. AL. SOCIO ORDINARIO
VEL EXTERNO · ORDINIS MAX. COR. BAV. CL. III MER. S. MICHAELIS CL. III EQUITE CET.

CAROLUS VOSSLER

PHILOSOPHIAE DOCTOR · PHILOLOGIAE Q. D. ROMANICAE PROFESSOR PUBLICUS ORDINARIUS · SEMINARII PHILOLOGICI
PRAESES · ACADEMIAE REGIAE LITTERARUM MONACENSIS SOCIUS ORDINARIUS · FACULTATIS PHILOSOPHICAE
SECTIONIS I P. T. DECANUS ET PROMOTOR LEGITIME CONSTITUTUS

PRAECLARO ET PERDOCTO VIRO DOMINO

CURTIO HUBER

CHURIENSI

DIE XXVI MENSIS IULII ANNI MDCCCCXVII

EXAMINIBUS RIGOROSIS

SUMMA CUM LAUDE

SUPERATIS DISSERTATIONE INAUGURALI SCRIPTA

IVO DE VENTO

DOCTORIS PHILOSOPHIAE GRADUM

CUM OMNIBUS PRIVILEGIIS ATQUE IMMUNITATIBUS ADNEXIS EX UNANIMI
ORDINIS PHILOSOPHORUM SECTIONIS I DECRETO CONTULIT.

IN HUIUS REI TESTIMONIUM HOC PUBLICUM DIPLOMA SIGILLIS MAIORIBUS REGIAE LITTERARUM UNIVERSITATIS ET
ORDINIS PHILOSOPHORUM SECT. I ADIECTIS ORDINIS DECANUS ATQUE RECTOR MAGNIFICUS IPSI SUBSCRIPSERUNT

(L. S.)   (L. S.)
DR. K. DE GOEBEL m.p.   DR. KARL VOSSLER m.p.

MONACI DIE XXII MENSIS FEBRUARII ANNI P. CHR. N. MCMLIII

RECTOR MAGNIFICUS   ORDINIS PHILOSOPHORUM DECANUS

The musicologist and member of the "Weiße Rose," Professor Kurt Huber, was stripped of his doctor title on March 8, 1943, shortly after his arrest on February 27. On July 13, 1943, Huber was executed. His doctorate was reinstated after the war by the rector Mariano San Nicolò, who presented Huber's widow, Klara, with this new certificate in 1953, on the 10th anniversary of her husband's execution.

Due to the anti-Semitic "Reich Citizens's Law" of September 15, 1935, a further eight professors and private lecturers lost their right to teach, and the university teachers Karl Wessely (1874–1953, opthalmology), Kasimir Fajans (1887–1975, physical chemistry), Friedrich Hartogs (1874–1943, descriptive geometry), and Fritz Wassermann (1884–1969, anatomy) were sent into retirement. Others, who faced the same fate in 1937, included the chemist Wilhelm Prandtl (1878–1956), the literary historian Walther Brecht (1876–1950), the Classical philologian Rudolf Pfeiffer (1889–1979), and the philosopher, psychologist, and educationalist Aloys Fischer (1880–1937). In this manner, at least 45 professors and lecturers had to leave the university by mid 1937 for "racist" or political reasons, including the Nazi opponent and well-known surgeon Max Lebsche (1886–1957) and the former rector Leo von Zumbusch.

The academic careers of many lecturers were thwarted in this or similar ways. The law passed on January 21, 1935, to release anybody from any position held, enabled the politically motivated early retirement of 15 renowned professors, after the Anglicist Max Förster (1869–1954) had already been forced to become professor emeritus in 1934.

A further tool of racial and political repression, already proposed by the student leader of Bavaria in 1933, was the revocation of doctorates. A regulation that was introduced across the whole Reich stipulated that expatriation would automatically result in the loss of a doctor title. Academic degrees were formally revoked by a university committee that had extremely little leeway in its decision-making process. 183 holders of doctorates at LMU were effected, the majority of whom were Jewish academics who had emigrated.

ANTI-SEMITISM AND AUTHORITARIAN INTERVENTIONS IN THE CURRICULUM

From 1934 onward, lectures on subjects no longer considered up-to-date were forbidden. At the same time, the number of politically biased, indoctrination courses in the fields of international affairs, military science, contemporary history, as well as ethnogeny and racial hygiene was increased. New examination and study regulations ensured that topics corresponding to the National Socialist ideology were given greater prominence.

The political grasp on the student body started straight away with a rigorous admissions regulation, which — within just a few years — turned the much bemoaned "overcrowding" at universities into a dearth of students and academics. A new student constitution that introduced the *Führerprinzip* and stipulated a number of obligations students had to take on, defined the political focus of university students.

Although the quota for Jewish students that was laid down in 1933 at five percent — or 1.5 percent in the case of freshmen — was not even reached at LMU, and up to 20 so-called "half and quarter Jews" were still studying during the war, the harassment of Jewish students and academics led to a continuous decline in their numbers. By the winter term in 1938/39, there were no German students still matriculated who were *Volljude* — solely of Jewish extraction — to use the terminology of the time.

Thanks to its traditional attractivity, LMU managed to maintain its numbers despite restrictive admissions regulations. In 1935, however, the fixing of quotas for universities in major cities caused a drastic slump in the number of students that could no longer be offset. In the winter term in 1934/35 it fell to 8,065; in the summer term in

The student in uniform was an expression of students' political engagement and enforced conformity as well as their "fighting ability" — one of the main tasks that lay in the hands of student leaders from 1933 onward.

EXERCIZING POLITICAL POWER ON THE UNIVERSITY

Students's extracurricular, time-consuming obligations such as fatigue, compulsory sport, pre-military training organized by the SA college bureau, work for the student council, comradeship training through communal living, and political education made an orderly course of study impossible. They led to an enormous additional burden and ultimately, even in 1934, to public student protests, clear demonstrations of disapproval, and to a limited extent, individual acts of resistance. Any initial sympathy for the regime soon dissipated and opportunistic assimilation, apathy, and increasing rejection took its place. The effect political education had was minimal even if, around 1938, some 30 percent of students at the university were in the National Socialist German Students's League, 40 percent in the Party, and more than 50 percent part of the Party's organizational structure.

Habilitations and appointments that were continuously cut short due to the influence of politics were aimed at helping a new class of professor to prominence. At LMU about half of the chairs were re-staffed between 1933 and 1939. The fact that some qualified scholars such as Fritz Terhalle (1889–1962), Heinrich Mitteis, Alfred Hueck (1889–1975), and Mariano San Nicolò (1887–1955) could be recruited despite the political pressure, was primarily due to the unerring attitude demonstrated by the majority of faculty professors, who kept to existing principles and the priority given to candidates proposed by faculties themselves.

Admittedly, that did not prevent the university from being forced to take on a number of professors. The majority of them, however, turned out to be scholars who carried out their duties reliably.

1935 to 5,480. Contrary to the general trend, the percentage of female students up until 1937 remained relatively constant at 18 to 20 percent, dipping slightly before rising to 50 percent during the war.

After 1933, the student leadership was no longer allowed to have its own independent student lobby. From that time onward, its main task was to ensure the organizational and political registration and "conformity" of the students as well as training them to be "willing to fight." The dynamism of Nazi student leaders, although somewhat curtailed from higher up, was manifested in individual campaigns and disruptive incidents, such as against the newly appointed legal historial Heinrich Mitteis (1889–1952), and through the suppression of student corporations. The winter term of 1935/36 saw an end to couleur-bearing fraternities. At the beginning of 1936, there were only twelve fraternities at the university, compared to more than a hundred just ten years earlier.

There were only a few, such as the philosopher Wolfgang Schultz (1881–1936) and the racial hygiene expert Lothar Tirala (1886–1974), appointed by the Minister for Cultural Affairs Schemm despite opposition from the faculties, and later the philosopher Hans Grunsky (1902–1988), who were not up to the task in hand and caused an inglorious furor.

COMPLIANCE AND NON-COMPLIANCE: THE SITUATION IN THE FACULTIES

Partially conforming, but principally in opposition, the faculties and the majority of their members formed the strongest of bastions in the face of political totalitarian claims. They often found themselves involved in serious disputes with a minority gathered around the politically active lecturers's representative. Few deans implemented the *Führerprinzip* to the full, unlike Walther Wüst (1901–1993, Faculty of Philosophy), Heinz Kürten (1891–1966, Faculty of Medicine), and Friedrich von Faber (1880–1954, Faculty of Philosophy II and Faculty of Natural Science), who — during the long-contested dispute about a successor to Sommerfeld — decided against existing representatives of the subject in favor of supporters of "Aryan Physics."

Influential Nazi party officials were represented in the Faculty of Medicine in Franz Wirz (1889–1969), the head of the Party's college committee, the *Reichsdozentenführer* honorary professor Walter Schultze (1894–1979), and Gustav Borger (1899–1989), head of the Nazi lecturers's league. By contrast, National Socialists could not gain a foothold in the Faculty of Political Science, that struggled to survive due to the unusual merging of forestry engineering and the economics department in 1934. Through the geographical proximity and personal contact to the Party official Hans Frank (1900–1946), the Faculty of Law on the

The Minister for Cultural Affairs and the Gauleiter Adolf Wagner ordered the closure of the university's Faculty of Theology in early 1939.

The chairs that became vacant as a result of the closure of the Faculty of Theology were to be made available to the Party ideologist Alfred Rosenberg for his "Academy of Higher Learning."

other hand agreed to collaborate with the *Akademie für Deutsches Recht*, founded in 1933, of which Frank was president.

The Faculty of Theology fell victim to the escalating struggle between the Church and the State, and was closed in early 1939 by the Gauleiter and Minister for Cultural Affairs Adolf Wagner (1890–1944). After the *Reichswissenschaftsministerium* (Reich Ministry of Science, Education and Culture) insisted on appointing the NSDAP member Hans Barion (1899–1973) as successor to the canon lawyer Eduard Eichmann (1870–1946), despite objections from Cardinal Michael von Faulhaber (1869–1952), and the cardinal's subsequent refusal to allow theology students to attend Barion's lectures, Wagner ordered the closure of the faculty on February 16, 1939, after consulting the ministries in Berlin. The Party and the Gauleiter Wagner in particular were the driving forces behind this. He wanted to make the chairs that had now become vacant available to the Party ideologist Alfred Rosenberg (1893–1946), for the so-called "Academy of Higher Learning" the latter planned to establish. In addition to the National Socialist elite university's main premises on Lake Chiem, branches were to be set up at universities, such as an *Institut für Indogermanische Geistesgeschichte* (Institute for Indo-European History of Ideas) in Munich. As a consequence, its designated head, Professor Richard Harder (1896–1957), was transferred to Munich against the wishes of the faculty. All in all, the univesity was however able to assert itself during the bitter chair-related struggle, not least also due to the fact that the Rosenberg project was dropped in 1943.

The Gauleiter Wagner demonstrated his hostile attitude to the church once again in February 1941, when — without any legal basis — he ordered the professors for philosophy and history, Joachim von Rintelen (1898–1979) and Max Buchner (1881–

1941), whose posts were tied to the terms of the "Concordat," to be suspended from office. Both chairs remained vacant.

Seen as a whole, extremes in the conduct of university teachers — in the form of unmistakable or militant Nazi partisans on the one hand, and blatant opposition or resistance on the other — were exceptionally seldom in the individual disciplines at LMU considering their disparity. Between these poles, a whole range of different reactions could be found. The safeguarding of subject-related academic primacy was demonstrated surpisingly often, however, despite political repercussions.

LMU MUNICH DURING THE WAR

The outbreak of war was also a major turning point at LMU. Although it was one of five German universities that were able to carry on teaching, the Faculty of Veterinary Medicine was closed and despite repeated attempts at the highest levels in Bavaria, it was not re-opened.

By 1939, many professors and lecturers had already been called up for military service — 16 in the Faculty of Philosophy alone. Normal classes could only be maintained by making a special effort. A report from 1943 paints a bleak picture of the Faculty of Medicine, burdened with additional tasks, radically understaffed — with a third to one fifth less than before the war — and antiquated. Of its 119 members, half were conscripted. Exemption for professors called up was always refused.

The intermittent closure of other universities resulted in a rise in the number of students matriculated in Munich in the first term of the war period from 4,057, in the summer term of 1939, to 6,734. Of these, 4,312 alone were medics. Between 1941 and 1944 the number of students remained constant between 3,000 to 4,000, whereby the

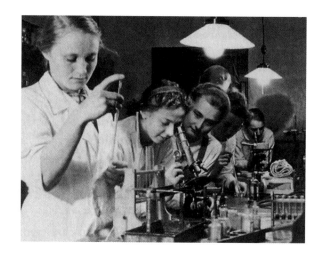

Between 1941 and 1944 the number of female students increased.

increase in the number of female students and medics was a characteristic trend in Munich as well.

THE WAR AND STUDENT LIFE

Virtually all male students took part in the war and took time off from their studies at short notice or were drafted into service. In addition, doctors-to-be were barracked in so-called *Studentenkompanien* — in Munich, five in all with 250 men. On top of this, came an increasing number of war invalids. As an emergency measure, vacation and special courses were offered, and long-distance supervision organized for students away at war; the Faculty of Law, for example, made use of the military post from 1942 onward. In this way, supervision was provided for some 3,500 students who were fighting in the war until the end of 1944.

Even during the war, celebrations that were good for publicity were held. The honorary doctor title given to the Italian Minister for Foreign Trade Raffaello Riccardi (1899–1976) was marked in the summer of 1942, and that of the Swede Sven Hedin

(1865–1952), the explorer of Asia, in January 1943 as part of the university's 470th anniversary celebrations. On both occasions the Reich Minister for Science, Bernhard Rust (1883–1945), and high-ranking Party functionaries were present.

Appointment procedures continued although they only resulted in a few new in-takes such as that of the psychologist Philipp Lersch (1898–1972) in 1942 and that of the surgeon Emil Karl Frey (1888–1977) one year later. In 1942/43, there was a fundamental political dispute and trial of strength concerning the successor to the Ancient historian Walter Otto (1878–1941), between the *Reichsdozentenführer* Schultze, who was a member of the Board of University Representatives, and the closed ranks of the whole university, which managed to force through the appointment of the renowned Ancient historian (Helmut Berve (1896–1979) even though, at that time, he was loyal to the regime. The Indologist Walther Wüst, rector since 1941, an active National Socialist, vice-president of the *Deutsche Akademie*, and director of the SS *Ahnenerbe* (ancestral heritage research institute) — ultimately holding the honorary rank of an *Oberführer* or senior leader — demonstrated his political influence in this instance which from time to time saw him backing traditional university interests.

Compulsory military service for all students announced in early 1940, permanent presence during the vacations in the armaments trade and help with the harvest, the threat of compulsory exmatriculation since 1943, and posting to the front, as well as the horrific experience of war, all weighed heavily on student morale. This came to a head in January 1943 during a major rally in the *Deutsches Museum* in the form of a protest and demonstration of strength, when the Bavarian prime minister and Gauleiter Paul Giesler (1895–1945) made disparaging remarks about female students — tumult broke out and was accompanied by fights.

THE COST OF CIVIL COURAGE WAS ONE'S OWN LIFE

Such protests and acts of both open and undercover resistance had also existed previously. However, the courageous example of active resistance displayed by a few select students in Munich at the time of the Stalingrad catastrophe in January/February 1943, was unprecendented. The *Weiße Rose* resistance group, centered around the siblings Hans and Sophie Scholl (1918–43 and 1921–43, respectively), Willi Graf (1918–43), Christoph Probst (1919–43), and Alexander Schmorell (1917–43), and the philosopher and musicologist Professor Kurt Huber (1893–1943) who became their mentor, had been distributing leaflets since summer 1942, calling for active resistance: "Nothing is so unworthy of a civilized nation as allowing itself to be governed without opposition by an irresponsible clique [...]."

The Scholl siblings were arrested on February 18, 1943, after distributing leaflets in the atrium at the university and four days later, on February 22, together with Christoph Probst, they were sentenced to death by the People's Court and executed. The death sentence was also passed in subsequent trials on Alexander Schmorell, Willi Graf, and ultimately also on Hans Leipelt (1921–45), as well as on Kurt Huber, whose speech in his own defence is an inspirational example of professorial confessional courage.

Although on that February 22, 1943, at a staged rally, over 3,000 students demonstrated their support for the Nazi state and against the "traitors," and although the rector tried to play down this incident for fear of further investigations, this act of resistance gained a huge symbolic significance. Its effect was not lost, despite the mood felt throughout the whole university which was suffering more and more from the impact of the war.

145

Members of the "Weiße Rose" paid for their courage in resisting National Socialism with their lives.

Sophie Scholl
b. 5/9/1921, executed on 2/22/1943

Hans Scholl
b. 9/22/1918, executed on 2/22/1943

Christoph Probst
b. 11/6/1919, executed on 2/22/1943

Alexander Schmorell
b. 9/16/1917, executed on 7/13/1943

Professor Kurt Huber
b. 10/24/1893, executed on 7/13/1943

Willi Graf
b. 1/2/1918, executed on 10/12/1943

The memorial to the "Weiße Rose" in the LMU atrium.

	1	2	3	4	5	6	7	8	9	10		1	2	3	4	5	6	7	8	9	10
A																					
B																					
C																					

Reichsministerium für Wissenschaft, Erziehung und Volksbildung

Zweitschrift!

Leipelt Reichs-Nr. ett. R.M. 3840

Familienname:

Hans Konrad *zum Tode verurteilt!*

Vornamen:
(Rufname unterstreichen!)

Geburtsdaten: Tag Monat Jahr Geburtsort:

jüd. Mischling Grades

(nähere Bezeichnung, falls notwendig) ③

Familienstand:

⑥

Anschrift am Hochschulort:

Postanstalt bzw. -bezirk

Schelling Straße *) Nr. 132

Platz

bei:

⑥

Heimatanschrift**):

Postanstalt bzw. -bezirk

Straße *) Nr.

Platz

**) Anschrift der Eltern, des Vaters, der Mutter, des Pflegevaters, des Vormundes oder eigener dauernder Wohnsitz. (Zutreffendes unterstreichen!)

Name des Vaters:
(falls verstorben, Name der Mutter oder des Pflegevaters oder Vormundes)

⑦ ⑧

Hochschulbildung: Beruf:

ja — nein*) ⑨

Berufsstellung:

Wohnung des Vaters:
(nur ausfüllen, wenn die gleiche Anschrift nicht schon unter ⑥ angegeben ist)

Straße *) Nr.

Platz

Geschwister:
(ohne den Studierenden selbst) Bruder, Schwester(n)

davon studieren bzw. haben studiert:

es sind erwerbstätig:

Form. HKK 1. 10. 5. 40. 30 000 —

Reichsdeutscher Student deutscher Volkszugehörigkeit

① Fakultät: Nat. Fachgruppe: Nat. Fachschaft: Chemie

㉗ Hoch-schulsem.: ㉘ Fachsem.: ⑰ Studienziel: ⑱ Berufsziel:

㉖ Frühere Studiengebiete: von bis einschl.

1. 3.

2. 4.

⑮ Schulvorbildung: in

Charakter der Reifeprüfung: Abiturientenjahrgang: Ostern*) Sommer als Schü Herbst Exte

⑯ Sonstige außerordentliche Zulassung, Art:

wann: Tag Monat Jahr durch (welche Stelle):

Immatrikuliert am: unter Hochschulnummer: Exmatrikuliert am: Grund:

/ /

/

Beurlaubt im Studienabschnitt: Grund: Beurlaubt im Studienabschnitt: Grund:

Studium im Ausland:
in zeitlicher Reihenfolge: von bis einschl. Hochschule Ort Land

⑬ Angehöriger welcher Gliederung bzw. welches ange-schlossenen Verbandes der NSDAP.: seit: Dienstgrad bzw. Amt:

Tag Monat Jahr

Mitglied der NSDAP. seit: Tag Monat Jahr Münchener Nr.: *) Nichtzutreffendes streichen

Shortly after the Scholl siblings and Christoph Probst, Willi Graf and Alexander Schmorell were executed, as were Professor Kurt Huber and the chemistry student and Wieland-pupil Hans Leipelt. Above: Detail taken from Leipelt's student register that has been invalidated and the words "sentenced to death" added next to his name.

148

THE END OF THE THIRD REICH ALSO MARKS THE END OF TEACHING

The list of university members in the institution's catalog who died "heroic deaths" became longer and longer as the war drew on. In the end it included more than 500 names. Continuous air raids hit the university badly. On July 13, 1944, the main building was destroyed and by the winter of 1944 many clinics and most of the natural science institutes had been obliterated or severely damaged.

The proclamation of a "Total War" on September 1, 1944, virtually brought teaching to a standstill, as only war invalids and widows of soldiers were permitted to matriculate as new students or to take exams allowing them to continue studying. LMU Munich registered 294 male and 1,292 female students for combat — from a total number of 3,965.

Following a decree put out by the Reich Ministry of Science, Education, and Culture on October 12, 1944, the Faculty of Law as well as the Faculties of Economics and Philosophy at LMU were to be shut completely, and the Faculties of Natural Science and Medicine partially.

The rector Walther Wüst exerted his influential contact to central positions on state and Party levels — from the Reich ministers Rust and Goebbels up to Reichsmarschall Göring and Reichsleiter Bormann — and was able to avert the de-facto closure that threatened the whole university.

However, following the destruction wrought in the summer of 1944 and the departure of "bombed out" lecturers, teaching could only be continued in the winter term of 1944/45 on a very rudimentary level and with considerable restrictions. The search for alternative premises and evacuation

The rector Walther Wüst, here talking to the rector of "la Sapienza" — Rome University — Piètro de Francisci, was the embodiment of the "Führerprinzip" at LMU. The arrest of the Scholl siblings also took place during his term in office.

plans — the medical clinics were to be moved to Haar — were of top priority.

The summer term in 1945 that was to begin on April 16 did not come about. Through the destruction of the war and the end of the dictatorship, 1945 — unlike 1918 — marked a clear break in the history of LMU.

The main university building was completely destroyed in an air raid in July 1944. Teaching could only be continued on a very rudimentary level, and in 1945, there was no summer term.

149

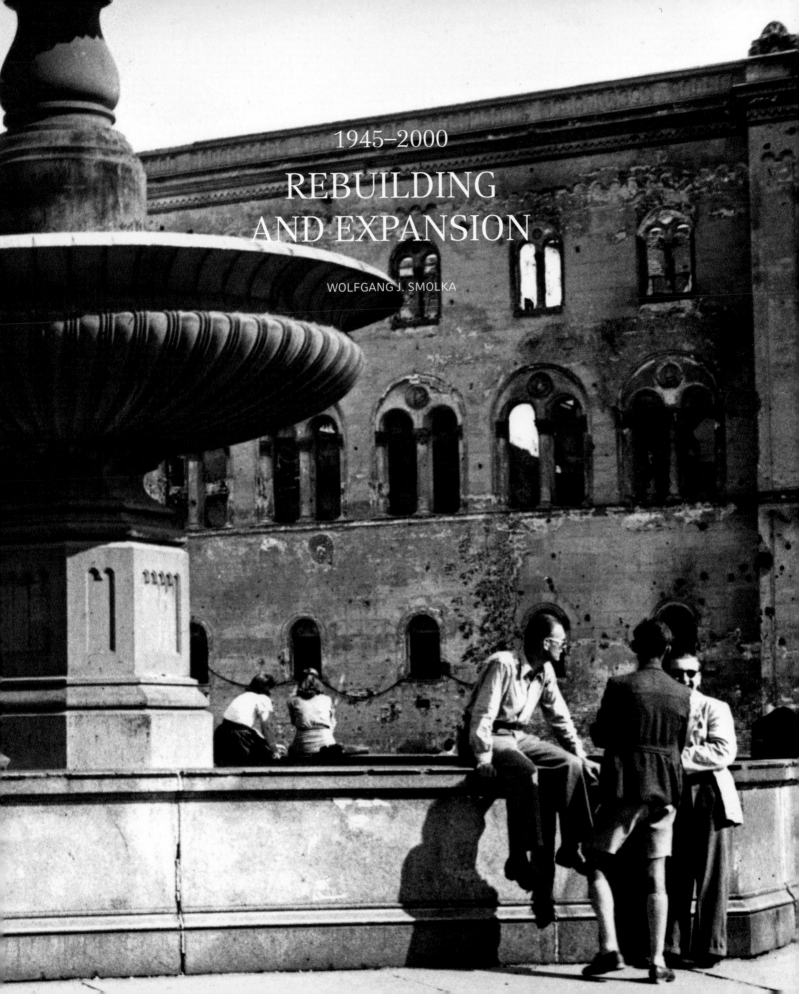

1945–2000

REBUILDING
AND EXPANSION

WOLFGANG J. SMOLKA

The city and university were both heavily bombed during the war. Rebuilding the university took twelve years.

previous double page:
Students around the fountain outside the main university building in the early 1950s. Student life only slowly returned to normal.

Rubble and ruin, hunger and material shortages, physical and mental suffering: For LMU Munich the war and its immediate impact also represented a formidable break in its almost 500-year history.

The first decade of the post-war period was indelibly marked by the immense reconstruction effort and by endeavors to put research and teaching back on track in the face of enormous difficulties. Nevertheless, at first, this all led to the re-establishment of the former, the familiar, and the known: The university was largely returned to the status quo in which it had been up until 1933.

Due to the influence the National Socialist regime had had, universities in West Germany were now consciously conceived as politically neutral "protective zones." The most profound changes they underwent, however, were only to be felt after the initial arduous years of rebuilding. Increasing bureaucracy and governmental reglementation were a challenge to the university's autonomy.

The next generation of students not directly effected by the war, the Nazi era or reconstruction efforts, vented its anger about political and social conditions within the previously sacrosanct walls of the university. It was in fact this politicization of the universities, the Higher Education Act on national and regional levels, the restricted admissions policy, academic reform commissions, and regulated student numbers that brought about greater — and, more significantly, longer term — changes to the general conditions experienced by lecturers and students from the 1970s onward, than the war and subsequent collapse many years previously.

DIPLOMACY OF A NEW START: QUICK REBUILDING OR UNIVERSITY REFORM?

On April 30, 1945, the city of Munich was handed over to the advancing US army. University life in the few months previous to this had only eked out an existence between ruins and in private houses. In fact, the winter term of 1944/45 did not really take place, even if exams were held in clinics and professors's apartments and doctoral canditates had to clamber over rubble and debris to hand in their disserations. The American military government ordered the university to cease all activity on May 14, 1945. In the days that followed, fifteen professors convened and designated the Classical philologist Albert Rehm (1871–1949) from among their ranks — the last rector from the pre-1933 era who could still be reached — to be the university's acting rector.

Albert Rehm was appointed acting rector of the university in May 1945. The entries in his diaries during his rectorship provide an insight into the university's history in the immediate post-war period. This picture shows him in his younger days, presumably during his first period in office as rector.

Rehm took up office without his position being confirmed by the US military government but with its acceptance. Both the Germans and Americans strongly felt that the university should start operating again as soon as possible, although the notion held by the occupying force was somewhat ambivalent. On the one hand, following a quick and thorough denazification of the teaching staff, those faculties in particular whose training facilities could provide the capacities needed to rebuild a democratic Germany, as envisaged by the occupying power, were to re-start operation as soon as possible. On the other hand, the reopening of the university was to be directly linked to a reform modeled on plans drawn up by the American military government. Since these plans started to take shape slowly and rather vaguely, Munich University — like all other universities in the American occupation zone — cut its own path towards re-opening its doors, caught between being a university corporation, the regulations of the US military government, and German ministerial bureaucracy.

LACK OF SPACE, SHORTAGE OF TEACHING MATERIAL, AND THE DENAZIFICATION OF TEACHING STAFF

The conditions under which Rehm took over the office of rector at LMU Munich were dismal in every respect. Nothing more than ruins of more than 70 percent of the buildings remained. The historical main building and the site of the clinics and natural science institutes were particularly badly effected. The university library reported a loss of around one third of a total of some one million volumes. And what was left, had been stored in more than 40 sites scattered in and around Munich.

Not only one third of LMU's books were lost, but invaluable archival material was also destroyed. The archive in the Institute of Journalism.

above and left:
70 percent of LMU's buildings were destroyed or no longer usable; the main building was cordoned off due to the danger of it collapsing.

What turned out to be much more problematic was the staff situation. In the course of "denazification" or "epuration" initiated after the war, the teaching staff — that had been reconfigured beetween 1933 and 1945 in the interests of the Nazi regime — was hit by a wave of dismissals, the extent of which was unique in its history. By the end of 1946, around 80 percent of the university teaching staff had been categorized as politically tarnished and removed from their positions. Frequently, minor formalities sufficed the military government. Denunciation also had its repercussions in many instances.

A more precise analysis of a large number of cases and the rehabilitation of individual staff members that ensued, ultimately reduced the quota of those suspended from office to around 50 percent. That was, however, still high enough to leave gaping holes in the staff structure that could only be filled with difficulty. Of those who had emigrated, some returned hesitantly to Munich while many emeriti resumed teaching to at least help compensate for the lack of university teachers for the time being.

DIFFICULT COMMUNICATION
WITH THE AMERICAN OCCUPYING FORCES

An internal university commission that formed part of the planning committee headed by the rector, Rehm, was established in 1945 as a "self-cleansing" mechanism, initially under the jurisdiction of the American military administration. This committee was to be the nucleus of a new university, as seen by the military government, and initiate the resumption of teaching and research work. Within a short space of time it was just this political cleansing process within the staff that became a central issue between Rehm and the Americans. The notion as to who was unencumbered, who was merely a follower, and who actively involved was completely different.

On top of this was the Americans's massive scepticism with regard to certain elements in the education tradition in Germany. This manifested itself for example in the stubborn criticism of syllabi that were considered too conservative, of a supposedly antiquated medical tuition, or of courses that conveyed too little democratic understanding. This resulted in several applications submitted by Rehm for the reopening of the university being turned down on a regular basis by the military government.

With the establishment of the first Bavarian post-war government under Prime Minister Fritz Schäffer (1888–1967) from the summer of 1945 onward, an operative Ministry of Education and Cultural Affairs under Otto Hipp (1885–1952) existed once again too. Both his first university advisor, Professor Reinhard Demoll (1882–1960), as well as ministers and the prime minister himself had previously been removed from their positions in September 1945 by the military authorities due to differences in denazification policies. The prerequisites for an uninterrupted period of work were finally established under the government of Wilhelm Hoegner (1887–1980) through the appointment of Franz Fendt (1892–1982) as Minister for Cultural Affairs. But even the latter could not completely dispel the fundamental disagreements between the rector, Rehm, and the American military government. In January 1946 Rehm resigned, and it was only with considerable difficulty that a successor, whom the occupying forces also approved, could be found in the person of the 73-year-old Romanist Karl Vossler, who had already proved his capabilities as rector in difficult times in 1926/27.

TEACHING CAN START AGAIN

In the spring of 1946, an agreement was finally reached for the reopening of the university under Vossler's rectorship: first of all for the Faculties of

Wilhelm Hoegner was Bavaria's first and only SPD prime minister since the war. Hoegner spent the years under National Socialist rule in exile in Switzerland, only returning to Germany in 1945.

The surgeon and orthopedist Georg Hohmann became rector at the same time as the official reopening of LMU Munich in 1946.

Philosophy, Law, Economics, and Natural Science; the medical and veterinary science faculties followed later. The theology faculty had already resumed operation in February 1946 ahead of the others. Overseen by the mathematics professor Kurt Vogel (1888–1985), special classes had, however, already been started in 1945 to put prospective students — especially those returning from the war — in a better position to cope with a regular course of study.

The Ministry of Education and Cultural Affairs named April 1, 1946, as the beginning of the first regular term since the end of the war. The official reopening of LMU Munich was on July 23, 1946, accompanied by the installation of the first elected post-war rector, Georg Hohmann (1880–1970) from Frankfurt am Main and his prorector Willibalt Apelt (1877–1965) from Leipzig. A conscious decision had thus been made to appoint two outsiders to top positions at LMU. Unencumbered by local events during the first few months after the war, they were to adopt an intermediary position between the three parties, the university, the ministry, and the military government. As such, Ludwig-Maximilians-Universität could claim the dubious honor of being the last university in the American occupation sector to start operating again.

The Triumphal Arch marking the transition between Ludwigstrasse and Leopoldstrasse was also a victim of the bombing, as were more than 40 percent of the buildings in Munich.

ADVERSITY AND HARDSHIP IN THE FIRST FEW YEARS

During the first two years after the war the Americans gave absolute priority to their re-education policy and to a rigorous denazification. Both the dismissal of those who were politically tarnished as well as sluggish reinstatement and rehabilitation measures resulted in an intolerable personnel situation in many areas in university institutions. Many academics hesitated about returning to Munich from exile, and it made it difficult for those in Munich in finding suitable outside scholars for the university, especially seeing that posts in the British and French zones had been filled much faster as working conditions there were more stable. The harsh living conditions of post-war Munich also played a role of course, which was why non-university academic institutions and organizations avoided Munich for many years too, on top of the generally poor local conditions.

The circumstances at that time are certainly difficult to envisage in this day and age: 45 percent of the buildings in Munich had been destroyed, there were around 300,000 homeless, many residents of Munich had to make do with temporary accommodation between rubble and ruins for many years.

Student "hunger demonstration" on Sophienstrasse (June 17, 1948). In the background, the building now occupied by the Bavarian state tax office.

Shortages of food, clothing, and fuel were omnipresent. 70 percent of those studying in Munich were considered undernourished.

Like the bodies of the younger generation, their minds were also craving for food. Even months before the university reopened, the institute's internal admissions board registered some 7,000 matriculation applications. Under the prevailing conditions only 4,000 students could be admitted at first (of whom 25 percent were female); this restriction however was lifted in January 1946. Two years after the end of the war, the Minister for Cultural Affairs, Alois Hundhammer, commented on the "worrying" increase in the number of students at all Bavarian universities; another two years further on, LMU Munich enrolled its 10,000th student.

REBUILDING THE STUDENT INFRASTRUCTURE

The material hardship among students was great. Even during the *Wirtschaftswunder* — the "economic miracle" — between 30 and 60 percent of students worked at the same time as studying so as to be able to keep up with the cost of living and pay course fees. The latter included "lecture

159

While the theologian Michael Schmaus was rector (1951–52), student fraternities were permitted again at LMU.

Studentenwerk students' union was one of its main priorities. Its premises in Louisenstrasse had been totally destroyed during the war, the halls of residence severely damaged, and what was still intact had generally been put to another use.

The rebuilding of the *Studentenwerk* started without delay, under changing management, as soon as the war was over. In 1948, it was run as a non-profitmaking institution under public law. As in other areas as well, reality soon caught up with the bold plans initially made — which included a premises located centrally between the various university institutes, comprising cafeterias, libraries, halls, and offices. These plans were sacrificed for mediocre partial solutions that nevertheless still provided students in Munich with some essential support. In 2010, the *Studentenwerk* in Munich attended to the needs of around 92,000 students at twelve university institutions in and around the city — almost as many as the total number of students at all German universities and polytechnics combined in 1950!

With the reopening of the university, the AStA was also reconstituted as a representative of the students' interests and joined up with other student bodies in Bavaria to form one umbrella organization. With an eye on the hardships experienced in the first few years, student accommodation and the cafeteria became the focus of attention much more than any other issues. After the monetary reform of 1948, more capacity was given to student self-representational interests as well as to restructuring academic life, with student exchanges, for example, as part of an international program for scholars.

After student fraternities were permitted once again from 1952 under the rector Michael Schmaus (1897–1993), their representatives made up a

money" or tuition fees up until 1969. Only the university board could waive this charge or approve a reduction. Complaints about too few grants and too little support for students were always to be found in the reports of post-war rectors just as much as those of student organizations — something that has become alarmingly topical once again today.

In 1945, the Ministry of Education and Cultural Affairs even set up a separate department for student matters that principally focused on accommodation, clothing, and books, and later on grants. In addition, the reconstitution of the

The university's damaged principal auditorium, the Audimax. A lot of reconstruction work had to be done — to which the "student construction gang" made an invaluable contribution.

large percentage of AStA functionaries. It was only from the 1960s onward, under the influence of the student protest movement and the politicization of universities, that the cleft between fraternity members, student representatives, and other students became larger once again.

NEW LIFE BETWEEN THE RUINS

A uniquely individual contribution was made by students in the years immediately after the end of the war through their work in the "student construction section," headed by the Egyptologist Hans Wolfgang Müller (1907–91). At first, it was run on a voluntary basis. From the winter term of

1946/47 onward, a six-month stint to help rebuild the university became compulsory — the completion of this duty being made into one of the prerequisites for admission by the Ministry of Education and Cultural Affairs. Starting with clearing rubble and provisonal repairs to the main university building in particular, the construction unit soon became an indispensable general factotum. Its tasks ranged from guard, emergency, supervision, and transport duties through to helping construction companies contracted to rebuild the main building and institutes. The construction gang was not dissolved until 1949. Among those who studied immediately after the war, its memory has become a legend.

There was actually a considerable amount of activity amongst the ruins. The large auditorium in the main university building had survived mostly unscathed and, as one of the few spacious rooms in Munich that could still be used, it was particularly coveted. Many post-war concerts given by the Munich philharmonic orchestra were held there from the summer of 1945 under the direction of Eugen Jochum (1902–87), Hans Knappertsbusch (1888–1965), and Wilhelm Furtwängler (1886–1954). The first commemoration held to honor members of the "White Rose" took place in the auditorium, and it was here that international literary figures and philosophers found an audience which was only too grateful to eavesdrop on the free development of thought.

The auditorium's role in the founding of the new Bavarian state is also noteworthy: The "Beratender Landesausschuss" (state advisory committee) and the *Verfassunggebende Landesversammlung* (state constitutional convention) both held assemblies there. This was where the new Bavarian constitution was agreed upon, and where the first elected post-war Bavarian parliament was convened. By 1953 the auditorium had to be closed for repairs. Since 1984, its Jugendstil interior has been shining again in all its glory.

NEW HOMES FOR FACULTIES AND INSTITUTES

The physical reconstruction of the university in the first twenty years of the post-war period obviously took prominence. At the end of the war, only twelve lecture theaters out of a total of 62 in the main university building could still be used. It was here that around 70 percent of the students had to have their lectures. Apart from the symbolic and historical importance of the building, this was a major reason why so much attention was paid to its restoration. However, it took twelve years before the

building regained the appearance it now has today. With its extensions to the north and south of the historical core, it is still representative of the university as a whole and, through its central location in the city, also integrates it into the urban municipality of Munich.

The severity of destruction triggered thoughts about a fundamental reassessment of the university's location in Munich. Consideration was given to moving the university beyond the bounds of the cramped inner city to a site outside the municipal area. Apart from the construction of the major new teaching hospital in Großhadern, such thoughts however were never put into practice. Nevertheless, the construction of new buildings was possible, especially where it was no longer feasible to rebuild one that had been completely destroyed and a replacement was needed. This can be seen today for example in the Faculty of Veterinary Medicine complex between Königinstrasse and the English Garden, erected in the typical utility style of the 1950s and '60s.

Within the area bordered by Sophienstrasse, Karlstrasse, Arcisstrasse/Katharina-von-Bora-Strasse, and Luisenstrasse, institutes for pharmacy, chemistry, biology, and zoology had already become established in the 1920s and '30s. Massive bomb damage made it necessary for building on the whole site to be done largely from scratch, which was then considerably expanded to include additional natural science facilities. In the meantime, all of these university institutes have made way for a modern urban district and moved to LMU's equally state-of-the-art "high tech campus" in Großhadern and Martinsried.

Despite careful planning already carried out during the pre-war period, the university library was not rehoused in a new structure, due to the main building's importance within the urban fabric as a whole.

The university's large auditorium, the "Große Aula," came through the war largely unscathed. Due to the lack of alternative venues, this is where the constitutive meeting of the Bavarian State Advisory Committee (above) was held in February 1946. The State Constitutional Convention also held assemblies in the auditorium; this was where the new Bavarian constitution was agreed.

Alternative accommodation was also needed for research and teaching; the hygiene institute taught in this pre-fab block.

Much of the rebuilding work at the university had to be utility in style: above, the new building for veterinary medicine on Königinstrasse.

The so-called "Salinenbau" (Ludwigstrasse 27) still houses the core of the university library today. The International Office and the Central Student Advisory Office are also to be found here. Damage to the masonry on the building's south façade has been left as a reminder of the destruction wrought in World War II.

Instead, it was allowed to move into the *Salinenbau* to the south of the main building, a red brick building fronting Ludwigstrasse and Schellingstrasse, which today is still the center of the university's mountain of books.

The Faculty of Medicine clinics and institutes, fanning out over a wide area to the west of Sendlinger Tor Platz, were all constructed in the 19th and at the turn of the 20th century. Even before the war, significant shortcomings with regard to their modern usage were already obvious. Nevertheless, they were rebuilt on their old sites. Thoughts about future problem-free expansion, however, especially with regard to the medical and surgical clinic, soon forced things to be reconsidered. In 1955, the Bavarian cabinet decided to have a new building erected on the edge of the city to house these clinics. The starting signal for the Klinikum Großhadern was given. The first building phase, however, could not be started until 1967/68, a fate that the clinic shared with many other university building projects. The reason for this was not just the limited

resources — by 1968 some 65 million German marks had already been spent on construction work with a further 314 million estimated — but also the fact that building measures had produced a formidable planning and administrative workload. At the topping-out ceremony for the teaching hospital's ward block on October 17, 1972, the rector at that time, Professor Nikolaus Lobkowicz (b. 1931), rightfully said that this undertaking was the biggest building project in the university's history.

More a footnote to events at the university, but still not unimportant within the history of post-war Bavaria as a whole, is the fate of the Maximilianeum. The representative building on the terrace above the Isar, generally known today as the seat of the Bavarian parliament, was originally used exclusively to house King Maximilian II's foundation for gifted pupils, administered by LMU Munich. As the foundation and the university were not in a position to finance the reconstruction of the badly damaged building on their own, the Free State was brought on board and it was leased to the parlia-

The philosopher Nikolaus Lobkowicz from Prague was rector and then president of LMU from 1971 through 1982. From 1984–96 he was president of the Catholic University of Eichstätt.

German marks, expenditure for education and research on both a national and regional level was downright despicable. In 1955, Köstler's successor, Alfred Marchionini (1899–1965), worked out that postponing the founding of the Federal Armed Forces by just one year could have financed the revamping of the university system throughout the whole republic in one fell swoop.

The university's rebuilding policy also tended toward spreading institutions out across different sites to an increasing extent, a trend that even today has not stopped. "New acquisitions" in the post-war era included the mountain observatory on Wendelstein as an extension to the university facility, which consequently became LMU's most southerly location. In 1960, the rector Eugen Ulmer (1903–88) could proudly claim: "Ludwig-Maximilians-Universität stretches from Wendelstein to the forests around Landshut."

ment. After constitutive sessions were held in the university's large auditorium, the university was able to offer the regional parliament a new home for the second time.

REARMAMENT INSTEAD OF INVESTING IN EDUCATION?

Sluggish building work, cramped conditions, and miserably equipped university institutes were the reason for a dramatic and equally indignant "status report" that the then rector Josef Nikolaus Köstler (1902–82) had distributed in 1954 to all influential instances and well-known public figures. In it, he not only complained about the frugal financing of universities but also the increasing and utterly stifling bureaucracy. At this time, rectors frequently criticized the cost of rearmament in the Federal Republic; compared to an annual defence budget of between nine and ten billion

The observatory on Wendelstein was originally a solar observatory built in 1941 for military purposes. After revamping, it has been used for night astronomy since 1989.

SELF-ADMINISTRATION AND A NEW CONSTITUTION

From the observatory on Wendelstein to the forests near Landshut owned by the university, from the symbol of modern scientific exploration to remnants of corporative independence: such was the spectrum in which the university had to hold its own in the post-war period.

The university was guaranteed the right to self-administration in the constitution of the new state of Bavaria on December 2, 1946, even though the state claimed the facilities and management were its responsibility. Albert Rehm's first draft of a new constitution made in September 1945 had recourse to the most important points in the old statutes of 1920/26, thus revoking the intrusion of the National Socialist state in the university's autonomy. Rehm's draft never became official even though university life was based on it in the first few years after the war.

This claim to autonomy gained all the more importance when, immediately after the war, endeavors to introduce reforms were made under the direction of the occupying forces aimed at curbing the university's corporative rights — something that failed, at least for the time being, due to the strong resistance of the restituted university itself. The Board of University Representatives at LMU passed a new draft constitution on July 27, 1953, albeit renamed "statutes," that was given ministerial approval. As such, LMU Munich had written history, as it was the first university in Germany to draw up its statutes as a public corporation thanks to its entitlement to independent jurisdiction.

DEPARTMENTS, TITLES, AND FUNCTIONS

According to these statutes, LMU comprised seven faculties, the affairs of which were managed in each case by a dean who was elected for one year.

His representative (the vice dean) was always the person whose term of office as dean had just finished. The principal of the university was the rector. He was elected for one year from the circle of all those who held official positions as professor ordinarius or professor extraordinarius and was given the honorary title *Magnifizenz*. At the same time he also held the chair of the two most important bodies within the academic self-administrative organization: the Board of University Representatives and the administrative committee. The Board of University Representatives, as the supreme decision-making body, comprised the rector and prorector, a delegate for the administrative committee, the deans, and several elected senators. In addition, representatives of professors without chairs and scientific assistants, civil servants, and students were also on the Board. The syndic, as head of the general administration of the university, participated in an advisory capacity. There were several committees with managerial and decision-making roles in the most varied divisions of academic life. Among the most important was the administrative committee already mentioned that continued to exist until shortly after the beginning of this century in the form of a budget commission.

In an environment with such a structure and which is — to a certain extent — autaric, some ritualistic dealings in academic life certainly still served a purpose. Today, these would perhaps come under the heading "corporate identity," if following generations had not taken action against "the mustiness of a thousand years." The highlights in the academic year at this time were the rectorship changeover, Founders's Day, and the matriculation celebration, at which freshmen were personally welcomed by the rector at a special function. At the beginning of each winter term, the festive handover of the chain of office by the outgoing rector to his successor, with official handshake and ceremonial pledge — at which the university regalia was also paraded — was attended by the professors. At the festival held every year at the end of June, the founding of the university was celebrated, a tradition that — like the rectorship changeover and matriculation celebration — fell victim to the riotous events in 1968 but was resumed in 1984.

Awarding honorary doctorates has been of particular importance to the academic image of the university since time immemorial. Apart from those titles given by the faculties, the whole university was proud to be able to call exceptional figures from science, politics, and economics honorary members of the university. These included Theodor Heuss (1884–1963) and Hans Knappertsbusch (1888–1965). Since the 800th anniversary of the city of Munich in 1958, the university has expanded this tradition to include the title of honorary senator, presented for the first time to Albrecht, Duke of Bavaria (1905–1996). And since 1983, the university has been able to secure the support of major figures in society through appointment to the board of trustees.

AMBIVALENT LOOK TO THE PAST

Thus seen, university life — from within and without — still takes place between centuries-old traditions, urgent present-day needs, and a future that is freqently regarded with a certain apprehension. In the first two decades after the war in particular it was very popular to look back to times long ago in the university's history, and such references can be found in speeches given by virtually all rectors and in the university's official publications. This form of recollection, however, was also deceptive as it drew attention away from a "present" that had only just become "past" — namely the twelve years under the National Socialists'. It was not just a question of coming to grips with Nazi involvement within the university's own ranks, but in the modern age certain things needed to be seen in a new

light. The final appearance of the main building after reconstruction is just one example: Aphorisms, such as the quotation from Horace *Dulce et decorum est pro patria mori*, that reflected the patriotic, humanistic educational ideals of the time, were once worked into the original railings in the atrium which were destroyed in the war. That it should be "sweet and fitting to die for one's country" was certainly no longer an ideal in the 1950s to be impressed upon young academics, and soon the question of restoring the metalwork ignited an international discussion which attracted considerable attention in the media. A public competition to include "replacement" aphorisms soon filled many binders but resulted in little that was satisfactory. The university ultimately had to come up with a suitably intellectual replacement from within its own ranks — even that was no easy undertaking.

Not always without its conflicts and problems, but nevertheless something that, on the other hand, has been upheld for almost seventy years, is the commemoration held for the members of the "White Rose." Ever since the very first year after the war, LMU Munich has succeded in keeping close to its most recent past. Beginning with the speech given by Romano Guardini (1885–1968), *Die Waage des Daseins* (The Balance of Being) on November 4, 1945, the memory of the "White Rose" is perpetuated every year in a ceremony held in February. In 1997, the White Rose Foundation's "White Rose Memorial Center" adjoining the atrium was inaugurated by the German President Roman Herzog, and in 2007, a bust of Sophie Scholl, created by the Munich-based sculptor Nicolai Tregor, was placed in the atrium itself. Together with the existing bronze relief by Lothar Dietz (1896–1976), an impressive ensemble in memory of the couageous resistance group against the Nazi dictatorship has been created within the university. When the competition for the design of the first memorial was announced in 1955, 275 artists from Germany and

The Guardini chair in the Faculty of Philosophy, Philosophy of Science, and the Study of Religion at LMU is named after the Catholic philosopher of religion, Romano Guardini.

A bust of Sophie Scholl in the atrium, made by the Munich sculptor Nicolai Tregor, is a reminder today of the famous member of the "White Rose."

abroad submitted entries. In 1958, Dietz's work was unveiled together with the inauguration of the renovated atrium, that very place where 15 years previously the Scholl siblings had scattered their leaflets. Once again, it was the philosopher of religion, Guardini, who held the commemorative address based on the tenor of the final words uttered by Hans Scholl "Let freedom live." Without any doubt, the historical main building at the university was and still is the "culminating point" in the life of the institution, and in its entirety, embodies the history of LMU in stone.

1958: A JUBILEE FOR THE CITY AND THE UNIVERSITY

A commemoration of quite a different kind was also held in 1958, namely the 800th anniversary of the city of Munich that had been planned with the active participation of professors from Munich.

Egon Wiberg (1901–76), the rector at that time, took the opportunity to point out that it was not only the 800th anniversary of the city's foundation but that its university was also celebrating its 500th anniversary as a seat of learning. Duke Louis the Rich decided to found a university in 1458. Fittingly, Wiberg cited from the foundation privilege granted by Pope Pius II, in which particular reference is made to the symbiosis between the town — at that time, admittedly, Ingolstadt — and the university.

A close co-existence between the local community and the university was not merely wishful thinking in the 1950s but a pleasing reality. Immediately after the war, the city had helped rebuild the university as far as it could by creating accommodation for students as well as providing work — some students, for example, were trained to be part-time tram conductors. The university once again became a popular venue for public cultural events and after the war the Lord Mayor, Karl Scharnagl (1881–1963) and his assistant for cultural affairs, Hans Ludwig Held (1885–1954), made a considerable personal effort toward attracting major academics to the city. Financial contributions to academic institutes and the students' union to hold international vacation courses, for example, show the city's solidarity with its university, which by the same token demonstrated its close connection to Munich through its huge contribution to the city's jubilee celebrations.

In Munich's anniversary year, the basis of a "city within the city" was even established: Egon Wiberg's long-cherished and vigorously pursued vision of a "cité universitaire" — an international student town along the lines of that in Paris — suddenly looked much more like becoming a reality within a surprisingly short while. In next to no time, the prime minister Hanns Seidel (1901–1961) made an 80,000 square-meter site available right next to the English Garden in the Freimann district of Munich, which was owned by the state of Bavaria. The Max Kade Foundation contibuted the substantial initial sum of one million German marks for this undertaking. Building work started in 1961 to plans drawn up by Ernst Maria Lang (b. 1916). The complex in Freimann, however, never

The chemist Egon Wiberg was rector of the university from 1957–58. A "cité universitaire" — a student town along the lines of that in Paris — was his long-cherished wish.
Photo: Felicitas Timpe (1923–2006).

developed into a "cité universitaire à la Paris," but simply evolved into the Freimann student housing district — fortunately, as many people believe. Nevertheless it was still the largest student residential area at that time in the Federal Republic.

INCREASING ATTRACTIVITY, BETTER REPUTATION, AND THE STRUGGLE FOR INTERNATIONAL ACCLAIM

The university itself could also brag about being the largest in Germany, certainly with regard to the number of staff and students. The standard of research and teaching at that time was and still is

On the occasion of the city of Munich's 800th jubilee in 1958, that was also the 500th anniversary of the university's "mental birth," the then finance minister of the Federal Republic, Ludwig Erhard (1897–1977), who also held an honorary professorship, visited the university. Erhard allowed himself to be photographed with the "Golden Ship." Whether he actually drank from this cup is not clear, and rather improbable, as such attempts generally resulted in stains on ties and shirts.

difficult to assess, despite the tendency to list universities around the world according to a ranking system, rather like the lending rates of international financial institutes. In times of the Excellence Initiative and competition in general, some of those in positions of responsibility may well look back longingly at the first decades after the war. Despite initial difficulties and without the competitive battles for graduate schools and "Clusters of Excellence," Ludwig-Maximilians-Universität regained the academic reputation it had enjoyed up until the war surprisingly quickly at that time — a reputation that it has been able to maintain at a high level to this day. Esteemed academics and all the different courses contributed toward this success immediately after the war. The historian Franz Schnabel (1887–1966), the theologian and philosopher Romano Guardini, as well as the biochemist and Nobel Prize winner Adolf Butenandt (1903–95), for example, should be mentioned in this respect.

The infrastructure of course also played a role. In the field of the arts, the treasures in Munich's libraries, for instance, regained their magical attraction, the natural science institutes were reinstated or founded from scratch, and even the prospect of possible work in a state-of-the-at clinic such as that at Großhadern attracted certain experts to Munich. Bold innovations were also risked: From 1965, an interfaculty "center for political science" at LMU Munich was planned. It was to be centered on its own political science institute, alongside which all those involved — as well as professors in the Faculties of Law, Economics, Cultural and Historical Science — were to be drawn on "to work together on problems in political research and teaching." The nucleus of this undertaking was a chair for political science that had been set up for Eric Voegelin (1901–85) in 1958 when he returned from exile, at a time when it was still being argued as to whether politics could ever be a matter of scholarship. Voegelin's professorship was soon

Eric Voegelin and Hans Maier held the two chairs that led to the founding of the "Geschwister-Scholl-Institute of Political Science."

The historian Franz Schnabel greatly influenced historical scholarship at LMU and beyond. His pupils include such renowned historians as Lothar Gall and Eberhard Weis.

joined by a second, filled by the later Bavarian minister of cultural affairs, Hans Maier (b. 1931). The center for political science as a massive research institute spanning all faculties, was never to become a reality. What did emerge, however, from the two political science chairs is the "Geschwister-Scholl-Institute of Political Science." That LMU now has more than a dozen research centers spanning all faculties — ranging from the nanosciences to ecumenism and Renaissance studies — would surely have filled the intellectual fathers of the political science center of 1965 with the feeling of utmost satisfaction.

Just as the young Federal Republic had to struggle for international recognition within the community of states after years of war and tyranny, so too did the universities in Germany. A visible sign of the effort made by Ludwig-Maximilians-Universität to forge a link to the international scientific community was the *Colloquium Europaeum*, inaugurated in 1955 with the "Paris University Week." Within this context, intellectuals from Scandinavia, Italy, Holland, and Scotland, as well as representatives from many other countries spent time at the "Munich University Weeks" colloquium up until 1964. Through the reopening of the office for foreign students in 1952, scholarship holders from abroad started to come to Munich once again. Around four percent of students at LMU in 1952 were non-Germans; this figure had risen to some nine percent by 1961. Since the beginning of the new millennium, the proportion has remained constant at around 12 to 15 percent. Conversely, more and more students from Munich have been able to study abroad on scholarships such as the academic exchange program initiated by the American senator James William Fulbright (1905–95) in 1946. Incidentally, Fulbright himself actually visited LMU Munich in 1964.

PROGRESSIVE POLITICIZATION AT THE UNIVERSITY

All in all, the Federal Republic's educational policy during the rebuilding period could not — by any manner of means — keep up with the requirements of teachers or students. Similar to the most recent sit-ins in lecture theaters in the winter of 2009/10, more than four decades earlier students also drew attention to conditions they found unacceptable. The nationwide "July 1st Campaign" initiative of 1965 addressed topics for the first time that have since been negotiated under the heading "educational crisis". They wanted to highlight a whole bundle of shortcomings in the educational system in West Germany, especially socially imbalanced educational opportunities at university level and the disproportionately low national and regional budgets in the light of rapidly growing students numbers. Demands for a fundamental restructuring, for a transition from an "ordinarius university" to a "group university" — i.e. with participation on equal terms — only became louder in the course of further discussions and the political mobilization of participating groups.

The "July 1st Campaign" also took place at Ludwig-Maximilians-Universität. Attended by some 4,000 students and with speeches by the AStA chairman Kurt Faltlhauser (b. 1940), later to become Bavarian finance minister, and the LMU professor and newly elected DFG president Julius Speer (1905–84), it passed off without incident. Students and professors had relatively similar aims and the university itself was not opposed to

reforms as such. AStA's endeavors for example resulted in student representatives being permitted to attend meetings in virtually all faculties. At LMU, the fear was not so much of a confrontation with the students as with the state. "It is often but a small step from state funding to state control," the rector Ludwig Kotter (b. 1920) prophesied when addressing university policies at Founders's Day celebrations in 1966.

Encroaching student and youth protest movements from the USA, demonstrations against the grand coalition in Bonn, the resentment of a new generation to the authority of the "middle-class state" and emergency legislation, the death of the student Benno Ohnesorg (1940–67) during the Shah's visit to Berlin in 1967: This was the background against which cracks in academic freedom first appeared in Munich and at LMU — initially in the form of disruptions to the rectorship ceremony and the Scholl memorial celebration.

Events escalated in April 1968 following the attempted assassination of Rudi Dutschke (1940–79) in Berlin: During the occupation of the publishing building in Munich by students and radical groups, the reporter Klaus Frings (1936–68) and the student Rüdiger Schreck (1941–68) were killed. Politicians and students succeeded in stemming the simmering violence potential, at least for the time being, at a rally on Königsplatz. The "psychological approach" taken during the police operation in Munich, which sought a dialogue between conflicting groups, was positively registered. This had evolved from experience gained from the "Schwabing Riots" of 1962. Despite this, the trenches had already been dug.

Student campaigns, which were frequently not clearly divisible from those of small, individual, radical groups, largely shifted to within the university. Disruptions to lectures, meetings of the

A stone thrown during the occupation of the publishing building in Munich in April 1968 killed the photographic journalist Klaus Frings (1936–68), who worked for AP and the Axel-Springer-Verlag, among others.

Board of University Representatives or faculties, the occupation of the rector's office or rooms in various institutes, AStA's "campaign weeks," as well as discussions of a more serious nature, teach-ins and sit-ins were part of everyday life at the university for some time. Pipe bombs in the Faculty of Law, police operations in the university's otherwise so carefully protected open spaces, and the violent interruption of the rectorship election in 1971, which then had to be held outside the university walls for the first time in its history, are some of the least happy memories of this unsettled period up until around 1974.

REFORMS CHANGE THE FACE OF THE UNIVERSITY

During this period, the face of the university also changed in a different respect. Independent of enforced state ordinances or group demonstrations, it initialized the most significant period of reform in its history — apart from during the Landshut era — with a number of changes being made to its classical structure. Following initial attempts made in 1961, LMU gained a chancellor as the principal administrative director in 1965, who was in charge of all administration instances

AUFRUF zur KAMPF-DEMONSTRATION

6. 7. 71

KOMMILITONEN,

heute um 15 Uhr versucht die reaktionäre Ordinarien-clique im zweiten Anlauf den Kandidaten ihrer Wahl, Herrn Dr. Nikolaus LOBKOWICZ zum REKTOR zu machen.

Herr LOBKOWICZ scheint entschlossen gegen den Willen der Studentenschaft Rektor zu werden und als Rektor gegen die Studentenschaft amtieren zu wollen.

Dieses Ziel kann er allerdings nur durch einen Großein-satz der Münchener Polizei erreichen: die Straßen um die Residenz sind ab 14 Uhr gesperrt.

Der ASTA hat einen Demonstrationszug zur Residenz an-gemeldet, der mittlerweile genehmigt worden ist.

Vor dem Beginn der Demonstration wird die Studenten-schaft auf einem teach-in noch einmal klarlegen, daß es ihr nicht um die Person des Herrn Lobkowicz geht, auch nicht um die Verteidigung jener "progressiveren" Variante kapitalistischer Bildungsplanung des Rektor Walter, sondern um die Wahrung und um den Ausbau jener Positionen der Studentenschaft, die sie benötigt zur politischen Arbeit an den Instituten.

14 UHR Demonstrationsbeginn vor der Universität

VORHER: 13³⁰ UHR Teach-in in der Großen Aula

Eigendruck im Selbstverlag
Verantwortlich: Theo Ebel, AStA, 8-München-23, Leopoldstr. 15

The AStA at LMU called upon students to demonstrate against the election of Professor Nikolaus Lobkowicz as rector of LMU in 1971. Accusations against him included "wanting to work against [the interests of] the students as rector."

Student agitation in the atrium: The late '60s and early '70s were turbulent years at LMU.

in the university. The administrative board (since 1970, the budget committee) then became the most important self-administrative body next to the Board of University Representatives, and could have direct recourse to the central administration in its executive function. As a move toward a "more professional" university management but also as a reaction to state planning measures, a full-time planning cadre and a planning commission were set up in 1970.

1969 was an even more significant year. After hundreds of year the rector relinquished his exclusive control. Munich was one of the first universities in Germany to introduce the collegial constitution. From then on, it came under the management of a committee comprising five members: the rector, prorector, two deputies, and the chancellor. The committee was also joined by a representative of the academic staff for the first time in 1969 —

something that was not repeated until 2001: the assistant and communication scientist Dr. Peter Glotz (1939–2005), who however soon moved on to take up a position in politics.

The spirit of change also stirred in the university's "extremities." In 1966, the fourteen physics chairs in the Faculty of Natural Science joined up to form one organizational entity — the "Physics Department" — to make better use of their resources. With this "department," the physicists were a good thirty years ahead of their time. It was not until 1999, following the refounding of the Historical Seminar, that a systematic departmental structure was introduced in all faculties at LMU.

In 1967, the Faculty of Protestant Theology at LMU was constituted and the first courses held in 1968. It was the second of its kind in Bavaria after Erlangen, and was to allow for changes in the denominational structure in Upper Bavaria and for the loss of Protestant theology colleges in East Germany. In 1969, the Faculty of Philosophy was divided into two, and in 1970 forestry engineering was separated from the Faculty of Economics and made into a faculty in its own right. In 1971, the Faculty of Natural Science was divided into five independent Faculties for Physics, Mathematics, Chemistry and Pharmacy, Biology, and Geosciences.

The integration of the newly founded "Munich School of Political Science" — proposed by the Ministry of Education and Cultural Affairs — as an "institutionally independent facility within the university" was, however, turned down by the Board of University Representatives, as this construct would give the school of political science a special status within the university as a whole. In the end, the ministry managed to push through its idea: The school was not to become a faculty but form an independent entity within LMU.

By contrast, all participants endorsed the incorporation of the Education College in the Pasing district of Munich. Putting this resolution into practice, however, soon became a bone of contention between the university and the ministry. The education college was to be annexed to LMU en bloc, which from the university's point of view — as in the case of the school of political science — would lead to a special status within the university and hamper integrated teacher training. In this case too, the university was compelled to compromise, resulting in a decree being passed on July 25, 1972, for the integration of the education college, initially as a whole, as the Faculty of Pedagogy.

After this process of expansion and integration over a period of several years, LMU Munich boasted fifteen faculties just prior to the Higher Education Act of 1973. With 28,500 students and a total of 9,255 employees, ranging from professors to porters, it was the largest university in Germany competing only with the Free University of Berlin, and the sixth largest employer in Munich.

It is possible that in those years, LMU's sheer size alone may have been alarming to one or other Bavarian education minister. Anyhow, in 1973, LMU narrowly escaped a catastrophe. In that year, a plan was put forward by the member of the regional parliament, Dr. Erich Schosser (b. 1924), to split the university into seven individual colleges of higher education — a scheme that LMU energetically fought against and that, fortunately, was not pursued. Soon afterward, when the Bavarian Higher Education Act came into effect in 1974, the university experienced further far-reaching changes as it was. Through the renewed division of the two Faculties of Philosophy, 21 so-called departments had been created, within which the individual academic facilities — institutes or clinics — then worked under collegial management. The term "department," however, soon reverted to the

The Historical Seminar, (re)founded in 1999, is housed in the "Historicum" on the corner of Amalienstrasse and Schellingstrasse. The older section of the building on Amalienstrasse previously housed the forestry research institute. The new part also includes the library of the Historicum, the glazed façade of which faces the Salinenhof.

traditional "faculty" and the Faculty of Pedagogy — the 21st — was dissolved as an entity as early as 1974 and merged into other divisions. In the meantime, the number of faculties has been reduced to 18 (as of 2010). The complete Faculty of Forestry Engineering for example was absorbed by the Technische Universität München and incorporated into its "Life Sciences" complex. In addition, the two philosophy faculties for linguistics and the study of literature were amalgamated.

By allowing representatives of the professors, academic staff, and students on departmental boards, assemblies, and the Board of University Representatives, as well as other staff members in the university as a whole, the first tentative steps were taken during this period towards a university group — something that LMU still endeavors to pursue today. In 1976, as a result of the Higher Education Act, the constellation of the university's managerial body changed. Instead of the rector, a president was appointed with a six-year term of office; instead of the prorector and deputies, there were three vice presidents. With the chancellor, that made five again.

The switch to a presidential constitution was not just a new label while keeping the status quo. What was significant was that the position of president was not tied to a professorship at the university; someone from outside the university could also be elected. The new president, however, was admittedly a long-serving member of the university, the previous rector who had been in office since 1971, Professor Nikolaus Lobkowicz. His two rival candidates, a graduate engineer and an attorney, on the other hand, projected a picture of the highest post in a university that was hitherto unfamiliar. Lobkowicz's successor was once again also a representative of the university: In 1982, Professor Wulf Steinmann (b. 1930) took on the position. In 1990, an amendment to the Bavarian Higher Education Act enabled the move away from a presidential back to a rectorate constitution. After that time, a rector who had to be a professor at the university, was elected for four years. Together with the rector and the chancellor, three prorectors — each with a two-year period of office — form the rectorate council. And today? The LMU executive board once again comprises a president and five vice presidents. The office of the chancellor was transformed into the office of the vice president for Finance and Administration. On top of this, the Higher Education Act of 1998 also introduced another far-reaching change: In the form of the *Hochschulrat* (university council), the university's executive board gained an additional committee that has considerable decision-making powers.

1974 saw the end of another centuries-old tradition at LMU Munich too, although this time it was of its own free will. It no longer considered it in keeping with the times to exercise its right to appoint priests to a number of different parishes — a tradition that formed part of the Ingolstadt and Landshut endowments — and handed this privelege over to the respective dioceses. The university forests around Landshut, however, are still in its possession to this day.

UNIVERSITY JUBILEE DURING THE OLYMPIC GAMES: CATALYST AND COMPETITOR

In keeping with the maxim "standing still doesn't get you anywhere," the 1960 and '70s were a particularly lively period for LMU, and during this eventful time — and obviously in its prime — it celebrated its 500th anniversary in 1972. Virtually at the same time, the summer Olympic Games were held in Munich. Reason enough for the city and the university to join forces to celebrate in full. As in former times, the university once again used this prominent occasion to award honorary memberships to the Board of University Representatives, and the Medal of Honor introduced in 1971.

The Olympic Games brought the university a number of bonuses. The main building could then be reached directly on the subway; after the athletes had left, part of the Olympic Village was turned into a second student housing area; and the Olympic sports facilities still form the backbone for sport practiced by all university institutions in Munich. For this, higher education had to pay one prestigious price: Ludwig-Maximilians-Universität was never honored with a special issue stamp — unlike all other major sister universities in Germany. With all the stamps brought out for the Olympics, Munich had been sufficiently showcased, was the laconic reason given by the Federal Post Ministry.

The reverse side of the Olympic medal was the Olympic price boom and a new awareness among local residents for changes in their municipality, which brought new constraints upon the university.

ASTA RUFT ZUM
BOYKOTT DER 500 JAHRFEIER AUF!
"TAG DER STUDENTEN" –
EINE PROVOKATION DER
• STUDENTEN!

29. Juni 1972

Eigendruck im Selbstverlag
Verantw.: Th. Welker
8-Mü-40, Leopoldstr. 15

Auf der gestrigen Studentenschaftsvollversammlung (Do, 22.6.72) wurde die umseitig abgedruckte Resolution angenommen, die den Boykott der 500-Jahr-Feier
der LMU durch AStA und Konvent legitimiert. Boykott der Feier heißt nicht, diese selbstgefällige Rückschau auf die Tradition bürgerlicher Wissenschaft als
problemlose Bestätigung ihrer selbst, diese Leistungsschau und "Bestandsaufnahme"
zu ignorieren. Diese bürgerliche Wissenschaft sieht sich explizit als ein aus
sich selbst entstehendes und autonom fortentwickelndes "Kontinuum des Geistes",
wobei die sie umgebende Gesellschaft nur als etwas äußerliches erscheint, was
sie nur gelegentlich tangiert - ihre Gesellschaftlichkeit erkennt sie nur formal,
wenn sie über ihre Wirkung oder Nichtwirkung in der sie umgebenden Umwelt
räsoniert, oder sich finanziell von gesellschaftlichen Instanzen abhängig fühlt
oder qua Gesetz eine "fortschrittliche" Organisationsform übergestülpt bekommt,
ohne daß diese Maßnahmen Wissenschaft als solche, ihre Methoden, Inhalte und
Ergebnisse betreffen würde. Ausdruck dieser Äußerlichkeit ist die scheinbare
Beziehungsllsigkeit zwischen BHG und der Wissenschaft und ihrer 500-jährigen
Existenz-Feier (Lobkowicz auf der gestrigen Pressekonferenz: er wisse gar nicht,
wieso man so eine Randerscheinung, wie das BHG anläßlich eines solch bedeutsamen
Jubiläums ins Feld führen könne).
Der AStA hat all dies als Grundlage seiner Politik stets auf die notwendige Trennung
der Wissenschaft vom kapitalistischen Produktionsprozeß zurückgeführt. Die
Funktion von Wissenschaft, allgemeine Voraussetzungen für die kapitalistische,
unsere Gesellschaft beherrschende Produktionsweise zu schaffen, läßt der Wissenschaft ihre eigenen Voraussetzungen unbewußt, die Reflexion ihrer widersprüchlichen
gesellschaftlichen Bedingtheit geht nicht in ihre Arbeitsweise ein.
Diesem Nachweis des Zusammenhangs von Wissenschaft und Gesellschaft leistet
der AStA und die AK-Fraktion tagtäglich im SOZIALISTISCHEN STUDIUM, dazu
bedarf es keines zusätzlichen Anlasses.
Im Rahmen der 500-Jahr-Feier wird von einem sog."Initiativ-Komitee" im Namen
der Studentenschaft ein "Tag der Studenten" durchgeführt (es handelt sich dabei
um einige RCDS-Mitglieder und Korporierte, die in "weiser" Voraussicht erkannten, daß die gewählten Studentenvertreter und ihre Organe einen solchen Tag

Not everyone viewed the university's anniversary as an occasion to celebrate. The AStA at LMU called upon students to boycott the 500th jubilee in 1972, as the festival was nothing but a "complacent look back at the tradition of bourgeois academia as a problem-free confirmation of its own self." What was especially criticized was the notion that the academic world saw itself as an autonomous self-furthering "continuum of the intellect," that largely excluded social aspects or merely acknowledged these formally.

Quite apart from the fact that it was looked on with mistrust by some as a hive of danger and source of revolutionary intrigue — an image that is as old as the university itself — it was also accused of following a seemingly unbridled expansion course over the previous few years in particular.

The university has long been seen as an unwelcome neighbor in the very district it was founded, the "Maxvorstadt," which the university has helped shape considerably since 1940. This could be seen in the controversy the new students' union and cafeteria complex in Leopoldpark unleashed, which found a sequel in the 1990s in the debates on the "Historicum" and the "Arnold-Sommerfeld House," the international center close to the main university building. On the other hand, luxury renovation schemes, soaring rents, and real estate speculation are not just a threat to the university itself since then, but more especially have hit a vital nerve of the students and staff. Things have become very cramped in the Maxvorstadt district.

BURSTING AT THE SEAMS

When the university was reopened in 1946, this dilemma was certainly something that could not have been envisaged to such an extent, although it was inevitable. By starting to build the Großhadern teaching hospital in good time, the situation in the downtown Faculty of Medicine buildings was eased. After the completion of the first phase in 1974, the 930 million German marks project was handed over to LMU Munich. This has contributed to the exceptional status now enjoyed by the Faculty of Medicine at LMU in the field of international research.

In the best possible company of LMU's HighTech-Campus, the Max Planck Institute, and other innovatively forward-looking research institutes in Großhadern and Martinsried, the aged clinic has

LMU's main building was linked directly to the subway system built for the Olympic Games in 1972 in Munich. Today, the U6 line runs from the HighTechCampus in Großhadern via the inner city clinic district and the central university site with its main building, to the Garching-Forschungszentrum stop at the far end, where LMU's physics institutes are located.

The building of the Medical Center of the University of Munich in Großhadern, nicknamed "the toaster" by students, greatly relieved the strain on the inner city clinics in 1974.

now become the subject of a costly renovation scheme. While the inner city clinics and Großhadern hospital were combined to form the financially completely independent LMU clinical complex in 1999, as is still the case, a way must now be found over the next few years to solve the major question of renovating both sites.

Several other institutes at the university that required a lot of space also managed to flee from the constraints of the city center. In 1972, in conjuction with the Technische Universität München, the physics division's Accelerator Laboratory was opened in Garching. Other examples are the Fa-

culty of Forestry Engineering move to Weihenstephan in 1992, and the Gene Center Munich opened in 1994 near the hospital in Großhadern, which was then joined in 1999 by the Faculty of Chemistry and Pharmacy. The central site originally planned for their expansion is now ruled by the world of art: This is where the Pinakothek der Moderne is located. Students of veterinary medicine are also being moved to a green-field site: To the north of Munich a completely new faculty campus is being built. The Faculty of Natural Science move away from the Sophienstrasse and Karlstrasse sites, and the new urban district that has been built, have already been discussed.

The Faculty of Chemistry and Pharmacy (to the right of Feodor-Lynen-Strasse) was built after the Gene Center Munich (top left corner in picture) in 1999 on the HighTech-Campus in Großhadern.

Gene Center Munich: Founded on the initiative of the biochemist Professor Ernst-Ludwig Winnacker (b. 1941) in 1994, it is now regarded as one of the most prestigious centers for biomolecular research and teaching internationally.

EXPANSION IN THE CITY CENTER

In the 1980s and '90s new construction projects were also started in the city center, and vacated buildings acquired by LMU. A new, centrally located building next to the cafeteria was erected in 1986 for education and pyschology. Historians, on the other hand, had to wait much longer for a similar home. The new-build project became bogged down in discussions between parties, residents, and administrative bodies, as well as in the financial misery surrounding Germany's building policy in the higher education sector. It only became a reality at the turn of the millennium.

On June 30, 1995, the university chancellor described the transfer of the extensive building complex previously occupied by Radio Free Europe next to the English Garden, to the university as like "winning the jackpot." The premises, vacated by the famous post-war broadcasting station when it moved to Prague, were handed back by the Americans to the Free State of Bavaria which fortunately made them over to the university. Many institutes have also been able to find a base near the main university site. These include the Geschwister-Scholl Institute, the Department of Communication Science and Media Research, the university's Japan Center, as well as the Institute of Social and Cultural Anthropology, and the Department of Computer Science. In this way, LMU Munich gained directly from the global political changes at that time.

EQUALITY IS PARAMOUNT

The broad spectrum of courses at LMU offered every term covers several thousand subjects for the good of mankind — or, more appropriately, womankind. In all, more than 60 percent of students at LMU Munich are female. However, just

less than 14 percent make it to the top of the long academic career ladder to become professors. To redress this imbalance, the position of women's representatives was introduced in 1988. In 1994, LMU passed a "commendation on the equal treatment of women and men in course studies, research, and teaching" in order to bring about a structural improvement of the situation for women — especially in the long term.

"The Alma Mater's Stepdaughters" was the name of an exhibition organized by the university's Women's Representative in 1993/94, which was also shown at other universities, to highlight the history of female university students in Bavaria that began in 1903. *Frauen-Studien* is the title of a brochure published every term, which for years has been calling for an interdisciplinary study on female and gender-specific subjects at LMU. The initiative is intended to be seen less as a competitor and more as a supplement to the traditional interdisciplinary *Studium Generale*, as has been the case again since 1949.

"Courses for Senior Citizens," initiated in 1983, are tailor-made for war-time and immediate post-war generations. Its prime aim is to provide those who, in their youth, could not take a normal degree course due to the hardships of the war and the post-war period, with an opportunity to attend a university. This is also intended to promote dialogue between the generations.

LESS POLITICS AND MORE RESEARCH

Since the 1980s, higher education policies have experienced a shift in emphasis that is also noticeable at LMU. The involvement of students and academic staff in university politics has declined appreciably and is reflected among other ways in a clearly lower number of students who go to the polls. Instead, research work at the university has

Women's Representatives at LMU (from left to right): The literary scholar Prof. Dr. Renate von Heydebrand was the first Women's Representative at LMU from 1988 until 1990.
She was followed by the linguist Dr. Hadumod Bußmann, who held the position from 1990 through 1997.
Dr. Edda Ziegler, also a literary scholar, was in office from 1997 to 2000.
Prof. Dr. Ulla Mitzdorf, professor for Medical Pyschology, was the Women's Representatives from 2000 until 2006, since when the theologian Dr. Margit Weber has held the position.

moved further into the foreground. Discussions about the lack of qualified people in technology and research in Germany as a whole have become widespread and are slightly reminiscent of the "Sputnik crisis" of the post-war era. Whenever state funding runs dry, third party financing suddenly becomes topical again. All the same, in 1994, scientists at LMU managed to generate 137 million Marks in this sector, rising to 196 million in 2000. In 2007, LMU attracted third party funding of 134 million euros (approx. 260 million German marks). In this respect, the *Gesellschaft der Freunde und Förderer der Universität München* — in short, the *Universitätsgesellschaft* — has regained its importance as a benefactor and helper to the university in times of need.

Despite all the rigors of the immediate post-war period, Munich itself has developed into a major center of the sciences. This has given LMU the opportunity to cooperate with a number of non-university research institutes in the Munich area such as the "Helmholtz Zentrum München – German Research Center for Environmental Health," or the twelve Max Planck institutes based here. Working together with the natural science technology facilities is just as important for LMU as the arts and social sciences, as for example with the Institute of Contemporary History, the Institute Technology-Theology-Natural Sciences as an independent organization affiliated to LMU, and the Rachel Carson Center, established in 2009, that bundles the expertise of the arts and natural and social sciences — a joint initiative of LMU and the Deutsches Museum focussed on pressing environmental questions and issues that will decide our future.

The work of the Bavarian Academy of Sciences and Humanities or the Bavarian Natural History Collections is by tradition inseparably interwoven with LMU's history, not only due to its links at staff level.

It comes as no surprise that throughout history leading figures in German scientific organizations have emanated from the teaching staff at LMU Munich, be it the president of the Max Planck Society, the DFG (German Research Foundation), or the Alexander von Humboldt Foundation, or be it chairmen of the German Council of Science and Humanities.

PRIZES, FOUNDATIONS, AND SCHOLARSHIPS

The "quality and quantity" of emerging academics are in direct correlation with demands for high-level performance in research, and are reflected in various academic prizes. Since 1984, the university has awarded research prizes every year on Founders's Day for exceptional doctorate and habilitation theses. On top of the awards funded by the *Universitätsgesellschaft* is one from the state capital, Munich, first given in 1993. LMU also leads the field in Germany with regard to awards from external institutions: It is, however, not possible to list all prizes and honorary awards here that are bestowed on both established and emerging research scientists, students, and employees at LMU.

The *Maximilianeumsstiftung*, on the other hand, provides sponsorship for up-and-coming academics at root level. Following the end of the Bavarian monarchy in 1918, the Bavarian state parliament acted as protectorate to this royal foundation against the founder's will. It was not until 1955, after negotiations that had been going on since 1926, that this right was finally transferred to LMU Munich. A new era for the foundation began in 1980, during the Wittelsbach jubilee celebrations, through the provision of a new foundation from the House of Wittelsbach that enables female students to benefit from this foundation for gifted pupils.

Since time immemorial, age has often been seen as synonymous with dignity and merit, be it with

Pupils of the Maximilianeum studying together. In 1955, the protectorate of the royal Maxi-milianeum foundation was transferred to the university. Since then the rector or president has also been head of the Maximilianeum. On the wall in the background, a copy of the foundation deed can be seen.

regard to princely dynasties or academic institutions — and with a history dating back more than 500 years, the university can certainly hold its head up high. Despite this, the focus at LMU is primarily on the future. Its image in the fields of research and teaching, as well as its profile in the city of Munich itself and on its outskirts, has con-sequently altered considerably. The appearance of the university today gives little hint at the enormous challenges and uncertainties in the institution's day-to-day operations that so marked the post-1945 period over a number of decades.

THE PATH INTO
THE NEW MILLENNIUM

REINHARD PUTZ

The "Speerträger" (Spear Bearer) hall in the main building as a study area — thanks to modern work methods and WLAN.

previous double page:
The setting sun is reflected in the glass façade of the biocenter completed in 2008. For the first time in more than 100 years all biology facilities at LMU are now to be found on one site on the HighTechCampus.

The face of the university has changed considerably since 2000. Alumni would recognize many familiar places from their student days and many renovated lecture halls, which would certainly conjure up a genuine feeling of being back home again. They would see that a new level of technology with beamers and modern sound systems has become standard in virtually all lecture halls, and see how students now concentrate on their laptops in the seminar rooms, on the steps, and in the corridors. They would however also notice that lectures and libraries are more crowded than before. And, in particular, they would be confronted with sometimes surprising new buzzwords: At LMU, talk is of "corporate design" and "corporate identity" which range from the printed letter head right down to the LMU Shop. Under the heading *Präsidialverfassung* (presidential constitution), the management structure and the way the university regards itself changed fundamentally in 2007. Politcally instigated cost-cutting measures have added a certain acerbity to the expression *Profilbildung* (cultivating a competitive profile) and have become the driving force behind an on-going structural reform. There is another word that has suddenly taken a hold on the Alma mater that outsiders used to consider rather introverted or perhaps even somewhat sedate: *Exzellenz*. This term has spread like wildfire throughout the university and become a permanent fixture in all divisions, even if under varying auspices. In keeping with the buzzword "Bologna," most course have now been restructured — and not always to the delight of the those concerned. A new awareness for constructively dealing with discrimination in any form has established itself throughout the university under the heading *Gleichstellung* (equality). Seen on an international scale, the number of female academics — especially those holding professorships — is still dis-

The library in the "Book Tower" includes all the works of the Faculties of Catholic Theology and Protestant Theology as well as the Faculty of Philosophy, Philosophy of Science and the Study of Religion. With more than 340,000 volumes it is the largest open access library of its kind in Germany.

gracefully low, even if an upward trend over the past few decades can be discerned, with their share rising from seven to fourteen percent.

Over the past ten years, LMU has certainly spruced itself up despite the massive space problem in some divisions. The main university building from 1840 is now gleaming again — and was even awarded the "Best Façade" prize by the city of Munich. In the north east tower, the so-called "Book Tower," a large central library for several divisions in the arts has been created. The success

LMU is not a campus university but is located on many different sites in the city, on its outskirts, and beyond. Economics, Social Sciences, and the Arts are to be found in the historical main complex and adjoining buildings in the city center. The biocenter with state-of-the-art laboratories and rooms for seminars and practicals is the most recent addition to LMU's HighTechCampus in Großhadern/Martinsried that has been growing continuously over the past thirty years.

The Faculty of Biology's Department II was already able to move into the new biocenter in Großhadern/Martinsried in 2004 after the first building phase was completed. Department I (botany) followed in 2009 after the completion of the second phase.

of a number of institutes has brought about a search for new quarters elsewhere, and buildings round about have been rented to accommodate a whole range of different facilities. In this way, a new base for the university archive has been found in Freimann, and in Garching a green LMU sign lights up a building for laser physics. Some of the clinics in the Faculty of Veterinary Medicine have moved to Oberwiesenfeld, while university life pulsates on the main site around Ludwigstrasse

both inside and outside the buildings, just as one would wish an academic center to be.

The past few years have finally led to a decision being taken on the future location of the clinics and institutes in the Faculty of Medicine. Renovation work on the lovely anatomy building has been started, while the other preclinical theoretical institutes are planning their move to the BioMedical Center in Großhadern. Biology followed the Faculty of

This bird's eye view shows a large part of the HighTechCampus in Großhadern/Martinsried. The Faculties of Biology, Chemistry and Pharmacy, the Gene Center Munich and the Faculty of Medicine, with the Medical Center of the University of Munich (in the background) are all located on the 250-acre site.

Chemistry and Pharmacy, that had already moved to the HighTechCampus in Großhadern/Martinsried in 1999, in two stages (2004 and 2008), and is now installed in two modern complexes. In 2009, a cafeteria and a kindergarten were opened in their immediate vicinity. Work on extending the Medical Center of the University of Munich on the Großhadern site is moving forward; the frame of a modern surgical wing is now going up on the northern side of the large main complex. Immediately opposite,

the site for a center for dementia and stroke patients has been prepared.

To the west of the city, a Life Science campus has been created together with Max Planck institutes, the Founder Center IBZ, and a series of biology company spin-offs — something that is beyond comparison with any other university in Europe, with the subway providing good connections to the main university site in the city center.

CHANGES TO THE GENERAL
POLITICAL FRAMEWORK

The most significant political decisions effecting universities were anchored in the Bavarian Higher Education Act of 2006, in which the classical rectorate constitution was changed to a presidential one and the *Hochschulrat* (University Council) assigned a new task. The presidents, now elected by the university council, have much more responsibility and greater possibilities to exert their influence than previously enjoyed by rectors — something that, especially considering general political and economic factors, has doubtlessly led to the university gaining greater visibility and influence. A suitable candidate from outside the university may now be elected president. With this innovative construct, a new picture and awareness of itself has invariably started to evolve within the administrative body, one that some professors of the old school do not always see as a welcome limitation in the light of their previous role within an autonomous administrative system. National and international competition, that has now become very much a matter of course, made such a reorientation and streamlining of management structures absolutely necessary. While the academic Board of University Representatives, previously the supreme decision-making body at the university, used to be able to make the final decision on appointments — a key function at the university — its involvement in the appointments procedure now is restricted to passing on recommendations to the university management. Whereas resolutions on the university constitution — the pivotal set of regulations for internal procedures at the university — previously lay in the hands of the broadly structured university assembly, it is now the responsibility of the university council. As such, its function is comparable to that of the supervisory board of a major company in industry. Half of its 16 members are from the Board of Uni-

The Public Finance expert, Prof. Dr. Bernd Huber, has held the top post at LMU since 2002 — initially as rector, and following the introduction of the presidential constitution in 2006, as president. In June 2010, for the first time in the history of LMU, the tenure of his position was confirmed by the newly established University Council. His third term of office began in October 2010 and lasts six years.

versity Representatives, the remaining external members are leading figures from business, legal or academic institutions. In 2010, in the light of challenging national and international competition, LMU called for the university management to demonstate greater leadership; the classical, collegial, academic policy of co-determination will have to take a step back by comparison, certainly much to the regret of many colleagues whose roots in the system run deep.

The number of courses offered at a genuine "universitas" like LMU is incredibly broad and diverse. At present, this offer has been taken up by 47,000 students. Spread across 18 faculties, around 700 professors and some 3,600 academic staff members are involved in teaching and research.

CULTIVATING A COMPETITIVE PROFILE

Since its foundation in 1472 in Ingolstadt, LMU has seen itself as a broad-based university covering all academic fields. In struggling to find the correct "brand name," it regards itself to be a classical *Volluniversität* (full university – i.e. offering a comprehensive range of disciplines), in which links can be found to all major contemporary areas of research, with the sole exception of technical subjects otherwise taught in the hallowed halls of the Technische Universität München, Munich's second major university. For top level research to maintain the profile necessary in a global competitive field, a focus on specific designated areas has become imperative.

The profile of such a large university has to try to find a balance between trail-blazing performance on the one hand and future-oriented fundamental structures that are sustainable in the long term on the other. In all events, cultivating a competitive profile means concentrating on so-called "beacons," i.e. fields of research of a particularly important character. This results in an often painful shift of resources, a process that began in 2004 just a few weeks after the state election and the far-reaching decision made by the Bavarian state parliament. The ruling that all state ministries had to make substantial cuts to their budgets led to a dramatic reduction in the number of professors and other staff at universities, as their costs were largely tied up with personnel expenses. Politi-

195

	**Competition round 2006**
	Competition round 2007

In October 2006, the DFG and "Wissenschaftsrat" (academic council) announced the results of the nationwide "Excellence Initiative". LMU was successful in all three lines of funding and, until 2011, can make use of funds of around 180 million euros to establish a Graduate Center for Systemic Neurosciences and three "Clusters of Excellence" (the Center for Integrated Protein Science Munich (CIPSM), the Nanosystems Initiative Munich (NIM), and the Munich-Centre for Advanced Photonics (MAP)), as well as for the "LMUexcellent" concept for the future. In the first round Technische Universität München and TU Karlsruhe were also successful along with LMU. In the second funding round in 2007 a further six German universities secured the title "Exzellenzuniversität."

cians, arguing the necessity of a budget consolidation to justify such a procedure as a whole, introduced expressions such as "efficiency reserves" and "cutting out dead wood" into the discussion. The commission set up by the state government under the heading *Wissenschaftsland Bayern 2020* (academic excellence in Bavaria 2020) sped up the process of establishing a profile after 2005. In between whiles, even the merging of the two major universities in Munich was discussed.

LMU faced these challenges positively and proactively, and embarked upon a process to establish a profile that is still ongoing. In a manner never seen before, the *LMUinnovativ* initiative introduced in 2004 has resulted in all faculties at the university analyzing their internal structures and making suggestions to cut back posts in certain areas, as well as establishing new focal points with the possibility of reinstating certain positions.

In an exemplary fashion, *LMUinnovativ* has shown how a very large university can equally well deal with fundamental structural reforms and hone its profile to meet new circumstances. The collective disclosure by all faculties has, in addition, largely contributed to furthering the university's common academic spirit.

In hindsight, the impulse to start such a restructuring process was — despite the problems it brought with it — actually something to be grateful for, as it could be taken as a generally accepted standard and used to meet the challenges of comparable processes in the years that followed. In this way, LMU was well prepared for the "Excellence Initiative" announced by the federal government in 2005. Through the success of three Clusters of Excellence, one Graduate School, and the "LMUexcellent" institutional strategy during the competition one year later, LMU was able to establish its position at the top of Germany's university landscape. What makes this success so special is that it is based on a continuous and long-standing cooperation between many academics at the university and surrounding institutes. One expression of this excellent area of cooperation at top research level is the award of the Nobel Prize in Physics in 2005 to Professor Theodor W. Hänsch for his research on the frequency comb.

The Excellence Initiative by the federal and state governments modelled the first decade of the new millennium to a considerable extent and led to changes at universities which would never have been thought possible before. Declared an "elite university" during the first round of this initiative, LMU gained an international reputation that has led to a sweeping upturn. With not inconsiderable means, it became possible to pursue the expansion of successful core areas, the success of which still seriously influences LMU's internal structure to this day. Sponsorship formats, aimed at the creation of larger work groups by joining forces, have also raised questions about the correct form of sponsoring. As one of the largest universities in Germany, LMU has always placed value on a broad subject basis in all faculties, especially in the arts and social sciences. It was, however, the natural science disciplines that were especially successful in the Excellence Initiative. The so-called institutional strategy, that was also backed by considerable funding in the excellence initiatives, has made it possible for development measures across the university to be established, from which, for instance, the arts were also able to profit. This could be seen in the research cooperation initiative set up as part of the LMUexcellent program in the late summer of 2008 with the University of California, Berkeley, that — among other things — deals with exchanges for visiting professors, a doctorate and post-doctorate program, and the sponsorship of joint research projects by scientists from both universities.

The LMU physicist Theodor W. Hänsch was awarded the Nobel Prize in Physics in 2005 for his research on the frequency comb, with which the frequency of laser light can be measured to a much higher precision.
Hänsch shared the prize with the two US American researchers John L. Hall and Roy J. Glauber.

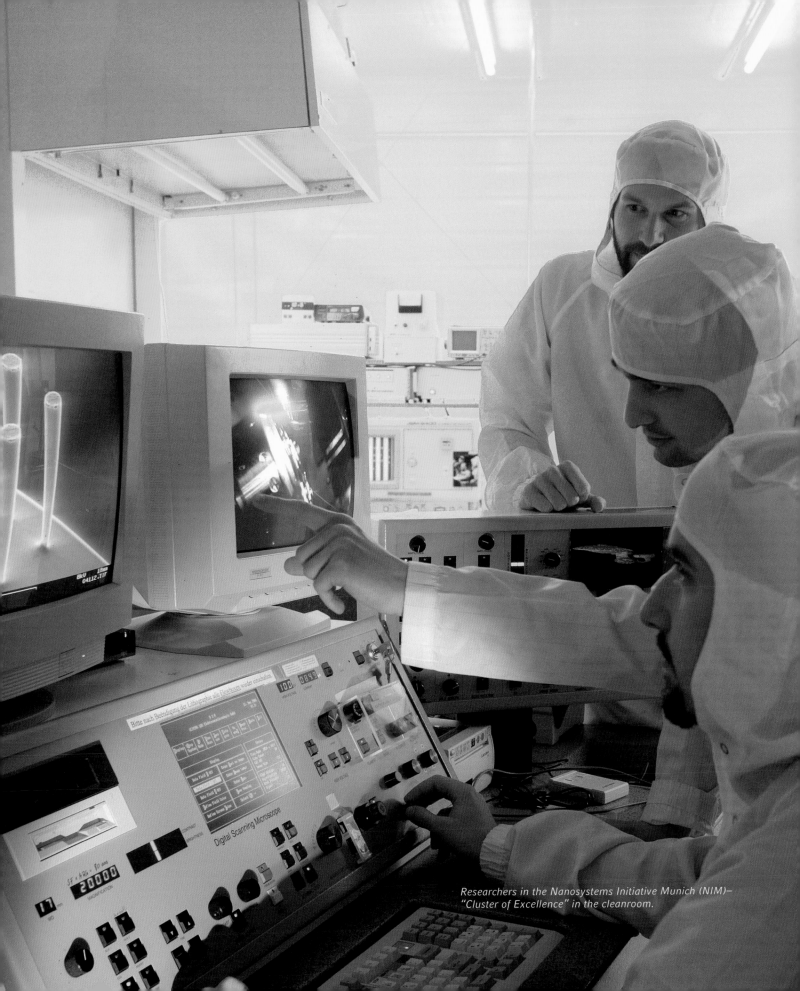

Researchers in the Nanosystems Initiative Munich (NIM)–
"Cluster of Excellence" in the cleanroom.

The Center for Advanced Studies (CAS) at LMU in Seestrasse in the Schwabing district of Munich sees itself as a forum for intensive academic interchange beyond established interdisciplinary boundaries. Through its activities, it promotes the most varied forms of cooperative research and interdisciplinary communication within the university; in addition, it assists in integrating visiting scholars into academic life at LMU.

The mentoring program supports highly qualified, young female academics pursue academic careers up to professorship level.
Renowned and experienced female professors in the various faculties act as mentors to the talented young scholars. The mentors adopt a role model character and advise and assist their mentees in an individual or group basis with regard to career planning and developing their own personal academic profiles.
An interdisciplinary mentee network enables participants to offer each other mutual assistance in reaching their academic goals.

In addition to creating professorships, the paticularly important promotion of women's careers through a special mentoring program, a dual career program, proposals for the personal development of communication and management techniques, and a program for young academics, also form part of the LMUexcellent initiative. The establishing of a Center for Advanced Studies (CAS) permits a focussed discussion on topics for the future and makes provisions for special interdisciplinary research projects.

As preparation for the next round of the Excellence Initiative in 2012, the faculties were called upon to define a stategy to take them through to 2016. This process, backed by all faculties after a series of detailed discussions, has led to the definition of future-oriented focal areas, many of which involve several departments and faculties.

FAR-REACHING AUTONOMY

There is hardly any other buzzword that whips up public opinion as much as "autonomy." Universities would only too gladly depend as little as possible on the direct influence of the state or ministries. However, it should not be forgotten either that they are largely financed by the state. Striking a balance between a justified involvement in fundamental decisions at the university and the university's equally justified desire for as much freedom as possible in the areas of research and teaching, is one of the major challenges of the collaboration between the state parliament, the government, and the university. In 2009, Bavarian universities were given the right to carry out appointments independently; the ministry of education and science's involvement to date — concerning the minister's right to summon someone to a chair — was moved to the beginning of the appointments procedure, namely to cooperation on the creation of posts and putting out tenders. New appointments to a chair are now made by the president. Decisions to create or modify courses are now made by the Board of University Representatives in consultation with the University Council. The move toward greater autonomy is only possible in small steps and with mutual respect, bearing the financial source in mind. Agreements on objectives are part of this process and how to deal with this instrument in the most constructive manner is still an ongoing process at the university.

TUITION FEES

After long public politcal discussions, students in Bavaria have had to pay tuition fees since the summer of 2007. Although this brought in a consider-

The practical clinical training center, "Zentrum für Unterricht und Studien" (ZeUS) within the LMU Faculty of Medicine, is funded by tuition fees. In communication training sessions with lay actors young medics can practice their skills talking to patients or work on dummies.
Such supportive teaching aids have been introduced in various divisions of the university, including, for example, a sonography practice lab in the Faculty of Veterinary Medicine.

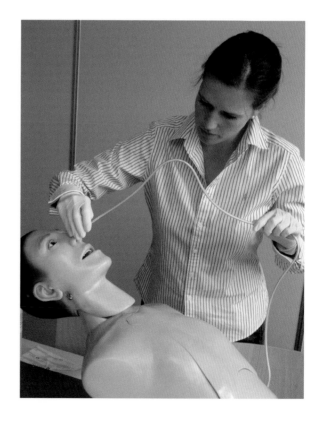

able sum of money for the university not everyone was entirely happy with the situation. By definition, tuition fees are only to be used exclusively to improve teaching — something that has since led to endless discussions between representatives of the university and students who are fully involved in the decision-making process. For these, the fees are naturally an additional financial burden; on the other hand, it has also become possible to finance real improvements to teaching, which could never even have been hoped for previously. In many faculties, the student/teacher ratio has been considerably improved by appointing new lecturers and tutors; in the Faculty of Medicine, a center for practical clinical training (ZeUS) for example has been established, and new and expanded facilities have been created for physics and chemistry practicals.

Discussions about whether tuition fees are justified and the amount to be paid will continue to accompany us as they touch on the fundamental issue of the status of public education. With their energetic claim for autonomy, universities inevitably find themselves at the heart of this conflict, which became one of the causes that triggered student demonstrations at universities nationwide. The protests at LMU that reached a peak at the end of 2009, were generally concentrated around the main building, where the principal auditorium, the Audimax, was occupied by mostly student groups during the last six weeks of that year, resulting in an acute disruption to scheduled university events despite the use of alternative venues. After many years of constructive cooperation, these protests represented an unpleasant, new experience for a university that is already stretched to its limits. Nevertheless, they led to a collective rethinking of the reasons behind this public display of discontent, many of which were caused by problems adapting courses to the Bologna Process. In dedicated work with the faculties concerned, additional suggestions to resolve the situation have been made.

Student protests in late 2009 were principally directed against implementing the Bologna Process reforms and tuition fees. They led to the Audimax at LMU being occupied over a period of several weeks.

201

THE BOLOGNA PROCESS

At the beginning of the new millennium countries throughout Europe set about opening up universities to a greater extent and on a mutual basis. The underlying declaration was drawn up in Bologna, home to the oldest university in Europe, and its name has accompanied us ever since with growing intensity. To begin with, it all sounded perfectly obvious: Degree courses should be brought in line based on three cycles, thus encouraging mobility among both students and lecturers. Achievement en route to a bachelor's or master's degree follows a system of points, the so-called European Credit Transfer System (ECTS), with reciprocal credits. The Bologna Process has started to influence our day-to-day life. Most courses — the only exception to date being those leading to state exams such as medicine, veterinary medicine, pharmacy, law, and teaching — were restructured in time for the winter term 2009/10. That this was not without its hitches is not really surprising given LMU's size. That protests by students effected would be so extensive was something however that nobody predicted. Of course there had been many a warning from both professors and students. For some, their heart was set on the tried and tested system of the classical diploma and master's degree course that permitted a considerable — and for many students too considerable an — amount of freedom.

It would seem that the Bologna Process cannot be reversed and will sucessfully accompany LMU on its path — even if it is not always smooth — to becoming an internationally recognized institution for forward-looking academic teaching.

Some may have the impression that with so much "excellence" and such a high level of performance in research that teaching at LMU is not given the necessary attention. That is not the case: in fact, quite the opposite is true — the university management has defined teaching as its number one priority. The most visible sign of this is the appointment of university representatives to implement the Bologna Process at LMU as well as for teacher training. An important accent is this field was set by LMU back in 2004 with the creation of the Teacher Education Center, that works on further developing the general principles of teacher training based on research, and putting these into practice.

LMU'S GLOBAL IMAGE

LMU has been thoroughly swept along by the momentum of the Internet and new media. A revamped website in LMU's modern design has long since established itself as something to be proud of, the image of LMU as it were on the Internet. As a platform for the university, however, it is not static at all, but an expression of the daily growing stream of information on offer and news of what is currently happening at LMU. The uniformly designed Internet presence has gradually expanded over the past decade to cover all institutes at LMU and, in the meantime, has become an indispensable data network for all organizational questions and as an important source of information on institutes and sub-divisions within LMU.

The possibilities opened up by new technology have made it easier for all members of the university to adopt one common corporate image and one common corporate design at LMU. The LMU logo has become an internationally recognizable trademark that we are all just that little bit proud to see on signs throughout Munich, on letter heads, and on presentation transparencies, and which we can even display on our lapels. The shop at Leopoldstrasse 13, that started out as a virtual online shop in 2007 before the real LMU Shop was opened in 2009, helps propagate the "LMU brand," selling correspondingly designed articles ranging from ballpoint pens to LMU T-shirts and LMU mugs. The T-shirt in particular has long since spread the name LMU to all corners of the globe!

Among the important signs to welcome young students, who are often rather apprehensive at first when they start at our university, is an event introduced some years ago. On this day, at the beginning of the first term, the main building is full to bursting! Party time with lively music, a welcome gift — a chic bag with the LMU logo on it of course, donated by our *Universitätsgesellschaft* — and a motivating speech to greet the

freshmen by the university president. An encouraging note that launches student life off on the right footing.

Every second year the university is filled with the sound of boisterous children for several days. Some hundred schoolchildren aged between eight and twelve surge through the main building to one of the other larger lecture theaters — their parents having to stay outside — and can spend an hour as "student kids." The *KinderUni* funded by the Munich association *Kultur und Spielraum e.V.* has become an event at LMU, or rather a series of events, that

LMU's website is usually the starting point for all those interested in the university, and is as such the image LMU presents the world.

In connection with the relaunch of LMU's central Internet presence, a uniform corporate design for the university was introduced for the first time in 2006. It was not just a question of finding a suitable and contemporary look. More importantly, all institutes and sub-divisions at LMU should be presented under one "roof" and yet, at the same time, they should be able to have enough freedom for their own presentations. The flexible "LMU box system" is the result.

attracts attention both within the university and without, even if does cause some colleagues to frown. Most, however, take part enthusiastically. And it's quite a challenge as well as an experience for a university lecturer to keep charge of an auditorium full of extremely lively children when they otherwise have to deal with more or less committed students.

At the other end of the scale, courses for senior citizens have firmly established themselves within the university structure. Several thousand men and women are matriculated, fee-paying students, for whom a series of courses has been specially devised. The courses offered meet the growing public interest in research and its increasing global significance. Occasionally of course the flood of interested people puts a strain on the space available at the university, and also has repercussions on regular lectures in various courses. On the one hand, a shortage of space has been created by our appealing courses for senior citizens, on the other, an intensive and positive interaction has developed between the university and the residents of Munich and the surrounding area.

Mugs, T-shirts, and stationery items with the LMU design have been available online since 2007. Since 2009 the full range of articles can also be found at the LMU Shop at Leopoldstrasse 13, in the immediate vicinity of the main university building.

The shop now has more than 70 products on offer — from conference products to leisure sweaters and LMU teddies.

Young "students" proudly show their student ID cards. The winter term 2004/05 kicked off with a series of lectures for 8 to 12-year-old at LMU's KinderUni Munich. Since then, it has been held regularly and has become very popular, both with children and professors.

With fascinating subjects from academia and teaching, student life and an interesting working day at the university, "MünchnerUni Magazin" (MUM for short) has been reporting now for more than 20 years.
Research findings also have to reach their public to make them come alive. This is ensured by the research journal "Einsichten" that is published once a year.

The spirit of the times found in the university's openness is also reflected in the way the *MünchnerUni Magazin* (MUM), LMU's principal publication, has evolved. Now more than twenty years old, it has developed into a journal with a contemporary design and a broad mixture of subjects. It reports on topical events at the university, on plans and progress made, and not least of all on success stories and awards. The publication *Einsichten* (Insights) has been reporting on the findings of our exceptional researchers since 2004.

INTERNATIONAL PRESENCE

A modern university is not least of all judged by its international reputation. Cooperation with colleagues abroad is something that is now taken for granted at LMU. There is hardly a research project in which international scholars are not involved. The majority of newly appointed professors can look back at sometimes several years of research at institutes abroad, and can now strengthen ties with established partners from their positions at LMU. To promote new contacts, LMU has established a bridgehead of sorts in the USA. As part of the German University Alliance and together with the Freie Universität Berlin, LMU has been running its own office in New York since 2005 that has made a name for itself as a central office dealing with queries from North American universities, on the one hand, and as an interface for our young academics seeking positions, on the other. Collaboration with Chinese universities is developing extremely satisfactorily too, and its continued expansion is helped by LMU's office in China, which also advises those in the Middle Kingdom interested in our university. Other institutionalized means for collaboration have come about through the Excellence Initiative. The cooperation with Berkeley already mentioned, for example, evolved in this way; the Faculty of Physics at Tokyo University is in close contact with that at

LMU. An innovative project has been launched together with Harvard University, aimed at bringing together young academics from various fields of Life Sciences (LMU–Harvard Young Scientists' Forum). That LMU is a leading member in the League of European Research Universities (LERU) seems to have become a matter of course in the meantime. LERU — with LMU as one of its founder memebers — is a network of European, research-oriented universities set up in 2002, with the objective of jointly defining higher education and research policies by having a direct voice and permanent influence at European level. 22 European universities with a comparable research performance were partners within this cooperation in 2010.

Over the past ten years, the number of students at LMU to complete part of ther course abroad — so-called "outgoings" — has multiplied quite considerably. In the meantime, LMU is acknowledged as being the most active German university in the Erasmus program. The number of foreign students to spend a term or a complete academic year with us ("incomings") is similar at a pleasingly high level. At around 6,700, this made up some 15 percent of the overall number of students in 2010.

In many areas, especially in *Magister*, master's, and doctorate courses, English is gaining more and more in importance as a means of communication in teaching and laboratory work, which in turn makes LMU that much more attractive for international students. Time and again, the representatives of our International Office have found that it is hardly necessary to advertise for LMU at the many international education fairs. The graduate program's informative and lucid homepages very effectively encourage closer inspection and attract the attention of young people around the world looking for somewhere to study.

PROSPECTS

LMU can look back on a turbulent past decade, during which momentum increased from year to year. Its image has changed faster than many outsiders would have considered possible. It has established itself as one of the leading universities in Germany and as one of the most successful centers of scholarship in Europe, and continues to pursue this promising course. A continuous examination of its strengths and weaknesses has ensured that LMU has kept its feet firmly on the ground, and has remained an open university. Placing its trust in its ambitious scholars, its many dedicated members of staff, and the students's openness to meet the social challenges of the future, Ludwig-Maximilians-Universität can look confidently ahead to the new decade.

At around 15 percent, the proportion of foreign students at LMU is surprisingly high.

THE MÜNCHENER UNIVERSITÄTSGESELLSCHAFT

MICHAEL KAMP / INA DEPPE

The rector Erich von Drygalski initiated the founding of the "Münchener Universitätsgesellschaft" in 1922. The geography professor is especially known for his leadership of an expedition to Greenland and the first German expedition to the South Pole.

During World War I and at the beginning of the 1920s university associations were founded in several German cities with the aim of providing local support to the respective university. The lack of space, the shortage of teaching staff and equipment, as well as the growing numbers of students left their mark on universities toward the end of the war and during the inflation-inflicted post-war period. The state suffered under the burden of trying to keep research and teaching at a high level, especially during the years of crisis.

On June 16, 1922, such an association was founded in Munich as well. The *Gesellschaft von Freunden und Förderern der Universität München e. V.* (Society of Friends and Benefactors of the University of Munich), as the *Münchener Universitätsgesellschaft* is officially named, was called into being. It was to provide assistance to Ludwig-Maximilians-Universität, especially in times of need.

The rector of the university at that time, Erich von Drygalski (1865–1949) — a professor ordinarius for geography since 1906 and internationally famous, having led numerous expeditions to the Arctic and Antarctic — initiated its establishment. Its founder members included representatives from politics, culture, academia, and commerce, including the Bavarian prime minister Count Hugo von Lerchenfeld, Thomas Mann (1875–1955), and Ricarda Huch (1871–1947). More than 100 individuals and companies joined the society. This initiative attracted the particular attention of the Munich Re (Münchener Rückversicherungs-Gesellschaft). Dr. Wilhelm Kißkalt (1873–1958), the reinsurance company's CEO, was elected to be the society's 1st chairman.

With the association's help, the aim was to "advise and support the university to fulfill its task, espe-

Thomas Mann was one of the founder members of the "Universitätsgesellschaft" together with the authoress Ricarda Huch.

Wilhelm Kißkalt, director of Munich Re, was elected 1st chairman of the "Universitätsgesellschaft" in 1922.

Satzung

der Gesellschaft von Freunden und Förderern der Universität München (Münchener Universitätsgesellschaft) e. V.

The statutes of the "Münchener Universitätsgesellschaft" were adopted at the foundation ceremony on June 16, 1922. Its aim was to "advise and support the university to fulfill its task, especially through funding academic research and teaching."

cially through funding academic research and teaching at the university," as laid down in the statutes "through the collecting of money." It was decided to establish graded annual contributions and a democratic structure, with every member having the right to vote at the annual general meeting. The board of directors was always to include the rector, the prorector, and someone from the university administration. Representatives of the faculties and the general student committee sat on a commission that was aimed at providing support for the board and recruiting new members. Both bodies were to be elected every three years. Revenue was to be used exclusively for the good of the university.

Very soon, interest in the association started to be shown from other fields. At the end of the business year, the *Universitätsgesellschaft* already had 600 members. By 1924 it was 1,680. Despite the shortage of means, it was still possible to provide important assistance: foreign literature — in short supply after the war — and new equipment were bought for the university.

From 1926 onward, greater funds were available. This was thanks to the publicity gained from LMU's 100th anniversary celebration of its move to from Landshut to Munich. Many professors drew attention to problems in the academic sphere in the press. A well funded jubilee foundation was set up through which specialist books were acquired. That same year, a new member joined the board of directors: Walther Meuschel, born in 1897, was a member of the board of directors at Munich Re and became the 1st secretary. Meuschel, who was to keep his position until 1978, left his mark on the association like no other. In 1929 he clearly stipulated the principles of the *Universitätsgesellschaft*, especially in the field of research, in a letter to the rector — an objective to which the *Universitätsgesellschaft* is still committed today.

LMU's 100th anniversary of its move to from Landshut to Munich: the Rector Karl Vossler at the head of the festive procession during the celebration. The "Universitätsgesellschaft" set up a jubilee foundation to include all donations received during the 1926 anniversary year. Revenue from the funds invested in shares and foreign currency were to be used for the benefit of the university.

The university observatory was given a photographic lens in 1929 for the large refracting telescope, financed by the "Universitätsgesellschaft".

In the 1920s and '30s, microscopes were among the objects most frequently donated by the "Universitätsgesellschaft".

When the National Socialists seized power in 1933, the *Universitätsgesellschaft* entered a phase of incisive change too. The long-serving Jewish board member, Max Weinmann, left the association "voluntarily." Even if no explicit force were used, one can hardly speak of "free will" in the light of such a change to political circumstances. Kißkalt, who had joined the NSDAP in March 1933, informed the board on May 23, 1933, simply that Weinmann had left on his own accord. There was no hint of any expression of solidarity. In 1936, Meuschel reported to the rector that the association had no Jewish members either on the board or in honorary positions in its ranks. From then on, no more reminders were sent out to members believed to be Jews. Such memberships were simply left to peter out without drawing any degree of attention. The ruling passed by the board on July 17, 1933, dissolving the committee followed similar lines. One of the reasons given for this move was "that the times conditioned that certain members should no longer retain their seats on the committee." It is not a far cry to assume that one wanted to rid the board of participation from "racially," denominationally, and politically undesirable members. With such measures the *Universitätsgesellschaft* was reacting in keeping with the rest of society, although unlike in the case of the association in Jena for example, Nazi officials did not have to be admitted nor did the society have to be structured according to the *"Führer"* principle. In 1934 it was ruled that enforcing the *"Führerprinzip* was not necessary for the *Universitätsgesellschaft"*, as its work comprised solely the collection and distribution of funds for academic and teaching purposes. There was also no politically conditioned change to the distribution of funds.

The board continued to be elected democratically by its members up until 1943, when in April that year, the ban by the Ministry of Justice for associations to hold assemblies prevented any further general meetings being called. The *Universitätsgesellschaft* was only able to execute its function in a limited fashion in the final years of the war. No general meetings were held, and the funds earmarked for the university became increasingly less. At the end of the war and the assumption of power by the US American military government in Bavaria, the activities of the *Münchener Universitätsgesellschaft* came to a complete standstill. The board of the *Universitätsgesellschaft* was dissolved, and any further activity was forbidden.

In 1945, 70 percent of the university was destroyed; only twelve lecture halls in the main university building could still be used. The university library had lost much of its holdings and there was a shortage of teaching staff. Compared to 1938, the number of students however had doubled, as many of those who wanted to study during the war but were unable to, matriculated to study. Against this back-

The philosophy professor Aloys Wenzl, who had been subjected to considerable repression under the Nazi regime due to his Christian faith, strove for the renewed founding of the "Universitätsgesellschaft" after World War II.

ground, the rector of the University, Aloys Wenzl (1887–1967), who had been dismissed from his post as professor of philosophy in 1938 for political reasons, pushed for the *Universitätsgesellschaft* to be reestablished and sent out invitations to a meeting to be held on May 12, 1948, for this very reason. Meuschel was elected 1st chairman and Dr. Heinz Böß, a director at Munich Re, 1st secretary.

At the beginning of the 1950s, funds started to come in again thanks to a number of different advertising initiatives. By 1955, 31,000 German marks and donations in kind were collected. As membership numbers had stagnated, a strategy to attract single donations from industry was adopted. In this way, significant sums were collected to be used, for example, for cancer research, and infectious dis-

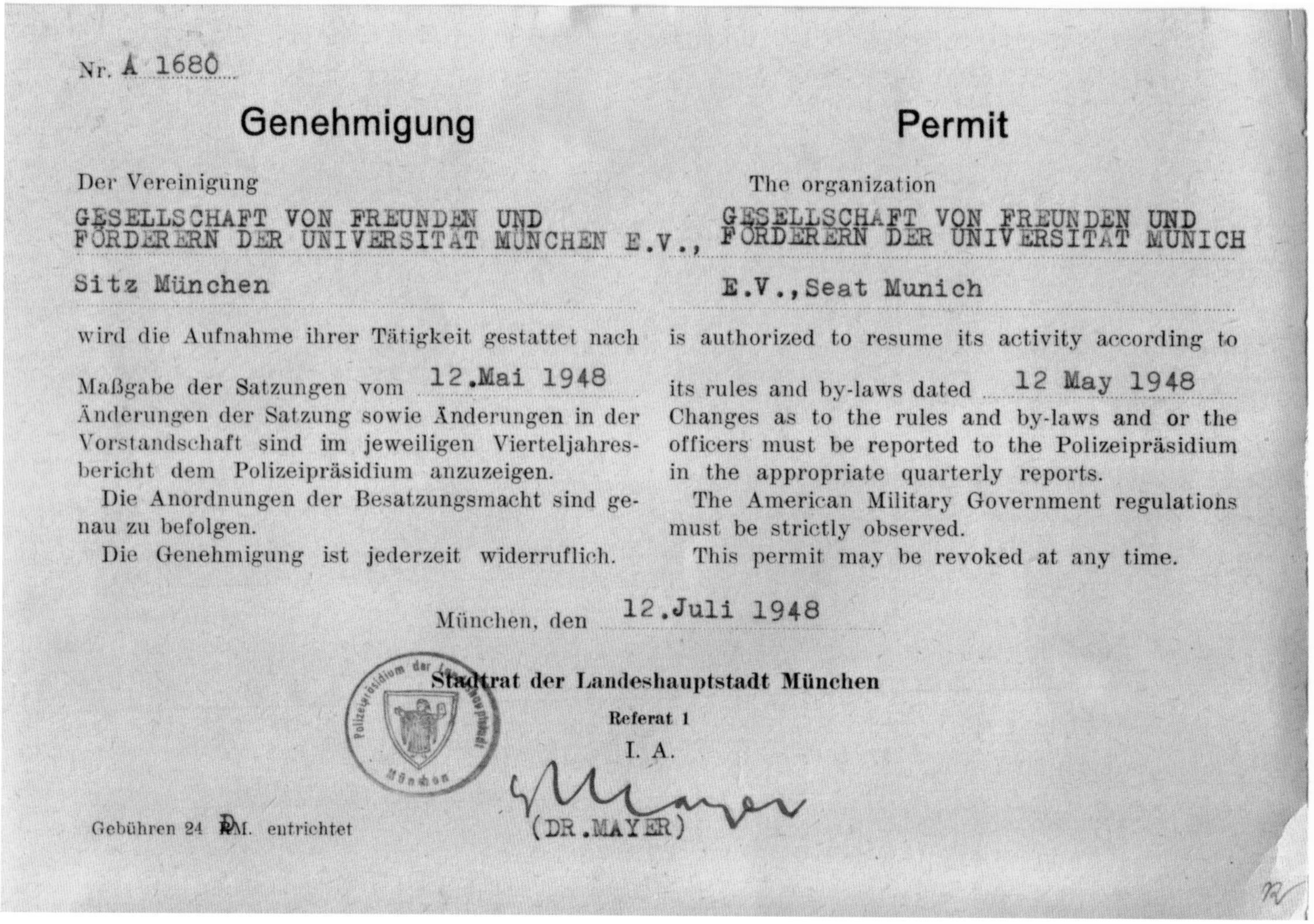

Nr. A 1680

Genehmigung	Permit
Der Vereinigung	The organization
GESELLSCHAFT VON FREUNDEN UND FÖRDERERN DER UNIVERSITÄT MÜNCHEN E.V.,	GESELLSCHAFT VON FREUNDEN UND FÖRDERERN DER UNIVERSITÄT MUNICH
Sitz München	E.V., Seat Munich
wird die Aufnahme ihrer Tätigkeit gestattet nach Maßgabe der Satzungen vom 12.Mai 1948 Änderungen der Satzung sowie Änderungen in der Vorstandschaft sind im jeweiligen Vierteljahresbericht dem Polizeipräsidium anzuzeigen.	is authorized to resume its activity according to its rules and by-laws dated 12 May 1948 Changes as to the rules and by-laws and or the officers must be reported to the Polizeipräsidium in the appropriate quarterly reports.
Die Anordnungen der Besatzungsmacht sind genau zu befolgen.	The American Military Government regulations must be strictly observed.
Die Genehmigung ist jederzeit widerruflich.	This permit may be revoked at any time.

München, den 12.Juli 1948

Stadtrat der Landeshauptstadt München

Referat 1

I. A.

(DR.MAYER)

Gebühren 24 RM. entrichtet

After official permission was granted by the US American military government, the "Universitätsgesellschaft" was approved by Munich's city council in 1948.

eases and tropical medicine. A board of trustees was set up to expand the *Universitätsgesellschaft's* sphere of action. Rupprecht of Bavaria (1869–1955) took on the position of chairman and was followed in 1955 by his son, Albrecht (1905–96).

Student numbers rose of the next few years to a degree never seen before. In 1948/49, 9,900 students were matriculated at the university; by 1968/69, there were 23,300. This development and a new political awareness among students who defended the democratization of the university, presented the university management with an utterly new challenge. The *Universitätsgesellschaft* offered its assistance here as well. So that the public could be kept informed about the higher education and academic reform, it provided the university management with funds to set up a press department in 1967 — the first at a university in Bavaria.

The funding provided by the *Universitätsgesellschaft* to support university operations rose in the years that followed. In 1976, for example, the figure was DM 1,264,375. Foundations for specific purposes to provide assistance to the natural sciences accounted for 87 % of this amount. The focus on the natural sciences was particularly pronounced which is why the *Universitätsgesellschaft* began to concentrate more closely on cultural studies and the arts using non-specified funds. Projects sponsored in the arts included lecture tours and archeological digs, for example, over the following few years. Important projects funded were the lecture series held from 1979 onward and the senior citizens's courses introduced in 1982. In 1984, an initiative was started to present prizes for doctorate and habilitation theses, which to this day still provides support for young academics. In the late 1980s, the purchase of the first personal computers and computer-aided equipment was financed. A large sum was set aside in 1990 to establish the *Internationales Begegnungs-*

zentrum der Wissenschaft München e. V. The funding that same year of the *Gastprofessur der Universitätsgesellschaft* scheme for visiting professors was also of particular importance.

Dr. Detlef Schneidawind, board member of Munich Re, became 1st chairman in 1993, taking over from Dr. Horst K. Jannott, board member of Munich Re since 1969 and 1st chairman of the *Universitätsgesellschaft* since 1978. At the time of this changeover in 1993, the association had 1,750 sponsors.

Under Schneidawind, sponsorship was largely concentrated on supporting the university in updating its communication media and on higher education's growing internationalization. This led to the

Detlef Schneidawind, former CEO of Munich Re, was 1st chairman of the "Universitätsgesellschaft" from 1993 through 2006. Under his aegis, the association provided the university with support especially in updating its communication media and in meeting higher education's growing need for internationalization.

Dr. Wolfgang Strassl, also a board member of Munich Re, has been 1st chairman of the "Universitätsgesellschaft" since 2006. He has continued the association's sponsorship policy along the same lines as his predecessor. Under Strassl, the "Universitätsgesellschaft" has also set its own special accent: In 2008, it awarded a 25,000 euros cultural prize for the first time.

Schneidawind frequently appeared in public and held lectures on behalf of the *Universitätsgesellschaft* within the university and elsewhere. Membership increased: In 1995, the *Universitätsgesellschaft* had 2,000 members, today there are even around 2,400. As such, it is one of the largest associations of its kind in Germany.

1st chairman Dr. Wolfgang Strassl, who has been in office since 2006, has continued the association's sponsorship policy along the same lines as his predecessor and the traditions of the *Universitätsgesellschaft*. Funded projects include a didactic chemistry research colloquium for prospective teachers, a research project in the Faculty of Catholic Theology, and the financing of a capsule endoscopic unit for clinical diagnostics of the gastrointestinal tract in children. However, under Strassl, the *Universitätsgesellschaft* has also set its own special accent, awarding a 25,000 euros cultural prize for the first time in 2008, based on a proposal made by HRH Franz, Duke of

Universitätsgesellschaft funding projects such as "Venice International University," in which Ludwig-Maximilians-Universität also participates, and the "LMU Virtual Campus," finalized in 2000, which also uses funds from the *Universitätsgesellschaft*. Urgently needed assistance was given to innovative projects in the arts as well. Only thanks to the rapid financial support given by the *Universitätsgesellschaft* was it possible for the interdisciplinary, structured courses for creative writing at Munich, that had been operating since the winter term 1999/2000 under the name MANUSKRIPTUM, to be continued in 2001 and 2005. The MANUSKRIPTUM courses are still part of the *Universitätsgesellschaft's* sponsorship portfolio.

The US American sociologist and historian, Mike Davis (b. 1945), was the first winner of the "Universitätsgesellschaft's" cultural prize. In 2010, the French sociologist and philosopher, Bruno Latour (b. 1947) received the award.

Bavaria. Exceptional figures from the humanities, literature, art, and culture who are honored with this award, have the possibility to present the findings of their research to a broader public in the form of inderdisciplinary lectures in the arts and social sciences, in addition to receiving the prize money.

Since its foundation in 1922, the *Universitätsgesellschaft's* office has been at Munich Re. The *Universitätsgesellschaft* sponsors some 60 projects annually and places around one million euros at the university's disposal. Ever since its foundation it has understood how to interpret the signs of the times and to react in a suitable manner to the

respective situation at LMU. In many cases, it has provided the initial impulse for innovative projects and contributed towards their being implemented with swift and unbureaucratic help.

münchener
universitätsgesellschaft
Gesellschaft von Freunden und Förderern der Universität München e.V.

Münchener Universitätsgesellschaft e. V.,
Königinstraße 107, 80802 München,
Tel.: 0 89/38 91- 56 07, Fax: 0 89/38 91- 7 56 07,
info@unigesellschaft.de, www.unigesellschaft.de

One of the LMU's department of arts's veejay events, funded by the Universitätsgesellschaft, held during the "Münchner Wissenschaftstage" in 2006.

Student life at LMU

CREATIVE BREAKS OUTSIDE

ANJA BURKEL

A lecture in the "Audimax," the main auditorium. Some 47,000 young people study at LMU.

K ing Louis I, in the casual pose of a ruler, is seated in the atrium. Chiseled out of marble, the larger-than-life figure of the monarch holds audience from his throne in the main building at Ludwig-Maximilians-Universität, vis-à-vis a statue of the Prince Regent, Luitpold. More than 200 years ago, when he was crown prince, he was a student himself at the Bavarian state university — at that time still in Landshut. In those days, snuff and secret duels were part of everyday life for his fellow students. The student life that he now looks down upon from his marble throne, is modern, vibrant — and extremely diverse.

One of the first events in the life of a student is the freshmen's party in Fall, organized by the students's representatives at LMU. Have a great time where otherwise lectures are held: The seminar rooms and lecture theaters in the historical main university building on Geschwister-Scholl-Platz are converted into a huge club. Between columns and statues, the start of university life is celebrated with live bands, poetry slams, cabarets, and discos.

Fellow students who meet at the freshmen's party only make up a small percentage of the overall number of students at one of the largest and most prestigious universities in Germany. Around 47,000 young men and women are working towards their degree in some 150 different subjects at LMU. They make up a large and interesting mixture of people: From Egyptologists to French teachers, lawyers to physicists-to-be and future dentists. 15 percent of them are from abroad, making LMU one of the most attractive universities internationally in the Germany. For students at LMU who are themselves interested in spending a period studying abroad, the university has exchange programs with a number of partner universities around the globe.

The porter's window in the entrance area to the main university building is where tips and assistance are given to help students find their way around.

The main university building, in which many of the students have their lectures, forms a picture postcard setting for a course of study. A cascading fountain stands in front of the pale yellow facade; students pour through the arches to and from lectures — and, inside, freshmen lose their way to start with in the endless corridors and marble staircases. Just as well that there is a friendly face behind the window with the word "Information" on it, who can point lost souls in the right direction. Outside the main entrance, many students carefully step over the stone leaflets set in the cobblestones — a work of art that is a reminder of the resistance group, the "White Rose," whose leaflets against the regime rained down inside the atrium during the period under the National Socialists. Here, a permanent exhibition is now devoted to them in the "White Rose Memorial Center."

Today, the address of the main university building is also a reminder of the Scholl siblings; the square on the other side of the road is named after their fellow resistance fighter, Kurt Huber. However, not all student life takes place here by a long chalk, and many students have to travel quite a distance between seminars and lectures. LMU is not a campus university — its faculties and department are widely scattered throughout Munich and the surrounding area like the grains of salt on a pretzel. Bright, angular, modern — such are the buildings on LMU's HighTechCampus in Großhadern/Martinsried, one of Europe's leading "Life Sciences" complexes. The Japanologists and political scientists are accommodated on the edge of the English Garden, the medics on Bavariaring. The university buildings that spread out from Geschwister-Scholl-Platz down Leopoldstrasse and Ludwigstrasse as far as the *Schweinchenbau* (Piglet Building), home to trainee teachers and psychologists, are a little closer together. This is where the LMU Shop can be found that has T-shirts, mugs, and USB sticks, among other things, on offer. Just behind it is the

The "Weiße Rose" memorial: Some 50 ceramic tiles embedded in the cobblestones outside LMU's main entrance on Geschwister-Scholl-Platz, are a reminder of the Weiße Rose group's leaflet campaign in the atrium in 1943, that led to the arrest of Sophie and Hans Scholl and their fellow resistance fighters. The tiles were designed by the sculptor Robert Schmidt-Matt and set in the ground in 1988. In April 2006, some of the tiles were pried out and stolen. They were replaced that same year.

LMU is scattered across the whole Munich city area, taking in the HighTechCampus in Großhadern/Martinsried, the city center, the Maxvorstadt district with the main university building, Oberschleißheim, and Oettingenstrasse 67, for example (photo), right next to the English Garden. Where students of Political Science and Computer Science now come and go, was home to the former US broadcasting station, Radio Free Europe (RFE) and Radio Liberty (RL), which have since moved to Prague.

largest cafeteria run by the Munich *Studentenwerk* which not only offers meals from one euro upward, but also has the largest pinboard in the world — or so it would seem, at least. The foyer literally rustles with new and well-worn pieces of paper. This is where everything under the sun can be found — from Icelandic housemates to "incredibly comfortable sofas" or test persons for medical studies.

Students can also find a huge choice of places to eat in the academic chill-out district behind the main building. In this bubly neighborhood, student pubs rub shoulders with small boutiques and copyshops; there is always one shop closing down somewhere and a new one celebrating its open-

"Alter Simpl" is a student pub with a long tradition. Its name is an abbreviation of the satirical magazine "Simplicissimus." It's caricaturist Th. Th. Heine (1867–1948) used his famous bulldog as a logo, which no longer has to pull at the chains of censorship but open champagne bottles with its sharp teeth.

ing. But there are some classic names that have kept going all this time: almost a whole semester can squeeze around one of the wooden tables in *Atzinger. Schneller*, the pastry shop and café with its floral wallpaper, seves good old-fashioned Black Forest Gateau and puff pastry palmiers. In *Alter Simpl*, that has been in Türkenstrasse for more than 100 years, budding literary geniuses such as Thomas Mann and Joachim Ringelnatz used to become lost in discussion. Today, freshmen take their visiting parents there for a roast pork lunch. The quarter behind the university is also a good spot for going out in the evening. This is where people especially like to meet outside — as in most districts in Munich. As soon as the sun

comes out, restaurant and café owners put out their tables and chairs on the sidewalks without delay. If the weather is a bit doubtful then heaters and fleece blankets are provided for guests. Of course, the pleasant — some would say — Italianate climate does help a lot.

Away from the main university building, one thing is within walking distance of almost all institutes: a beer garden for those creative breaks outside. Bring your own picnic and wash it down with a *Maß* of beer; the waft of pricey *Steckerlfisch* (grilled fish on a skewer) is for free. When beer gardens close at 11 p.m., that marks the end of partying outside just as in traditional Bavarian

The Tollwood Festival first took place in 1988 on the southern edge of the Olympic Park. Apart from the summer festival there is now also a winter festival with a wide range of cultural events including concerts, cabarets, and theater productions.

films. It's then time to seek out one of the count-less bars and pubs in Munich, from the chic to the run down. The stage in the Atomic Café, for example, decked out in '60s style, was where the rock group *Sportfreunde Stiller* first came together. Munich's "official" party zone is the Glockenbach district, where students rub shoulders with the rest of the world at retro bars that are often compared to those in Berlin. The choice of leisure and cultural activities in Munich is so vast that it can even become a bit stressful: which of the many museums or cinemas to visit, soccer or music festival, opera or theater?

For the creatively minded, LMU offers many possibilities: The majority of those seated at the microphones at "M94.5" — the radio training channel — are students at one of Munich's universities. The MANUSKRIPTUM course for create writing has even produced a recipient of the Ingeborg Bachmann Prize for German literature. The UniGalerie^LMU mostly exhibits works by alumni and current students. And to find a placement in the field of media or publishing, nobody in Munich has to leave the city. But the "student and job market" at LMU's Career Service can also help find interesting jobs and work experience.

Munich could be perfect — if it were not for the housing problem. Rooms in the Bavarian capital are among the most expensive in Germany. And student house-sharers have a difficult time up against professional couples with overflowing bank balances and sports cars. Bizarre stories are part-and-parcel of every student's search for a place to live. There is hardly a student party without anecdotes about long queues to view the classic "broom cupboard" at an exorbitant price. Many different attempts have been made to solve the accommodation problem. The sought-after bungalows from the '70s in the Olympic Village, with balconies and sleeping galleries, were rebuilt and insulated, and

"MANUSKRIPTUM – Münchener Kurse für kreatives Schreiben" aims to give an insight into literary writing and provides the opportunity to discuss one's own texts with well-known authors and experienced writers. The doctor and author Jens Petersen (b. 1976), completed LMU's MANUSKRIPTUM course in 2001/2002. Since then he has published two prize-winning novels, "Die Haushälterin" and "Bis dass der Tod." He was awarded the Ingeborg Bachmann Prize of the city of Klagenfurt for "Bis dass der Tod" in 2009.

The *"Studentenwerk München"* provides rooms and cafeterias. Students can also seek out advise here on an extensive range of issues.

halls of residence extended. Many students live rent-free with senior citizens, thanks to the "Board vs. Help" initiative, "paying" their way by doing the housework. And on the edge of the English Garden, near the student housing district in the north of Munich, the metallic finish of the "live-in cubes," sponsored by a cellphone provider, glistens in the sun. Inside, students squeeze into an ingeniously planned seven square meters, which — depending on whether the furniture is folded up or down — is perfect for sleeping, studying or hosting guests.

Whoever needs to escape the confinement of student accommodation can enjoy the expanse of one of Munich's many green spaces. From a bridge on the edge of the English Garden, surfers in wetsuits can be watched riding the perfect wave in the Eisbach, while horses from the university's riding school gallop along the sand tracks that wind their way through the park. Reading up for university work lying in the grass in the English Garden is

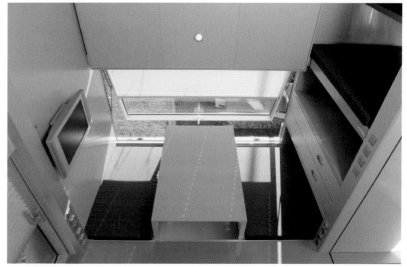

Cooking, sleeping, showering, studying, eating, watching TV, and hosting friends — every corner of the seven-square-meter "live-in cube" is used to the full. There are a total of seven of these sited on the edge of the student housing area in the "O2 Village."

Life in Munich has many facets: Surfing on the Eisbach or watching the sun go down from the Monopteros in the English Garden.

Leo von Klenze (1784–1864) designed the Königsplatz for King Louis I. The square forms a classical architectural Gesamtkunstwerk, with the Ionic Glyptothek, the Corinthian State Collections of Antiquies, and the Doric Propylaea, which is shown in the photo. In the summer, the Königsplatz is the venue for various open-air festivals from classical music to pop.

almost as pleasant as on the man-made beach on the renaturalized Isar. But be warned: on summer evenings there's no peace to be found along Munich's river, with barbeques everywhere on the *Flaucher* pebble beaches, jetties, and water meadows, the beer being kept cool in the Isar. And perhaps somewhere nearby a group of partygoers on a raft is about to stop on the river bank. The larger lakes to the south west of the city are a welcome place to cool off, such as Lake Starnberg with its student bathing area. And on the beach volleyball courts at the university's main sports complex in the Olympic Park, sports enthusiasts try to hit the ball into the each others's halves.

More breathing space can be found in the nearby Alps: Many students relax at the weekend with a hike or climb on one of Munich's local mountains such as Wendelstein, which by the way is crowned by LMU's observatory. Lush green meadows, the sound of cow bells in the background — this is the best way to clear one's brain for the term ahead. In winter, students can weave their way down the ski-runs in Lenggries or Garmisch-Partenkirchen, both ski resorts being reachable by train from Munich in less than one-and-a-half hours. The proximity of the mountains is also reflected in the range of courses of the university sports's center, with cave exploration and avalance survival courses or ice climbing up frozen waterfalls.

In September, things can get even more crowded in Munich's student rooms. That's when the Oktoberfest gets going, and with it the traditional stream of visitors from elsewhere who want a place to stay. The *Wiesn* dates back to the wedding of Crown Prince Louis — later King Louis I — and his bride, Theresa. Their celebration in October 1810 included a horserace on "Theresa's Meadow" — the precursor of the Oktoberfest. Nowadays, many young people also don *Lederhosen* and candy-colored *Dirndl* before heading for the big wheel, beer tents, and gingerbread hearts. But Munich also has its own carnival tradition. The classic *Fasching* events in the spring are the dancing at the central market and the parties in the basements of the student halls in Biederstein.

Perhaps Munich also provides such a lovely setting to study in, because the climate complements it so perfectly. Icy winters give it that "snow globe" charm; hot summers highlight its delights. When the city has really heated up in July, the university summer festival takes place at the end of the lecture season. Also organized by the students's representatives, many an inner courtyard in the main building is turned into a beer garden, the atrium into a bar. Students sip cocktails between the columns and historical sun dial, and King Louis I looks down upon the scene from his marble pedestal.

NOBEL PRIZE WINNERS

WILHELM CONRAD RÖNTGEN (1901)

Wilhelm Conrad Röntgen (1845–1923) was awarded the Nobel Prize in Physics in 1901. He was the first scientist to be presented with the prize in this discipline. Röntgen received the award primarily for his research into x-rays discovered by and named after him. This discovery, made while working at the University of Würzburg, opened up completely new possibilities in medical diagnostics and prepared the way for further important innovations and research, for example into radioactivity.

Between 1900 and 1920, Wilhelm Conrad Röntgen was professor at Ludwig-Maximilians-Universität. He retired in 1920.

ADOLF VON BAEYER (1905)

WILHELM WIEN (1911)

The chemist Adolf von Baeyer (1835–1917) was awarded the Nobel Prize in Chemistry in 1905, primarily for the synthesis of indigo and dyes made using triphenylmethane.

After the death of Justus von Liebig he was called to LMU Munich, and established a highly regarded chemistry laboratory where he worked until his retirement. The "Adolf-von-Baeyer-Medal," donated by Carl Duisberg in 1910, has been awarded by the Gesellschaft Deutscher Chemiker (German Chemical Society) since 1911 to chemists whose research has led to outstanding results and discoveries.

The Nobel Prize in Physics in 1911 went to the pysicist Wilhelm Wien (1864–1928) in recognition of his research into the laws of thermal radiation. This research was motivated largely by a question of economics as to whether gas or electrical lighting was cheaper. Wien started measuring emissions, that in 1896 culminated in a formula in which the majority of values measured could be accurately interpreted.

Wien was awarded the Nobel Prize while at the University of Würzburg. In 1920 he moved to Munich to Ludwig-Maximilians-Universität, where — as in Würzburg — he took over as Wilhelm Conrad Röntgen's successor. Wilhelm Wien was rector of LMU from 1925 to 1926.

MAX VON LAUE (1914)

RICHARD WILLSTÄTTER (1915)

Max von Laue (1879–1960) was awarded the Nobel Prize in 1914, also in physics. During his time at the University of Frankfurt am Main, the scientist discovered the diffraction of x-rays by crystals. This enabled him to prove both the wavelength of these rays as well as the structure of the crystals.

Laue came to LMU Munich in 1909 initially as a *Privatdozent*, and held lectures on optics, thermodynamics, and the theory of relativity. In 1912, he took up a position at the University of Zurich; in 1914 in Frankfurt am Main.

The chemist Richard Willstätter (1872–1942) received the Nobel Prize virtually at the same time as he decided to accept a position at Ludwig-Maximilians-Universität. The prize was in recognition of his study of plant pigments, especially of chlorophyll, the pigment essential for photosynthesis in plants. In addition, he proved that this green pigment, that allowed plants to convert luminous energy, contains magnesium.

Willstätter resigned his position as professor ordinarius in 1925, as he believed that anti-Semitism had gained the upper hand in the appointments procedure. Although he continued his research work in Munich, he left the city in 1939 for Switzerland due to the intensified persecution of Jews.

HEINRICH WIELAND (1927)

WERNER HEISENBERG (1932)

Willstätter's successor at the Institute of Chemistry at LMU in 1925 was Heinrich Wieland (1877–1957). Wieland received the Nobel Prize in Chemistry in 1927 for his research into the composition of bile acids and related substances. As his research was classified as being of strategic importance, several attempts to denunciate him during the National Socialist dictatorship came to no avail; he even managed to take on a number scholars burdened by the anti-Semitic "Nuremberg Laws" as guests in his work group, thus protecting them from persecution by the Nazis. Wieland had three children — one of his sons became a professor of medicine at LMU; his daughter, Eva, married Feodor Lynen, who was also a professor at LMU and the winner of the Nobel Prize in Medicine in 1964.

Werner Heisenberg (1901–1976) studied at LMU on a scholarship of the Maximilianeum Foundation under Arnold Sommerfeld, who acted as his mentor. He received the Nobel Prize in Physics at the early age of 31, "for the creation of quantum mechanics, the application of which has, inter alia, led to the discovery of the allotropic forms of hydrogen," as stated in the speech given in his honor. Heisenberg formulated the uncertainty principle named after him. This is a statement in quantum physics that maintains it is impossible to measure position x and momentum p of an electron simultaneously to arbitrarily high precision.

ADOLF BUTENANDT (1939)

FEODOR LYNEN (1964)

The Nobel Prize in Chemistry in 1939 went to Adolf Butenandt (1903–1995) for his research in the field of sex hormones. He shared the prize with Leopold Ružička, a researcher at ETH Zurich. Butenandt was called to the Institute of Pysiologic Medicine at LMU in 1952, that now carries his name.

From 1955 to 1960, when he took up office as president of the Max Planck Society, Butenandt was simultaneously chief executive of the Institute of Physiologic Chemistry at LMU and director of the Max Planck Institute for Biochemistry. An additional tenured professorship for physiologic chemistry was created especially for Butenandt, that he held until his retirement.

Feodor Lynen (1911–1979) was a pupil of Heinrich Wieland at LMU. His research into metabolic processes, especially how an organism breaks down fatty acids, injected a significant impulse into research and the therapy of metabolic diseases. The biochemist Lynen received the Nobel Prize in Medicine together with the German-American researcher Konrad Bloch (1912–2000) for their discoveries concerning the mechanism and regulation of cholesterol and fatty acid metabolism.

Lynen remained faithful to LMU where he was Professor Ordinarius from 1953 until his retirement in 1979, even turning down a call from Harvard University.

KARL RITTER VON FRISCH (1973)

KONRAD LORENZ (1973)

Karl Ritter von Frisch (1886–1982) was one of the most prominent German-speaking ethologists. In 1910, he joined the Zoological Institute at LMU. Following interim periods in Rostock and Breslau, he became professor at LMU in 1925. He retired in 1958 but still continued to carry out research. This was largely focussed on the western honey bee, centering his investigation on their senses of smell and taste and especially on their sense of orientation. This led to his discovery that bees can retain directions using the sun as a compass.

Frisch was awarded the Nobel Prize in Physiology or Medicine along with Konrad Lorenz and Nikolaas Tinbergen (1907–1988) "for their discoveries on the organization and triggering of individual and social behavioral patterns."

Konrad Lorenz (1903–1989) is considered the founder of comparative ethology. Until his retirement in 1973, he was head of the Max Planck Institute for Ornithology in Seewiesen. In addition to that, he was honorary professor at Ludwig-Maximilians-Universität. Lorenz proved that animals have a repertoire of instinctive behavior patterns according to which they react to certain stimuli or signals. When these patterns are irrevocably determined during a precisely restricted phase of an animal's life, this is called imprinting. Graylag goslings, for instance, accept the first living being they see after hatching as their mother — even if this being is a human. Lorenz also found the same was true for jackdaws.

GERD BINNIG (1986)

THEODOR W. HÄNSCH (2005)

Gerd Binnig (b. 1942) was awarded the Nobel Prize in Physics in 1986 together with Heinrich Rohrer (both at the IBM research laboratory in Zurich at that time) for developing the scanning tunneling microscope. During this process, an extremely fine tip examines the surface of an atom. A constant distance between tip and surface is regulated using a so-called tunneling current that flows between the tip and the surface to be examined when a bias is applied between the two. As opposed to an electron microscope, the scanning tunneling microscope is easier to operate and more reliable.

Gerd Binnig has been honorary professor at Ludwig-Maximilians-Universität since 1986.

Theodor W. Hänsch (b. 1941) was awarded the Nobel Prize in Physics in 2005. The scientist shared one half of the award with the US American researcher John L. Hall. The second half was awarded to the US American researcher Roy J. Glauber, who also works in the field of quantum optics. The Royal Swedish Academy of Sciences honored the contributions made by Hänsch and Hall to the development of laser-based precision spectroscopy with the help of which the optical frequency of atoms and molecules can be measured with extreme precision.

Hänsch holds the Chair of Experimental Physics at LMU and is director of the Max Planck Institute of Quantum Optics in Munich.

THE AUTHORS

PROF. DR. LAETITIA BOEHM, born in 1930, gained her doctorate in 1954 and her habilitation in 1959 in medieval and modern history. From 1969, she held the chair for medieval and modern history with special emphasis on the history of the university and teaching at LMU. From 1969 onward, Laetitia Boehm was senior executive of the University Archive, initially together with Prof. Dr. Johannes Spörl, and from 1977 through 2000 on her own.

DR. HELMUT BÖHM, born in 1946, completed a teacher education program in German, History, and Social Studies at LMU, where he also gained his doctorate. After working as an academic staff member and assistant he moved into school education in 1977. In 1981 he received a position in the Bavarian Ministry of Education and Cultural Affairs before becoming head of a secondary school in Untergriesbach. Since 1992, he has also been teaching modern and contemporary history at the University of Passau.

ANJA BURKEL, born in 1975, works as a journalist in Munich. She majored in journalism at LMU with minors in politics, sociology, and law, and completed editorial training at the Deutsche Journalistenschule. She then worked for five years in the editorial department at the Süddeutsche Zeitung in Munich, as well as for the Neue Zürcher Zeitung, among others. Anja Burkel has been a regular contributor to LMU's university magazine since 2007.

INA DEPPE, born in 1980, is an academic staff member and editor at the independent Munich institute for social research MPS. After studying modern and contemporary history, social and economic history, and ethnology, she gained editorial experience at various publishing houses. She is a freelance author specializing in cultural and educational history.

DR. MICHAEL KAMP, born in 1966, studied history and political science at LMU and University College, London, between 1991 and 1996. He is a freelance historian and runs a company specialized in historical projects with colleagues in Munich. His publications include the history of MAN Nutzfahrzeuge AG, the history of the clinics in Munich, and the history of Munich Zoo. He has also written the biographies of a number of benefactors.

PROF. DR. RAINER A. MÜLLER, born in 1944, died in 2004, studied history and German in Münster, Innsbruck, and Munich. The last position he held was as professor for early modern history at the Catholic University of Eichstätt. After gaining his doctorate (1971) he initially became an academic assistant at LMU, before his habilitation in 1982. In 1983, he became curator, working at the Haus der Bayerischen Geschichte, among others, before moving to the University of Eichstätt in 1988.

PROF. DR. WINFRIED MÜLLER, born in 1953, studied history, German, and political science at LMU, where he gained his doctorate in 1983 and his habilitation in 1991. After working as an assistant, he held deputy professorships at LMU and the University of Bonn. In 1999, he became the chair of regional Saxon history at the Technische Universität Dresden. Since 2000, he has also been director of the Institut für Sächsische Geschichte und Volkskunde in Dresden.

PROF. DR. REINHARD PUTZ, born in 1942, studied medicine at the University of Innsbruck, where he also gained his doctorate and habilitation. In 1982, he became professor of anatomy at the University of Freiburg, before taking up the call from LMU in 1989. From 2003, he was a member of the university management at LMU, and from April 2008, full-time vice president and representative of the president. At the end of September 2010, Reinhard Putz celebrated his retirement.

DR. WOLFGANG SMOLKA, born in 1955, is head of the University Archive at LMU. He studied educational and university history, modern history, medieval history, and ethnology at LMU, gaining his doctorate there in 1991 on a doctorate grant from the Studienstiftung des Deutschen Volkes (German National Academic Foundation). He has worked as a freelance historian and publisher as well as an academic member of staff in the University Archive and at the Historisches Kolleg.

PICTURE CREDITS